Political Power and Economic Inequality

Political Power and Economic Inequality

A Comparative Policy Approach

Charles F. Andrain

ROWMAN & LITTLEFIELD
Lanham • Boulder • New York • Toronto • Plymouth, UK

Published by Rowman & Littlefield
4501 Forbes Boulevard, Suite 200, Lanham, Maryland 20706
www.rowman.com

10 Thornbury Road, Plymouth PL6 7PP, United Kingdom

British Library Cataloguing in Publication Information Available

Library of Congress Cataloging-in-Publication Data

Andrain, Charles F.
Political power and economic inequality : a comparative policy approach / Charles F. Andrain.
pages cm
Includes bibliographical references and index.
ISBN 978-1-4422-2946-4 (cloth : alk. paper) — ISBN 978-1-4422-2947-1 (electronic)
1. Income distribution. 2. Capitalism. 3. Economics—Political aspects. 4. Social movements. 5. Policy sciences. I. Title.
HC79.I5A527 2014
339.2—dc23
2013047606

∞ ™ The paper used in this publication meets the minimum requirements of American National Standard for Information Sciences Permanence of Paper for Printed Library Materials, ANSI/NISO Z39.48-1992.

Printed in the United States of America

Contents

Acknowledgments

Numerous individuals have played a significant role in producing this book on income distribution. Robert J. Gormley read the first draft, offered valuable insights about ways to improve its quality, and suggested changes for making it more comprehensible. Professor Myunghee Kim served as an informal copy editor who not only corrected stylistic errors but clarified ambiguous passages. As a journalist and long-time professor of political science, Julie Sullivan indicated changes that would broaden the manuscript's appeal to readers. Professors David W. Dent and Jeffrey J. Sallaz reviewed the project for Rowman & Littlefield. With his extensive publications on Latin America and his experience teaching comparative politics classes, Dent recommended using specific information to explicate general assumptions. An expert on contemporary social theory and comparative labor issues, Sallaz stressed the importance of linking income distribution with a persuasive theoretical explanation that includes cultural values. The late David E. Apter was a professor, mentor, and coauthor. Examining diverse political systems throughout the world, he inspired this study of income distribution. At Stanford University, several librarians provided assistance: Veena Bhargava, Cheryl Caccialanza, Eric Heath, Mihoko Hosoi, James Jacobs, Suzie Kim, Hoang Le, Molly Molloy, Miriam Palm, Regina Lee Roberts, and Becky Ruelas. Rowman & Littlefield editors Susan McEachern, Carolyn Broadwell-Tkach, Jehanne Schweitzer, and Michele Tomiak transformed the manuscript into a book that probes the impact of political power and public policies on economic inequality.

Introduction

Not only in the industrialized societies but also in developing nations, the gap between rich and poor widened beginning in the early 1970s. Income disparities affected all aspects of life: health care, education, nutrition, employment, housing, child care, retirement, crime. When the income gap increased, the prospects diminished for upward economic mobility from one generation to the next. Youths experienced fewer opportunities to gain a high-paying job with social benefits. Government officials who supported egalitarian policies, such as generous, inclusive, comprehensive social-service programs, encountered opposition from right-wing political parties, social groups, and private corporations. They encouraged policymakers to enact austerity decisions that reduced equality. Low-income persons suffered the greatest damage from government actions that relied on fossil fuels and expropriated poor farmers' land for industrial development. Pressured by stagnant wages and high unemployment rates, labor unions struggled with corporations over pay, working conditions, and managerial control. Social movements protested poverty, land deprivation, high food prices, personal debts, unemployment, austerity policies, corruption, and police repression.

Highlighting the complex explanations for income distribution, *Political Power and Economic Inequality: A Comparative Policy Approach* makes several assumptions about the impact of public policies on inequality. First, just as the economy influences government decisions, so political power affects economic distribution. The book probes the specific policies that most effectively secure greater income equality. How does the political power of government institutions, political parties, corporations, labor unions, and social movements help produce these policies?

Second, economic equality during the twenty-first century stems from not only national conditions but also from global patterns of foreign trade, overseas investment, labor migration, and worldwide communications media. National institutions interact with such international organizations as the International Monetary Fund (IMF), World Bank, World Trade Organization (WTO), multinational corporations, and several nongovernmental voluntary associations. They operate in all regions, including Western Europe, Central and Eastern Europe, Asia, North America, and Latin America. Besides comparing specific nations in these regions, the book explores the income of different occupations, ethnic-religious groups, and women and men. How much political power do they exert? To what degree do they secure desired outcomes from the public policy process? Economic data, mainly from the 1990–2010 period, indicate the effects of fiscal, monetary, ownership, regulatory, and labor-market policies on income distribution.

Third, *Political Power and Economic Inequality* adopts an interdisciplinary perspective toward public policies. It integrates theories and information from political science, economics, and sociology. By linking cultural values and individual preferences to the structural assumptions of resource mobilization theory, this conceptual framework helps explain cross-national patterns of income distribution. Resource mobilization designates the opportunities and constraints experienced by key political organizations. Cultural values toward egalitarianism, individualism, hierarchy, and efficacy express distinctive notions of justice. Perceptions about the costs and benefits of egalitarian programs influence personal choices to support or oppose them.

The book's chapters focus on the general explanations behind the process of making policies about income distribution in several different nations. Chapter 1 compares the perspectives of John Maynard Keynes with contemporary neoliberals. Upholding the private provision of social services, they view income inequality as incompatible with an efficient market economy, price stability, and rapid growth. By contrast, Keynes, who wrote mainly from 1920 through the end of World War II, stressed the need for an activist government to stimulate demand, lower unemployment, and lessen income disparities. His perspective remains relevant for understanding the effect of public policies on income distribution during modern times when uncertainty, rapid change, and political turbulence face people all over the world.

Chapter 2 compares income distribution in the wealthy economies of Western Europe, North America, Australia, New Zealand, and Japan. Why did greater income equality emerge during the 1950–1975 period than after 1980? The priority placed on Keynesian and neoliberal beliefs partly explains this trend and cross-national differences. More egalitarian outcomes emerged from expenditure, tax, monetary, regulatory, and labor-market policies. Redistribution from wealthier to poorer individuals occurred because of generous, comprehensive, universal social-service programs. Progressive income taxes had a weaker impact. Policies that deregulated government control of private corporations and especially financial institutions produced greater income inequality. When corporations increased their power over labor unions during the late 1970s, neoliberal policymakers supported this change, which affected workers' wages, social-service benefits, and rights to participate in management.

Exploring income inequality among different political systems in Central and Eastern Europe, Asia, and Latin America, chapter 3 compares three types of political systems: elitist mobilization, bureaucratic-authoritarian, and reconciliation. These models highlight a society's basic features, especially values, power structures, and individual preferences. Led by party-state managers, elitist mobilization systems attained extensive income equality in Maoist China and the Soviet Union under Stalin, even though party-state elites and urban residents gained the most benefits. Aiming to achieve rapid industrialization, bureaucratic-authoritarian systems followed a program of developmental capitalism. After Mao died and the Soviet Union collapsed, the bureaucratic-authoritarian regimes in China (1978–2010) and Russia (1991–2010) placed a higher priority on rapid industrial growth than on income equality. A similar trend occurred in Latin American military dictatorships that governed from the end of World War II until the 1980s. However, the military officers who ruled South Korea and Taiwan secured not only rapid industrialization but also greater economic equality. Reconciliation systems differed across developing countries, but all of them merged pluralist arrangements with elitist features. Policies toward income equality originated from political leaders' value priorities and the power relationships among government institutions, competitive political parties, private corporations, and unions.

As chapter 4 emphasizes, global interdependence interacted with domestic policies to affect the income gap. Elites who dominated nation-states, multinational corporations, global development banks, and the mass media conglomerates exercised the power to translate their policy preferences into binding public policies. Their power extended to the cultural, economic, and political arenas. The media communicated information and cultural values. Economic decisions revolved around foreign trade, overseas investment, and labor migration, mainly to wealthier countries. The most powerful nation-states influenced these cultural and economic policies, particularly the stand toward immigration as well as fiscal programs that affected foreign investment and trade. After 1980 most policies reinforced the trend toward greater inequality within specific countries. Besides multinational financial institutions, the International Monetary Fund, World Bank, and World Trade Organization upheld the interests of wealthy creditors more than debtors, particularly low-income consumers and small businesses. Austerity programs preferred by financiers heightened national income differences. Neither global union organizations nor worldwide leftist movements had sufficient power to mobilize resources for more egalitarian outcomes.

Chapter 5 relies on the resource mobilization perspective to illuminate the goals, tactics, and outcomes of protest movements. What values motivate people to participate in protests? How do the movement's tactics influence the policy process? Why are some protests more successful than others in attaining egalitarian policies? A comparison of China, India, three Latin American societies (Mexico, Brazil, and Argentina), Western Europe, and the United States indicates that an egalitarian protest movement most effectively mobilizes resources when structural opportunities exceed constraints. An appealing ideological vision rallies support behind the cause, which combines material interests with cultural values affirming social justice. Political leaders use pragmatic tactics adapted to the changing historical context. Government agencies refrain from coercing protesters. Under these conditions, the prospects for successful goal attainment rise.

Reconciliation leaders confront three policy dilemmas about the relationships among capitalism, democracy, and economic inequality. First, how does procedural justice that stresses equal justice under the law shape distributive justice programs seeking more egalitarian outcomes? Chapter 6 shows that Norwegian government leaders more effectively coped with this dilemma than did British or US officials. Second, how do policies for rapid economic growth affect workers' wages? Giving precedence to land distribution, inclusive public education, and labor-intensive capital investment for manufactured exports, South Korean policies achieved more equal results than did Indian government decisions. Third, what conditions shape elected leaders' perceptions about the interactions between representative democracy, which emphasizes competitive elections, and participatory democracy that strives for greater popular involvement over the policy process? Focusing on social democratic governments in Chile and Uruguay, chapter 6 explains why Uruguayan leftist officials combined participatory with representative democracy but still obtained higher income equality through their fiscal policies.

The concluding chapter 7 summarizes the impact of public policies on income distribution, highlights cross-national attitudes about economic equality, and explores the role of social scientists as they try to influence government decisions. Mobilizing support for egalitarian policies requires a blend of cultural values with effective mobilization by left-wing political parties, unions, social movements, and the media, particularly radio, television, and the Internet. Particularly when these organizations communicate clear, persuasive messages about feasible solutions for narrowing the income gap, government leaders will more likely adopt egalitarian proposals. Small group networks of relatives, friends, neighbors, and workmates who share inclusive cultural values seek generous expenditures for social services. According to cross-national sample surveys, individuals prefer public social-service programs that supply universal, generous benefits for employment opportunities, health care, education, and retirement. Yet when right-wing groups, international financial institutions, and major corporations oppose these programs, governments often enact austerity programs that reduce income equality. Through greater cohesion and more extensive social networks, these elitist organizations can more successfully attain their goals than the general public, especially its poorer sector. Plagued by fiscal deficits, even governing social democratic and labor parties implement austerity policies to receive loans from the dominant financial sector. When lower growth, higher unemployment, and greater inequality ensue, incumbent parties lose popularity. Despite the negative effects of austerity, social scientists who prefer a Keynesian rather than a neoliberal approach toward job creation faced limited influence over the policy process during the early twenty-first century.

Chapter One

Perspectives on Income Distribution

Keynes and Neoliberalism

F. Scott Fitzgerald took a caustic view of wealthy individuals. Published in 1926, *The Rich Boy* told the story of a young man who viewed the rich as superior to other people. Born into a wealthy Connecticut family, Anson Hunter had the money to graduate from Yale University and become an investment banker on Wall Street. As a stockbroker during the 1920s, he dined at the Yale Club, drank excessive amounts of alcohol, dated beautiful women, and took vacations in Palm Beach, Florida. Trips to London, the leading financial center along with New York City, expanded Anson's understanding of global financial capitalism. His lucrative salary and commissions led not only to an extravagant lifestyle but to high status. Despite Anson's social prestige, Fitzgerald held a skeptical attitude toward the rich: "Let me tell you about the very rich. They are different from you and me. They possess and enjoy early, and it does something to them, makes them soft where we are hard and cynical where we are trustful. . . . Even where they enter deep into our world or sink below us, they still think that they are better than we are" (Fitzgerald 1926, 28).

Misinterpreting Fitzgerald's outlook on the rich, Ernest Hemingway in his 1936 story "The Snows of Kilimanjaro" mocked his rival's "romantic awe" of the "glamorous" rich: "He had started a story once that began, 'The very rich are different from you and me'. . . . Someone had said to Scott, Yes they have more money" (Hemingway 1936, 200). Yet Fitzgerald actually criticized rich people's behavior. Writing to his daughter Frances during 1940, he labeled advertising businesses and brokerage firms as "rackets" that make no "constructive contribution to humanity" and "pay a big price in human values for their money." He even recommended that his daughter marry a lawyer, journalist, or politician rather than a business executive (Fitzgerald 1945, 299–300).

How does economic inequality affect poor Americans today? In her book *Nickel and Dimed*, Barbara Ehrenreich described how their conditions differed from the wealthy lifestyle of Anson Hunter. Ehrenreich took jobs as a waitress, house cleaner, and Walmart sales clerk. She earned low wages, worked long hours, and received few benefits such as overtime pay or health insurance. Repressive managers, who expected obedience to their hierarchical authority, showed little respect for workers, mainly women. Intimidation threatened those few who tried to organize a union. Without any public social-service benefits, employees had to rely on their families for support. During the 2007–2009 financial crisis, people lost their jobs, homes, and access to food. Local government agencies delayed granting food stamps and minimal cash benefits to needy families. The punitive bureaucracy charged the poor with laziness, addiction, and promiscuity. Case workers stigmatized the poor as "bums" who deserved no aid. State and municipal policies decreased expenditures for public transportation, public schools, and public housing. Police harassed street vendors, beggars, and the homeless. Under these conditions, low-income persons depended on informal social networks—family, friends, neighbors—for assistance. Those without any network affiliations gained food by shooting squirrels, rabbits, or raccoons (Ehrenreich 2009).

During the early twenty-first century, many poor people protested their economic deprivation, as indicated by the Occupy movements that spread across cities throughout the United States. These movements recalled the populist struggles that occurred in the 1930s depression. At that time, Yip Harburg wrote a song titled "Brother, Can You Spare a Dime?" The lyrics perceived labor as a benefit, not a cost. Affirming the need for worker solidarity, Harburg praised workers who fought in wars, farmed the land, and built railroads. Today many wealthy corporate executives give few dimes to the working poor but receive billions from the US government.

Social scientists have used several indicators measuring the degree of economic well-being: wealth, poverty, income, and such resources as technical skills, educational achievements, and cultural values that parents transmit to their children. All societies experience greater differences in wealth than disposable income because wealth comprises ownership of cash, private transfers, retirement accounts, a home, landed property, stocks, bonds, and jewelry minus a family's debts. Hence, the richest 10 percent enjoy the most wealth. Cross-national poverty rates depend on techniques for measuring this variable. When poverty refers to one-half the median income, it bears a close correlation with the gini coefficient, a standardized measure of inequality that controls for the number of individuals in each household and facilitates comparisons across different countries (OECD 2008, 125–54). Named after the Italian statistician Corrado Gini, the gini compares the percentage of households in a nation with the proportion of total disposable income possessed by them. Disposable income includes the following types: earnings (wages, salaries), self-employment income, capital assets (interest, dividends, rent), and public cash transfers minus direct taxes and social security contributions. If each tenth of the national population holds 10 percent of the income, a society demonstrates full equality. When 1 percent of households possesses 90 percent of income, high inequality results. The gini ranges from 0 (all households have an equal income) to 1 (one household retains all income). During the early twenty-first century, ginis throughout the world ranged from around .25 to .60, with higher ginis in most developing nations than in Europe or the United States. As table 1.1 shows, the least inequality occurred in Denmark, Norway, Finland, Belgium, and the Czech Republic (Milanovic 2011, 3–36, 149–97).

Sizable income differences prevail in Asia and Latin America. Because of the large informal sectors and rural populations in these countries, economists cannot ascertain precise quantitative indicators of poverty or income distribution. Surveyors have collected the most extensive data from individuals in Organization for Economic Cooperation and Development (OECD) countries, which have urban, literate populations with greater access to information than held by individuals of most developing nations. Fewer surveys take place in the less industrialized societies, especially among low-income, less formally educated rural residents. Throughout the world, neither tax records nor sample surveys provide accurate information about the whole population. Not only self-employed businesspersons and workers in the rural sector but particularly wealthy people fail to report their total income. Given the understaffed administrative organization for revenue collection, extensive tax avoidance occurs. Longitudinal analyses become difficult because evidence about income distribution in most developing countries first appeared during the 1980s. Despite these qualifications, table 1.1 shows that high-income nations in Central Europe experienced the greatest equality around 2005–2010. Their ginis resembled ones in Northern Europe. South Koreans had slightly fewer income disparities than did the Japanese. Among the most industrialized societies, the United States faced the widest income gap. Measures of income inequality remain particularly tentative in China, Russia, and India. Nevertheless, the largest income differences probably occurred in these nations and Latin American countries with the highest gross domestic product (GDP), such as Mexico, Argentina, Chile, and especially Brazil (ECLAC 2011b, 70, 79; Korzeniewicz and Moran 2009, 1022; Milanovic 2011, 29–31; 2012, 8–12; OECD 2011a, 45, 51; 2013a; World Bank 2011, 68–71).

How can we best explain income distribution among rich and poorer nations? The distinction between "developed" and "developing" countries

Table 1.1. Income Inequality among Nations

Nation	*Date*	*Gini*
Denmark	2010	.25
Norway	2010	.25
Belgium	2010	.26
Czech Republic	2010	.26
Finland	2010	.26
Austria	2010	.27
Sweden	2010	.27
Hungary	2009	.27
Germany	2010	.29
Netherlands	2010	.29
France	2010	.30
Switzerland	2009	.30
Poland	2010	.305
South Korea	2010	.31
Canada	2010	.32
Italy	2010	.32
New Zealand	2009	.32
Australia	2009	.33
Ireland	2009	.33
Greece	2010	.34
Japan	2009	.34
Portugal	2010	.34
Spain	2010	.34
United Kingdom	2010	.34
United States	2010	.38
Turkey	2009	.41
Uruguay	2010	.42
Mexico	2010	.47
Russia	2007	.48
China	2012	.49
Chile	2011	.50
Argentina	2010	.51
India	2005	.54
Brazil	2009	.58

Sources: Economic Commission for Latin America and the Caribbean, *Social Panorama of Latin America* (Santiago, Chile: United Nations, 2011), 75–76; OECD, "Crisis Squeezes Income and Puts Pressure on Inequality and Poverty" (Paris: OECD, 2013); OECD, *Divided We Stand: Why Inequality Keeps Rising* (Paris: OECD, 2011), 45, 51; OECD, *Society at a Glance: Asia/Pacific 2011* (Paris: OECD, 2011), 64–65; Edward Wong, "Survey in China Shows a Wide Gap in Income," *New York Times*, July 20, 2013, A9.

Note: Ginis for disposable household income range from 0 (when all households have the same income after personal taxes and government expenditures) to 1 (when one household in a nation possesses all income). Data include income after taxes and social service expenditures.

underestimates some shared cultural values, organizational networks, and public policies. However different their income levels, societies throughout the world feature similar values and power structures that produce programs affecting income inequality. This book explores the degree to which generalizations about policy impacts in the most industrialized countries also hold true for Central and Eastern Europe, Asia, and Latin America. How do cultural values, structural conditions, and individual preferences within each society and the global arena explain support for egalitarian policies? Which specific policies most effectively secure greater equality?

Several assumptions guide this investigation about political power and economic inequality. Reciprocal interactions underlie each assumption. First, just as the economy shapes political life, so political power influences economic development. Today capitalism thrives throughout the world. The different forms all experience market exchanges, private production for profit, and bank credit. Some individuals work as self-employed entrepreneurs. Particularly in the industrialized nations, most workers earn a wage or salary. Few people control productive resources and the distribution of a firm's revenues. Even though the market society retains some degree of autonomy from the government, public policies affect the exchanges in producer, consumer, financial, and labor markets. Market exchanges depend on expenditure, tax, monetary, ownership, regulatory, and labor-market programs implemented by government officials. Private corporations receive government subsidies, tax credits, licenses, and contracts. Policies toward wages and collective bargaining shape the income of workers. Interest rates set by central banks determine opportunities for businesses to accumulate capital, for families to purchase a home, and for consumers to buy a TV set. Ownership and regulatory policies influence employee salaries and corporate profits (Wolff 2012, 19–26).

Capitalism not only transforms the economy but also produces changes in political power. The service sector gains dominance over manufacturing. Whereas manufacturing unions lose political influence, financial institutions increase their influence over the policy process. Changes linked to business cycles and uneven capitalist development spur inequalities among diverse occupations, economic groups, and geographic regions. The policies to handle these inequalities often wield a greater effect on income distribution than do technological innovations and demographic changes. Not just disposable income after government expenditures and taxes but market income partly stems from policymakers' decisions. Under all these conditions, the distinction between the public political sector and the private economic sector becomes blurred (Ingham 2008, 52–62, 92–118; Panitch and Gindin 2012, 1–21; Stanford 2008, 17–39; Volscho and Kelly 2012).

Second, national conditions demonstrate an interdependence with global patterns of trade, foreign investment, labor migration, and communications.

Domestic life depends on decisions made by multinational corporations, the International Monetary Fund, the World Bank, the World Trade Organization, regional development banks, and their allies. Multinational investors, financiers, and traders especially affect the income of those in developing nations. The reserves and exports by China, Brazil, and oil-producing Middle Eastern nations lead to income changes among more developed countries. In this era of capitalist globalization, the multinational ExxonMobil oil corporation advertises about "leveling the playing field for women around the world." Appeals to women in the developing world consider them "a vast, largely untapped reservoir of economic potential." Exploring the connection between national and global trends, this book inquires, "Sister, can you paradigm?" Three theoretical perspectives—cultural values, resource mobilization, and rational choice—offer tentative answers.

Third, cultural values about justice interact with structural opportunities to affect individual choices in the policy arena. Each variable depends on the other. Several organizations—government agencies, political parties, corporations, unions, lobbies, nongovernmental associations, social movements—transmit discourses about the justice of specific public policies. These organizations provide the resources for mobilizing the public behind a cultural vision that gives general meaning to specific persons. Even if groups have extensive access to resources and structural opportunities, preferences toward income distribution policies will never succeed unless individuals take action to realize goals. From the individualist perspective favored by Fitzgerald, motives, preferences, perceptions, attitudes, and expectations become crucial guides to behavior. They influence individuals' decisions about the most effective ways to achieve their policy preferences.

EXPLANATIONS OF INCOME INEQUALITY

Approaches toward resource mobilization, cultural values, and individual preferences help us understand the causes of public policies as well as the impact of specific decisions on income distribution. Among the several theoretical perspectives—symbolic discourse, Marxism, modern world-systems, rational choice—resource mobilization provides the clearest insights that explain specific interactions among such general variables as structural conditions, cultural values, and personal preferences. Stressing general trends about cross-national patterns of income inequality, the book highlights the complex relationships linking political power, public policies, and economic inequality.

Resource Mobilization

No matter how egalitarian their cultural values or policy preferences, political leaders cannot transform their beliefs into government action unless they mobilize resources behind effective organizations. Mobilizing structures include government organizations, political parties, private business corporations, labor unions, media, and social movements. These organizations must accumulate resources, motivate supporters to participate in political action, and effectively use resources to rally followers but demobilize opponents. Several types of resources become valuable assets: general information, technical expertise, communication channels, organizational skills, weapons, finances, usable time, energy, popular enthusiasm, morale, authority that derives from high status, leadership, moral righteousness, and personal charm. When an organization possesses a high volume of resources, its leaders try to transform one type of resource into another kind. For example, leaders may convert money into communication channels or information into high status.

Effective mobilizers realize their egalitarian goals when structural opportunities exceed constraints. A unified political discourse rallies supporters behind an egalitarian cause that affirms moral and material values. Idealistic purists ally with pragmatists. Through widespread media, leaders frame a discourse that communicates an ethical vision of economic justice. Written and particularly oral stories promote similar ways of thinking about the causes of injustice, possible solutions, and strategies for goal attainment. Shared emotions, such as anger against injustice and hope for reduced income differences, motivate supporters to participate in political action. Because of expected moral and material benefits that may result from egalitarian policies, supporters assume that mobilization will achieve a successful, desirable outcome.

Mobilizing structures show a high cohesion based on powerful social networks. Small groups like personal friendships permeate the larger organization. Sharing similar information, values, interests, and policy preferences, they promote a strong collective solidarity. High interpersonal trust enhances a common identity. Leaders who maintain connections with several other networks wield the greatest influence over policymakers.

Committed to greater equality, the mobilizing organization obtains support from key allies. It forms coalitions with sympathetic government agencies, leftist political parties, unions, consumer groups, populist social movements, ecological associations, and overseas institutions. Voluntary associations ally with political parties and government agencies to back egalitarian policy preferences. Through consensual strategies, mobilizers in democratic societies expand their support, encouraging potential recruits to join the movement. Under more authoritarian conditions, leaders use greater coercion to recruit followers and intimidate opponents.

When structural constraints overwhelm opportunities, egalitarian mobilizers gain less policy influence. Neither moral nor material motives form part of a political discourse that frames stories about the need for increased income equality. Proclaiming a moral vision, purists disdain working with pragmatists who seek to negotiate compromises. When social changes occur, strategies remain the same. No effective communication channels transmit optimistic messages to followers about the favorable prospects for mobilization. Widespread political apathy dissuades individuals from taking risks. Diverse interests and values hinder the opportunity to rally behind a common cause. No unified small group networks supply cohesion to the larger organization. Supporters who prefer egalitarian policies remain atomized, isolated, demoralized, and distrustful of others. Extensive repression by groups opposed to economic equality intimidates potential joiners. Allied with hostile government officials, private corporations reject egalitarian policies. Unions have limited power. Stressing the need for order, security, and obedience to established authority, police deter protesters from engaging in political action. Confronting numerous restraints, egalitarian mobilizers secure few alliances with either government officials or leaders of influential political parties, voluntary associations, and social movements. Because the costs of mobilization appear to exceed the benefits, political leaders need to communicate cultural values that motivate, educate, and energize supporters behind the cause of economic justice (Andrain and Apter 1995, 207–302; Joas and Knöbl 2009, 110–15; McAdam, Tarrow, and Tilly 2001; O'Hearn 2009; Ormerod 2012, 96–192; Starr, Fernandez, and Scholl 2011; Stinchcombe 2005, 214–27; Tarrow 2011).

Cultural Values

Four cultural values—equality, individualism, hierarchy, and fatalism—shape interpretations of economic justice. These values frame the basic problems facing a society, influence crucial policy options that may help resolve problems, and justify selected policies. When key leaders regard poverty and ill health, rather than fiscal deficits, as major problems, they reject austerity policies during periods of low growth. Larger public expenditures for social services become a primary policy option. Appeals to social solidarity, job security, and personal freedom enhance egalitarian policies. If a society's dominant values uphold cooperative individualism, minimize fatalism, downplay deference to hierarchical elites, and affirm the shared, universal qualities of all persons, policies will seek more equal opportunities and income. When anger against economic injustice arises, high political efficacy strengthens hope for greater social equality. Opposite hegemonic values hinder the emergence of egalitarian programs. Atomistic, passive individualism prevails. Hierarchical values espoused by ruling elites justify inequality. Fatalism regards maldistribution of wealth as natural, inevitable, and undesirable. Egalitarian justice seems infeasible (Douglas and Ney 1998, 96–185; Jones 2011; Wildavsky 1998).

Neither individuals nor societies uphold only one core value. Instead, diverse values compete for dominance and combine to influence public policies. For example, corporate executives often synthesize individualist support for entrepreneurial freedom with hierarchy that justifies secret operations, government subsidies, and low taxes on business. From 1950 through the early 1980s, when social democratic parties governed Scandinavia, they reconciled bureaucratic hierarchy with implementation of egalitarian social benefits. After promarket values gained appeal in the 1980s, the greens, socialist left, and left-wing social democrats linked equality to expanded individual choice as ways to retain many egalitarian programs that provided universal benefits but in a decentralized way.

Even if general values remain stable, specific interpretations of the four values often change when societies face war, economic crises, and global competition. Under the different historical context, individuals abandon old interpretations and seek new meanings that help them understand social change. New coalitions of government agencies, political parties, interest groups, and popular movements arise to mobilize resources for new policy preferences. For instance, equality assumed a different meaning in 1973, when Socialists and Communists governed Chile with President Allende, than during the early 2000s, when the Socialists allied with the Christian Democrats to control cabinet ministries. Whereas the Allende administration tried to implement a transformative redistribution program, thirty years later Socialist presidents backed incremental policies for expanding equal opportunities (Andrain and Smith 2006, 94–104; Sandel 2009, 31–102, 140–66, 265–69; Swedlow 2011).

Individual Preferences

Besides cultural values and structural conditions, individuals play a crucial role in political life. Individual preferences, motives, expectations, perceptions, emotions, and beliefs affect policy performance. The specific person interprets cultural values and seeks information from various organizations. She retains some freedom from cultural and structural restraints to make independent choices. Instead of an organic whole, society functions as an aggregate of individuals who have diverse interests, values, and preferences. They often hold divergent interpretations of such values as equality. Some persons prefer policies that facilitate greater equality before the law and more equal opportunities for upward social mobility. Other individuals place priority on a reduced income gap between rich and poor. Although references to nations, governments, political parties, private corporations, and market institutions identify them as singular entities (artificial persons), individuals head them all. Their leaders reveal heterogeneous opinions about collective group interests, policy preferences, and the most effective strategies for realizing desired outcomes, such as enhanced income equality.

Taking a strategic orientation, individuals often try to estimate the usefulness of alternative ways for attaining a desired outcome. Participants in the policy process—government officials, corporate executives, union leaders, media personalities, activist citizens—calculate the costs and benefits of egalitarian programs. If they estimate that the benefits to the self, group, and nation outweigh the costs, they will back these policies. Particularly when individuals place a high value on equality, feel politically efficacious, take advantage of structural opportunities, and secure information that allies have greater power than opponents, effective actions to obtain egalitarian income policies become more likely (Andrain and Apter 1995, 160–65; Becker and Posner 2009, 4–8; Bresser-Pereira 2012; Cassidy 2009, 151–204; Dewan and Shepsle 2008a, 2008b; Elster 2007, 191–231, 460–65; Hardin 2009; Sheena Iyengar 2010, 74–140; Kahneman 2011, 276–309, 411–18; Rueschemeyer 2009, 40–106, 152–227).

As John Maynard Keynes recognized, rational choice and material gain hardly comprise the only motives that explain personal preferences. Faced with uncertain outcomes, individuals often base their preferences not just on rational calculations but on their ideological biases, conventional opinions, habits, hunches, peer group norms, and emotions. Even though material gains, such as wage increases and lower taxes, form an important personal incentive, moral-spiritual values often affect an individual's policy agenda. Leaders may pursue ethical values—justice, civic virtue, procedural fairness—for society, not only enhanced material rewards for the self and a particular group. They use these values to frame their preferences, justify their policies, and thereby widen support for specific programs focused on income distribution (Keynes 1973c, 149–54, 383–84).

PERSPECTIVE OF KEYNES

John Maynard Keynes (1883–1946), who wrote most of his books and articles from 1919 through the end of World War II, explained the causes of income distribution and recommended tentative policies that would reduce economic inequalities. Even though policymakers departed from some of his more specific recommendations, his general beliefs won widespread support in democratic industrialized countries from World War II until the 1970s, when both inflation and unemployment increased. Keynes functioned as a political economist who blended general theory with reliable statistical evidence. Opposed to doctrinaire, rigid theories, he formulated general explanations that applied to changing conditions. When the historical context changed, Keynes believed that theorists should not only write reports that analyze a problem but recommend new practical solutions to reduce high unemployment, low wages, trade imbalances, and unstable prices (Keynes 1972, 335–66). According to him, economic analysis must have relevance for government decision making. As his student and later Cambridge University colleague Austin Robinson (1947, 10) commented, "His absorbing interest in politics and government made Keynes, in the very best sense of those words, a political economist." Along with a focus on incremental reform, pragmatism and feasibility guided his policy proposals. Skeptical of closed minds in all persons, whatever their social status, Keynes took a pragmatic, tolerant position when formulating his policy preferences. Because theories must adapt to the dynamic, volatile conditions within capitalist societies, future effects of specific policies remain uncertain. Hence, his policy positions, like the desirability of free trade, changed as the international context changed.

Keynes showed scant deference to ruling elites, even though he wanted the highest achievers with superior knowledge, education, and competence to govern society. Perceiving politics as the "survival of the unfit," Keynes (1978, 147) assumed that economists who advised politicians should function as dentists, as humble specialists who diagnosed social ailments and recommended tentative treatments (Keynes 1972, 311, 332; 1981a, 222; 1982a, 87–88; 1982b, 36). In 1944 he mentioned his difficulty keeping a "straight face" when negotiating with US Treasury officials: "I try to prepare and sustain myself by repeating the three vows which I always make before a visit to America, namely, one that I will drink no cocktails, two that I will obey my wife, and three that I will never allow myself to be betrayed into speaking the truth" (Keynes 1980d, 134).

Rather than a specialized economist who wove logical deductive theories, Keynes played several roles that linked his analyses to practical issues. Educated at Eton and Cambridge, he was a Cambridge University lecturer beginning in 1909 and lasting until World War II. There he gave lectures to the brightest undergraduate students and advised them in the Political Economy Club. As a civil servant, Keynes held a position at the India Office (1906–1908), functioned in the British Treasury during both world wars (1915–1919, 1940–1946), collaborated with Bank of England officials, and after World War II served as Britain's governor on the International Monetary Fund and the World Bank. Through all these administrative positions, Keynes concentrated on devising policies that would secure loans for Britain during the two wars, promote prosperous postwar economies, regulate investment, and secure fixed but adjustable currency values designed to facilitate balanced world trade. From 1943 to 1946, he served as a Liberal member of the House of Lords. With his persuasive rhetoric and clear thinking,

Keynes helped persuade his fellow lords to approve in early 1946 the Bretton Woods agreement that established the International Monetary Fund and World Bank. As senior financial administrator of King's College, Cambridge, he invested in equity stocks that yielded high long-term dividends. His experiences also involved work as chairman of the National Mutual Life Assurance Society and as director of several investment companies. Through these activities, Keynes gained knowledge of practical economic problems, particularly the distinction between the most desirable options and the most probable results (Chambers and Dimson 2013; Keynes 1983, 1, 219).

Keynes sought to persuade public opinion through writings that reflected clear, logical analyses. He wrote numerous books, edited the *Economic Journal* (1911–1946), and published articles in the *Manchester Guardian*, the *Evening Standard*, and the *New Statesman and Nation*. As close friend of authors Virginia Woolf, Lytton Strachey, and E. M. Forster, he incorporated insights from literature, philosophy, ethics, history, sociology, political science, and economics into his works. Married to the ballerina Lydia Lopokova, he promoted music and the arts, particularly ballet. His wife helped ensure that his beliefs about economic justice reflected humane moral values. Keynes wanted government officials to unite practical reforms with ethical ideals: social justice, public service, scientific knowledge, intellectual freedom, and civic virtue (P. Clarke 2009; Keynes 1981a, 639; 1982a, 233–46; A. Robinson 1947; Skidelsky 2009, 133–53).

The interpretations of economic justice expressed by Keynes focused on equality and individualism. Whereas Keynes supported economic and cultural equality, he placed lower priority on political equality. From his viewpoint, government should narrow income disparities caused by speculative corporations that gamble people's money, exploit their ignorance, and take excessive risks. Rejecting hierarchical domination, he condemned corporate actions that restricted credit, produced higher unemployment, and lowered wages for workers, who faced the choice of starvation or submission to wealthier classes. For him, women as well as men deserved higher wages. Opposed to discrimination against women and ethnic groups, Keynes showed lower regard for populist political equality. Perceiving most voters as too ill-informed about complex issues, he wanted educated professionals and competent experts, especially civil servants, to govern the society along with a strong elected parliament. His belief in the personal liberties of thought, expression, and faith combined with a moral concern for service to the community (Keynes 1971b, 281–83; 1972, 222–23, 291–93, 302–3, 373; 1973c, 157–60, 372–81; 1981a, 444; 1983, 239).

Although Keynes praised competitive capitalism for its efficient use of resources to achieve material prosperity, he criticized its ethical failings. Short-term material gains, such as high profits, took priority over long-term regard for social well-being: justice, beauty, and scientific knowledge. For many corporate executives, traders, and entrepreneurs, capital accumulation became an end, not a means to higher growth. Speculation triumphed over investment in schools, hospitals, and transportation that would expand employment and reduce income inequalities. When depression, joblessness, and income disparity increased, the poor, unemployed persons faced low morale, little self-confidence, and humiliating treatment by others. Capitalism needed an activist government to promote not only stable capital investment, lower unemployment, and reduction of income disparities but also civic virtue that transcends private economic interests (Backhouse and Bateman 2011, 47–75, 139–59; Keynes 1972, 222–29; 1973c, 157).

Resource mobilization theory helps explain the influence of Keynes over British government policies. A high-ranking civil servant during both world wars, Keynes possessed the resources to shape government decisions. With his wealth, general knowledge, technical expertise, and discursive skills, he could persuade diverse audiences and gain numerous allies: political leaders, government officials, writers, intellectuals, university professors, economists. His small group networks strengthened interpersonal trust, social cohesion, and shared values. As an idealist concerned to uphold moral obligations and a pragmatist who could devise innovative policy solutions when conditions changed, Keynes mobilized his resources to lessen unemployment and income inequality.

Keynes wanted government institutions to play an activist role in coping with economic problems such as high unemployment, rising prices, and trade imbalances. When public programs curtail the booms and busts in a market economy, they help ensure a more prosperous, egalitarian society. To avoid this economic volatility, governments should enact policies that effectively adapt to changing conditions. By providing accurate information, government can reduce uncertainty and help people manage economic decisions, especially during periods of rapid change. Rather than rely on private enterprises to stimulate capital investment, Keynes supported a central government board of public investment to plan this state-financed investment through low-interest loans. Higher investment would not only expand productive supply but also increase aggregate demand. Particularly when investment occurs within the nation, rather than overseas, employment rises as workers build houses, roads, public transportation, post offices, and electric power facilities (Keynes 1972, 146–48, 292; 1973c, 94–95; 1981a, 223–27, 444, 692; 1982a, 109, 182–83, 394).

Although during the 1930s Keynes placed priority on securing full employment, he also backed policies that aimed to reduce income inequality. He favored redistributive programs—education, health care, family allowances, pensions, unemployment assistance—that stimulate consumption by poorer people. His tax preferences supported higher income taxes on the wealthy but lower sales taxes paid by consumers. Opposed to government-mandated wage reductions during a depression, he believed that the resulting decline in aggregate demand (purchasing power) would forestall a recovery. By causing increased expenditures by consumers and businesses, low interest rates not only prevent creditors from earning lucrative rewards from expensive loans but also provide incentives for consumers to purchase more goods and for businesses to produce them. When treasury department officials accountable to an elected legislature retain some government controls over the central bank, financiers feel less inclined to make speculative, risky investments that enrich the wealthy, especially executives heading multinational corporations (Keynes 1972, 148, 394–97; 1973b, 132; 1973c, 158–63, 321–26, 372–83; 1978, 58; 1981a, 121, 221, 676–77, 689; 1982a, 131).

Even if these policy recommendations involved a more extensive scope of government power, including greater state planning and regulation of private businesses, Keynes wanted practical results, not a doctrinaire application of laissez-faire practice, to determine the interaction between public and private enterprises. As partners, both must pursue wise, efficient management that serves the community, not merely the private advantage of their directors. Monopolistic industries endanger the competitive economy because their managers operate in secret and fail to provide accurate information about assets. According to Keynes, large corporations operate as lotteries exacerbating income inequality. He recommended that semiautonomous agencies with partial independence from the central government check monopolistic power. Along with government organizations, they should undertake most capital investment planned by national policymakers.

Dedicated to a competitive but regulated market economy, Keynes rejected the repressive type of state socialism in Stalin's Soviet Union. From his perspective, its dogmatic interpretation of Marxism venerated the official hegemonic ideology as a secular political religion promising eventual human equality in a classless society. Egalitarian goals justified dictatorial means. The zealous converts spread their ideological vision through bribery, intolerance, violence, and persecution. Stalin's coercive tactics purged Communist Party members who had worked as missionaries for the transformative cause (Keynes 1972, 256–94; 1973c, 380; 1980b, 322, 326; 1981a, 695–98; 1982a, 88–92; 1982b, 72).

Taking a pragmatic view of labor unions and political parties, Keynes had scant regard for doctrinaire organizations. During the 1920s he criticized the Labour Party and its allied trade unions for operating autocratically, inciting class warfare, and demanding excessive wage increases when the economy boomed. He saw the Conservative Party as committed to contradictory, dogmatic programs. It upheld a laissez-faire ideology but enacted high protective tariffs. Committed to the individual liberty associated with the Liberal Party, Keynes gave it stronger support, particularly during the immediate post–World War I decade. He worked closely with Liberal Party government officials, such as David Lloyd George, who enacted egalitarian social-service policies for health care, pensions, and unemployment insurance. Late in the 1920s Keynes taught at the Liberal Summer School. When the Depression struck Britain in 1929 and lasted until the outbreak of World War II, he backed a Liberal government alliance with the Labour Party. Before the war, Keynes also maintained close ties with Conservative Party leader Harold Macmillan. As prime minister from 1957 to 1963, Macmillan implemented more egalitarian public policies than did later Conservative and Labour government officials (Cardim de Carvalho 2008–2009; P. Clarke 2009, 59–92; Hakhverdian 2009; Keynes 1972, 295–311; 1982a, 33–35; A. Robinson 1947, 37–38; Sheehan, 2009; Skidelsky 2009).

When advising British governments and corporations, Keynes doubted the extent of rational behavior among individuals, whether political leaders, business executives, or voters. Rather than assume that rational calculations guide all actions, he believed that nonrational attitudes also affect behavior. Conventions, peer group conformity, emotions, whims, and what he labeled "animal spirits" scarcely facilitate precise mathematical formulas: "Most, probably, of our decisions to do something positive . . . can only be taken as a result of animal spirits—of a spontaneous urge to action rather than inaction, and not as the outcome of a weighted average of quantitative benefits multiplied by quantitative probabilities" (Keynes 1973c, 161).

Keynes doubted that economists can accurately predict the long-range consequences of current policies. Values, structural conditions, perceptions, and expectations change. When economists advise government officials, uncertainty about future outcomes confounds attempts to estimate the precise economic benefits or costs that will result from present decisions: "This *long run* is a misleading guide to current affairs. *In the long run* we are all dead. Economists set themselves too easy a task if in tempestuous seasons they can only tell us when the storm is long past the ocean is flat again" (Keynes 1971a, 65). Under the changing historical context, the most rational proposals for public policies reflect tentative judgments. Although trained as a mathematician, Keynes felt that algebraic formulas cannot fully explain how most choices arise from complex variables: values, expectations, peer group interactions, the cohesion of elite networks.

According to Keynes, private investors do not always choose rational strategies that promote the public good or bring advantages to the general society. If such investors hoard their money, a disequilibrium emerges between capital investment (supply) and expenditures for consumption (demand). This imbalance produces high unemployment and income inequality over a lengthy period. Because capitalist markets do not automatically restore an equilibrium between supply and demand, they need activist government policies that will stabilize capital investment, expand jobs, and enhance consumer purchasing power (Akerlof and Shiller 2009; Backhouse and Bateman 2011, 113–37; Keynes 1972, 268–69; 1973b, 109–24; 1973c, 153–63, 321–25, 372–83; 1980b, 427–46).

From the end of World War II through the early 1970s, Keynesian beliefs shaped public policies in most democratic nations throughout Western Europe, North America, Australia, New Zealand, and Latin America. The 1930s depression deprived many rich people of their wealth. The need for collective action promoted a strong government during World War II. Seeking to avoid the high unemployment that marked the Depression, political leaders after the war pursued reconstruction policies that stimulated high aggregate demand by consumers and workers. Soviet domination over Eastern Europe created fears among Western European democrats that excessive inequality in their societies would undermine political stability. Latin American countries faced prospects of revolution that might endanger both domestic and foreign private corporations, particularly US ones. Communist Party revolutions in China and Korea led South Korean and Taiwanese governments to enact egalitarian programs for land redistribution, inclusive public education, and a labor-intensive export manufacturing sector. Upholding a promarket capitalist economy, all these policymakers wanted governments to expand capital investment, lower unemployment, set interest rates, regulate banks, discourage financial speculation, and encourage businesses to pay workers wage increases that matched labor productivity. These Keynesian policies produced fairly high income equality.

PERSPECTIVE OF NEOLIBERALS

When world developments during the late 1970s weakened preferences for Keynesian policies, neoliberal beliefs attracted greater support from political elites. The Organization of Petroleum Exporting Countries (OPEC) raised oil prices in 1973–1975 and 1979. Lower economic growth, more unemployment, and higher inflation occurred. Unlike the 1950–1975 period, during the late 1970s labor productivity, capital investment, and corporate profits declined. When wage increases exceeded gains in labor productivity, unit labor costs rose. Business hostility to labor unions intensified. The economic stagnation plaguing the wealthiest capitalist societies after 1973 spread to Latin America and Eastern Europe. Discontent arose against nepotism, corruption, lower growth, and higher prices, especially for food and oil.

Neoliberals blamed Keynesian public programs for the economic stagnation. National government regulation of financial institutions waned. Private corporations assumed the main responsibility for capital investment. With increased globalization, central, retail, and investment banks invested more of their funds overseas. Global competition surged among multinational corporations. Seeking lower costs, they expanded foreign trade and overseas capital investment. As the manufacturing sector declined in the industrialized societies, manufacturing spread to developing nations like China, India, South Korea, Mexico, and Brazil. Everywhere the service sector, especially private financial services, became more prominent. Large banks, private insurance companies, hedge funds, equity firms, and mutual funds operated all over the world. These financial institutions speculated in risky activities. Corporations dominated labor unions, which exerted limited influence over collective bargains with employers. Families, private firms, charities, and local governments provided more social benefits than before to needy individuals. Taxes became more regressive. As a result of these neoliberal programs, most nations, particularly in Europe and North America, experienced less income equality after 1980 than during the 1950–1973 period (Andrain and Smith 2006, 24–30; Crouch 2008, 2009; Duménil and Lévy 2011, 1–169, 297–334; Genschel and Schwarz 2011; OECD 2008, 24–27, 52–53; OECD 2011a, 22–25, 45; OECD 2011e, 80–81; OECD 2011f, 66–67; Panitch and Gindin 2012, 133–42).

Why did neoliberal organizations succeed in mobilizing their resources behind programs that lowered economic equality? First, they possessed extensive resources, such as wealth, information, expertise, organizational skills, and close ties with government leaders. Second, neoliberals formed alliances with key elites, such as civil servants, cabinet ministers, jurists, probusiness political parties, corporate executives, and heads of mass media. Third, strong personal networks linked neoliberal organizations outside the government to public policymakers. Shared values, interests (power, wealth), and policy preferences reinforced cohesion. Fourth, a hegemonic discourse united neoliberals behind the cause of enhanced corporate power over government and greater independence of private businesses from direct political control. Research institutes propagated promarket neoliberal beliefs that gave precedence to economic freedom over equality. National think tanks included the Cato Institute and American Enterprise Institute (United States), Fraser Institute (Canada), Institute of Economic Affairs (Britain), Liberales Institut (Germany), and Instituto Liberal y Desarrollo (Chile). Economists in several intergovernmental organizations—International Monetary Fund, World Bank, World Trade Organization, Organization for Economic Cooperation and Development, European Commission, and regional development banks—communicated the same neoliberal positions as did private research institutes. Anti-Keynesian economists Friedrich Hayek, Ludwig von Mises, and Milton Friedman in 1947 founded the Mont Pelerin Society to uphold promarket programs throughout the world (Carroll 2009, 2010; Freeland 2012, 229–75; Gwartney, Hall, and Lawson 2010, 235–47; Wapshott 2011, 211–14).

Compared with Keynes, neoliberal economists showed less support for activist government policies that redistribute incomes in an egalitarian way.

For Friedrich Hayek, Milton Friedman, Robert Lucas, and Gary Becker, all of whom taught at the University of Chicago, government should reject policies that redistribute income to public sector workers, unionists, and poorer individuals. According to Hayek, present economic growth stems from past inequalities: "Even the poorest today owe their relative material well-being to the results of past inequality" (Hayek 1960, 44). Like neoliberals, Hayek placed the highest priority on strengthening private businesses in a market economy. Neoliberals doubted the desirability or ability of government officials to rectify market failures. Instead, they relied on voluntary associations and private entrepreneurial activities to realize economic justice. Rather than preferring egalitarian programs, neoliberals assumed that these policies stifle innovation, deter flexibility, and destroy personal freedom. Entrepreneurs who maximize production should gain the highest rewards (Cassidy 2009, 49–107). Procedural justice based on stable contracts and on rules ensuring private property rights became more important than substantive justice that produces more equal incomes.

Even if not all neoliberals held identical policy preferences, they shared similar beliefs about economic justice. As individualists, they equated justice with extensive personal freedom, especially the opportunity to operate private enterprises, expand productivity, and achieve success. Entrepreneurs must demonstrate individual virtues: innovation, hard work, achievement, ambition, and risk taking. The emphasis on personal choice combined with a preference for hierarchy. Subordinates should defer to expert authority by directors, managers, supervisors, and chief executives. Displaying high personal and political efficacy, these managerial elites enforce labor discipline over employees (Gwartney, Hall, and Lawson 2010, 219–29; Hayek 1960, 42–48, 136, 265–84, 305; K. Roberts 2008; Wade 2012, 31–36; Wapshott 2011, 207–25, 247–96).

Neoliberals wanted the central government to play a different role than it had performed during the postwar Keynesian era. Opposed to government activism supported by Keynes, they advocated a limited government that relies on market incentives, decentralization, private provision of most social services, and legal protections for individual economic freedom (J. Taylor 2012, 18–49, 59, 97). Private power took precedence over government power. Fearing gigantic government bureaucracies that exacerbate costs, neoliberals wanted individuals, families, voluntary associations, private enterprises, and local governments to finance such services as pensions, health care, education, and day care. State-owned enterprises should become privatized.

The neoliberal emphasis on the need for market autonomy and freedom from government control strengthened corporate power. Along with deregulated controls over financial flows, freer trade gave private corporations greater independence. Operating in hierarchical, secret ways, they gained generous subsidies, tax credits, licenses, contracts, and other incentives that expanded their resources. Overseas investment rose. Mergers and acquisitions enhanced the power of multinational corporations. Interchanges of personnel between government administrators and corporate executives allied private businesses with political leaders. Especially in dictatorial states, the police, military, and security forces quashed labor unions and populist movements that resisted corporate dominance. Even in more democratic regimes, these coercive agencies sided with private business. The market system gave private firms extensive freedom to hire employees, fire them, supply goods to consumers, and provide services. Threats of dismissal and capital flight deterred citizens from challenging the neoliberal discourse that dominated the private mass media.

Under the neoliberal agenda, neither leftist political parties nor labor unions wielded extensive policy influence. Unlike private corporations, they lacked the resources to organize their supporters behind a program of lower taxes on consumers, higher taxes on the rich, more generous government-financed social-service benefits, and tighter regulation of private business transactions. Neoliberal officials especially sought to weaken the power of unions that organized public employees. Allied with corporate heads, pro-business parties took a stand against unions. Even some European social democratic parties adopted a neoliberal program that gave more incentives to private enterprises than to their allies in trade unions. Fragmented by divergent interests, unions and left-wing parties lacked the organizational influence that they exerted during the Keynesian era from 1950 through 1975. Flexible labor market policies produced lower wages. More part-time, temporary jobs emerged. Workers received fewer private benefits (health care, pensions) but paid higher fees for them. Union influence in corporations declined. Managers gained greater ability to dismiss employees. By enhancing incentives for private corporations to decrease labor costs, these neoliberal programs reduced income equality (Albo 2007; Harvey 2005, 2007; Palma 2009; Pötzsch 2012; N. Thompson 2008).

Neoliberals have greater confidence than Keynes in their ability to calculate future outcomes with mathematical precision. Focusing on such variables as gross national product (GNP) per person, inflation rates, interest charges, capital investment ratios, and trade deficits, they elaborate formal deductive models with logically consistent assumptions. Computer specialists presumably possess sufficient information to make accurate predictions about long-range consequences. Hence, they can calculate the probability of achieving high returns for risky investments. According to neoliberals, egalitarian programs lead to irrational effects. Progressive taxes on the rich and comprehensive social-service expenditures for the whole population stimulate "free rides" that hinder innovation, flexibility, and productivity. Corporate profits fall. Investment and growth decline (Lawson 2009).

CONCLUSION

When the resource mobilization approach incorporates cultural values and individual preferences with structural conditions, it offers the most persuasive explanations for income distribution policies across several nations. The power of institutions and organizations dominating the policy process influences decisions about income equality. If organizations with egalitarian values govern the nation-state, the opportunities to implement generous, comprehensive, universal social-service policies rise. Along with allied unions, left-wing political parties mobilize a high electoral turnout, which facilitates their prospects for controlling the policy agenda. When they form an effective coalition with other political parties or factions of the dominant party, they can enact progressive income taxes. People receive high benefits for public health care, public education, government-financed day care, elder care, pensions, and public transportation. Sympathetic public media reinforce the egalitarian structures. Greater income equality results. Yet if unregulated private corporations, rightist political parties, and elitist media wield the most power over the policy process, structural constraints mount against egalitarian income distribution. Government officials feel little inclination to introduce new laws that would produce more equal outcomes (Brady 2009).

Relying on the resource mobilization perspective, the following chapters emphasize key issues about the causes and outcomes of income distribution policies. Chapter 2 probes the effect of several policies—expenditure, tax, ownership, regulation, labor market—on national income distribution in wealthy countries. The third chapter examines these policies in Central and Eastern Europe, Latin America, and Asia. Focusing on different types of political systems, it explains the power relationships among government institutions, political parties, private corporations, and labor unions. Chapter 4 on global capitalism explores the power of multinational corporations, dominant nation-states, and numerous intergovernmental financial institutions, including the International Monetary Fund, the World Bank, and the World Trade Organization. Chapter 5 considers activities outside formal government institutions, especially the impact of protest movements on support for egalitarian programs. Reviewing the relationship between economic inequality and political democracy, the sixth chapter highlights the dilemmas faced by government leaders who want to enact egalitarian policies under capitalist constraints. The concluding chapter 7 analyzes the impact of public opinion, social science research, and government decisions on income distribution.

Chapter Two

Policies and Income Distribution in Wealthy Nations

During the nineteenth century, Charles Dickens portrayed the impact of public policies on people's incomes. At a time of rapid industrialization when Britain emerged as the dominant global power, debtors suffered a cruel fate. After Dickens's father incurred unpaid debts, government officials sentenced him to Marshalsea Prison for three months. At age twelve, Charles had to leave school and work in a factory where he pasted labels on pots that contained black shoe polish. Even if this experience lasted only a year, it shaped his outlook the rest of his life. Several novels told stories of individuals who lost incomes after falling into debt. *Little Dorrit* had two parts. The first part on "Poverty" recounted the dark prison life of William Dorrit, who spent twenty-five years in the Marshalsea Prison. The second part about "Riches" depicted the brighter, happier times of Mr. Dorrit and his younger daughter Amy—Little Dorrit—as they traveled through Western Europe after his release from prison and the inheritance of a fortune. After leaving the blacking factory, Dickens from 1827 through the early 1830s worked as a junior law clerk, stenographer, and reporter who covered proceedings at Parliament. These experiences sensitized him to the legal obfuscations used by government officials to harass debtors.

Dickens denounced government officials for their inaction, obstructionism, and inefficiency. When Mr. Dorrit's partnership became bankrupt after supplying materiel to British troops fighting the Russians in the Crimean War (1853–1856), his major creditor, the Circumlocution Office, detained him for failing to repay his debts. Guided by the slogan, "HOW NOT TO DO IT," its officials used ponderous language to disguise their unwillingness to provide social services that would help reduce poverty. Assuming no responsibility for social misery, the Circumlocution Office blamed these problems on lack of private charity and on poor people's failure to demonstrate self-reliance. Middle-income persons who depended on financial speculation for their income were ruined when stocks collapsed.

Given the high unemployment rates and low wages facing England during the 1850s, many poor had to live in Bleeding Heart Yard, a neighborhood slum. Whereas they longed for "bread of comfort," rich elites feasted on luxurious dinners attended by all the "magnates" from the City of London, financial institutions, the House of Commons, the House of Lords, the Treasury, and the Church of England. Personal connections linked heads of private corporations and banks—"England's world-famed capitalists"—with members of Parliament, government ministries, and civil service. This alliance of economic and political elites strengthened cohesive social networks (Dickens 2003, 119–38, 148–58, 264–69, 427–29).

Protesting this elitism, Dickens expressed contempt toward cabinet ministries, Parliament, civil service, and financial elites who controlled the highest public positions. During the early 1850s, Britain endured cholera epidemics and a mismanaged war in Crimea. Immobilized by partisan squabbles between Tories and Whigs, parliamentarians refused to act. Instead, they deferred to cabinet ministries, especially the Treasury Office, which Dickens satirically labeled the "Circumlocution Office." Heading the most powerful government institution, Treasury officials constituted over 90 percent of government employees and controlled nearly all expenditures. Most senior Treasury posts went to aristocratic families. Many first and junior "lords" lacked competence to lead Britain in domestic or foreign affairs. Under direction of the Treasury, the Commissariat failed to support the British troops in the Crimean War. Troops suffered low pay, little food, ill health, and insufficient weapons, uniforms, and armed vehicles.

Adopting a laissez-faire attitude, the Treasury took little responsibility for resolving basic domestic problems. Sickness, inadequate sanitation facilities, starvation, unsafe housing, and deficient public education plagued the nation. Rather than provide social services, the government repressed workers who protested their dire conditions. Complacency, evasive discourse, and bureaucratic routine deterred attempts to change the policy process. Wealthy bankers became high-ranking officials in the Treasury. Conducting speculative investments, financiers swindled stockholders, forged documents, embezzled money, and defrauded the public (Douglas-Fairhurst 2011, 124; Easson 1999; Lund 1982; Philpotts 1993; Slater 2009, 387–431; Wall and Small 2003; Weiss 1982).

Forty years later, the novelist Anatole France described a similar elite-mass gap facing French society. According to him, although the French Revolution affirmed the value of equality, it established a political "empire of wealth" dominated by moneyed classes who acted like lords and masters. Citizenship meant maintaining the power of the idle rich. In *The Red Lily*, the poet Choulette attacked the chasm between political equality and economic inequality: "The poor must work under the majestic equality of the laws, which forbid rich and poor alike to sleep under bridges, to beg in the streets, and to steal bread" (France 1964, 110–11).

Even if Charles Dickens and Anatole France wrote their novels over one hundred years ago, their insights remain relevant today. Poor people still struggle to secure jobs, food, inexpensive health care, low-cost housing, and relief from debt. Particularly when high unemployment, low wages, and lack of credit occurred, these problems grew more severe. In France widespread homelessness forced many poor individuals to join *les misérables*. French youth, even the highly educated with university degrees, experienced joblessness, worked as unpaid interns, or could secure only part-time, temporary contracts. In Greece personal and government debts soared after 2008. Under pressure from financiers, bondholders, central banks, and international financial institutions, policymakers imposed austerity programs that reduced wages, limited union power, decreased the number of public-sector employees, lowered their salaries, and cut spending on pensions, education, health care, subsidized food, and other social services. The police used coercive tactics, such as tear gas and stun grenades, against Greeks who protested austerity. Finance and justice ministers supported a debtors' prison for those who owed tax authorities over 5,000 euros.

Similar dire conditions emerged in Spain. Unemployment soared to over 25 percent of the labor force. Over 50 percent of young people and immigrants lacked jobs. Public hospital wards closed. Children lacked teachers and science laboratories. After the housing boom collapsed, banks evicted homeowners who could not pay their mortgage-interest debts. Old people suffered from reduced pensions. Starving Spaniards searched garbage bins for food. Faced with declining public services, Catholic charities served more individuals in soup kitchens. In southern Spain, some mayors and union leaders staged raids against supermarkets (Buck 2012; Daley 2012; Hope 2012; Kouvelakis 2011; Tremlett and Roberts 2012; Trilling 2013). To cope with these problems, technocrats from the banking community became leading government officials, including prime minister. For many critics, these trends paralleled similar tendencies shown by the Circumlocution Office, which demanded austerity from the poor but no sacrifices by the rich.

The priority given to Keynesian and neoliberal beliefs shaped policymakers' decisions about income distribution. More specifically, egalitarian outcomes stemmed from expenditure, tax, monetary, regulatory, and labor-market programs. Redistribution from wealthier to poorer individuals resulted from generous, comprehensive, universal social-service benefits and to a lesser degree from progressive income taxes. When banks won greater independence from government control, deregulation policies helped intensify the financial crises that erupted during 2008. The politics of collective bargaining—the power of unions and businesses over working conditions—influenced wage settlements, pensions, health care, and rights to participate in management. National income equality depended on the effective implementation of these policies, which stemmed from the power of egalitarian elites to mobilize resources that commanded support from government officials, political parties, group allies, and the general public.

EXPENDITURE AND TAX POLICIES

Expenditure programs for social services secured the most egalitarian impact on people's income. Social scientists compared market income with disposable income after expenditures and taxes. Even market income, mainly salaries and wages for most individuals, derived partly from such public policies as property rights, stable contracts, product competition, sanitation facilities, and minimum wages. Yet in all industrialized nations, greater income equality emerged after public expenditures for social services. These included pensions, health care, education, disability payments, sick pay, family allowances, parental leaves, unemployment benefits, housing allowances, food subsidies, and active labor-market programs, including employment services, training, job relocation, and subsidized jobs (see table 2.1 for data on social services as a percentage of gross domestic product). Among these policies, public pensions and to a lesser degree child, family, disability, and social assistance benefits redistributed the most income to the poor. The impact of public pensions, unemployment compensation, and sick pay depended on coverage, replacement rates, qualifying periods, and duration of benefits. When the qualifying period shortened and the time period for securing these benefits lengthened, the income gap narrowed.

Not only generous benefits but their comprehensiveness and inclusiveness reduced inequality. Particularly when governments enacted universal social services applicable to all people, regardless of their income, equality increased. Lower administrative costs resulted from less bureaucratic surveillance. Instead of incurring stigma, recipients of universal services felt fewer social pressures when applying for health care, child care, and elder care. Individuals gained greater autonomy from family patriarchs. Middle-income persons perceived a balance between benefits and tax costs.

Noncash public services also decreased the income gap. If individuals had access to universal, government-financed health care and to public preprimary, primary, and secondary education, lower-income persons benefited, particularly children and the elderly. Private university education as well as privately financed health care brought greater gains to wealthier citizens (Garfinkel, Rainwater, and Smeeding 2010, 39–101; Kenworthy 2011, 5–17,

Table 2.1. Government Expenditures for Social Services in OECD Nations, 2010

Nation	*Total Expenditures for Social Services as % of GDP*	*Expenditures for Cash Benefits and Services as % of GDP*	*Expenditures for Education as % of GDP*
Denmark	38.9	30.1	8.8
France	38.1	32.2	5.9
Finland	36.2	29.4	6.8
Belgium	36.1	29.5	6.6
Sweden	35.1	28.3	7.0
Austria	34.7	28.8	5.9
Italy	32.3	27.8	4.5
Norway	31.8	23.0	8.8
Germany	31.6	27.1	4.5
Spain	31.5	26.5	5.0
Portugal	31.2	25.6	5.6
Ireland	30.2	23.7	6.5
United Kingdom	30.0	23.7	6.3
Netherlands	29.5	23.5	6.0
New Zealand	28.7	21.5	7.2
Greece	27.4	23.3	4.1
Japan	26.2	22.4	3.8
United States	25.5	20.0	5.5
Switzerland	25.2	20.0	5.2
Canada	23.9	18.6	5.3
Australia	23.1	17.9	5.2

Sources: OECD, *Education at a Glance 2012: OECD Indicators* (Paris: OECD, 2012), 246; OECD, *Education at a Glance 2013: OECD Indicators* (Paris: OECD, 2013), 219; *OECD Factbook 2013: Economic, Environmental and Social Statistics* (Paris: OECD, 2013), 213.

Note: Government expenditures for cash benefits and social services include pensions, health-care benefits, child allowances, parental payments, disability benefits, unemployment compensation, employment measures, housing allowances, rent subsidies, and food subsidies. Japanese spending on these benefits occurred in 2009. Public expenditures for education include all levels: primary, secondary, and tertiary. Data on education refer to 2009 for Germany and Canada and to 2005 for Greece.

63–69; OECD 2008, 97–121, 223–51; OECD 2011a, 309–34; Scruggs 2008; Wang, Caminada, and Goudswaard 2012).

Governments more effectively reduced market income inequalities after cash transfers and in-kind benefits (health care, education, housing) than after taxes. The most progressive taxes comprised those on personal income and corporate profits, which gained the highest revenue from the richest citizens. Sales and value-added taxes imposed greater burdens on poorer individuals. Tax policies benefited the richest 1 percent more than the poorest fifth. Wages and salaries incurred higher tax rates than did income from dividends and capital gains received mainly by wealthier persons (Wilensky 2012, 263–69).

Tax credits, exemptions, deductions, and evasions hardly lessened inequality. Most widespread in the United States, tax credits particularly benefited middle- and upper-income individuals who deducted mortgage interest payments, state income taxes, and local property taxes from their tax returns. Employers deducted health insurance premiums paid to workers. Corporations, including the largest banks, secured tax deductions for paying interest on their debts. Poorer Americans gained from the earned income tax credit (EITC) for care to children, disabled persons, and low-income people. Yet this means-tested program reduced credits when incomes rose. The complexities of filing the tax forms also discouraged many eligible employees from applying for the EITC. Because workers in Britain, Canada, Australia, France, and Germany could deduct only a low share of their wage as tax credits, their effect on income distribution remained limited (Atkinson, Piketty, and Saez 2011; Carbaugh and Ghosh 2011; Garfinkel, Rainwater, and Smeeding 2010, 52–58; Howard 2009; Ide and Steinmo 2009; Kenworthy 2008, 136–98; OECD 2008, 109–15; 2011a, 343–73; Prasad and Deng 2009).

Despite the weak impact of most taxes and tax credits on income distribution, a fairly strong cross-national correlation did prevail between economic inequality and all taxes as a share of GDP. As table 2.2 shows, Northern European governments implemented the highest level of taxes. Enacting lower overall taxes, policymakers in other countries secured larger income disparities (Kenworthy 2011, 71–88; OECD 2011c, 64; OECD 2012c, 96–100; OECD 2013c, 225).

Tax havens reinforced the trend toward less equality. Supported by neoliberals, these havens, or what the French call *paradis fiscaux*, enabled wealthy individuals and multinational corporations, especially financial institutions, to escape paying taxes and to avoid regulations enacted by national governments. Hierarchy and secret operations resulted. Multinationals moved their financial assets to low-tax nations but left their liabilities in higher-tax countries where they could deduct their losses. The most famous tax havens included several small island states mainly controlled by the British: Bermuda, the Bahamas, Cayman Islands, Isle of Man, Jersey, Guernsey, Malta. As a global tax haven, the City of London Corporation, a municipal authority, has long functioned independently of the British government. In the United States, Delaware, Nevada, and the New York island of Manhattan allowed wealthy corporations to avoid paying taxes. A similar process took place on the European continent among Switzerland, Liechtenstein, and Luxembourg. As a result of the globalized flow of mobile financial capital throughout the world, national tax policies produced only limited effects on domestic income distribution. Multinational bankers, lawyers, accountants,

Table 2.2. Taxes in OECD Nations, 2010

Nation	*Total Tax Revenue as % of GDP*	*Taxes on Income and Profits as % of Total Taxation*	*Taxes on Goods and Services as % of Total Taxation*	*Social Security Contributions as % of Total Taxation*
Denmark	47.6	61.6	31.9	02.1
Sweden	45.5	35.6	29.4	25.0
Belgium	43.5	34.3	25.6	32.4
France	42.9	21.9	25.0	38.7
Italy	42.9	32.9	25.9	31.3
Norway	42.9	47.0	27.6	22.5
Finland	42.5	35.7	31.5	29.8
Austria	42.0	28.3	28.0	34.6
Netherlands	38.7	27.9	30.8	36.3
Germany	36.1	28.7	29.5	39.0
United Kingdom	34.9	37.5	30.8	19.0
Spain	32.3	28.3	26.7	37.6
New Zealand	31.5	53.7	39.5	0
Portugal	31.3	26.9	39.4	28.8
Canada	31.0	46.8	24.3	15.3
Greece	30.9	22.2	39.0	35.2
Switzerland	28.1	46.2	22.6	23.8
Ireland	27.6	36.2	37.0	20.1
Japan	27.6	30.2	18.7	41.1
Australia	25.6	57.1	28.4	0
United States	24.8	43.6	18.0	25.7

Source: OECD, *Revenue Statistics: 1965–2011* (Paris: OECD, 2012), 100, 104.
Note: Social contributions include payments by employees and employers. Taxes on goods and services come mainly from value-added and sales taxes.

public-relations experts, and lobbyists gained the major rewards from the tax havens, which held the income of the world's richest individuals (Henry 2012; Palan, Murphy, and Chavagneux 2010; Shaxson 2011).

REGULATION OF FINANCIAL INSTITUTIONS

From the end of World War II to the early 1970s, Keynesian programs helped avoid financial crises. Finance and treasury ministries controlled the central bank, which implemented stable interest rates and fixed currencies. Along with private financial institutions, the central banks focused on postwar reconstruction through making loans for capital investment that financed capital goods, consumer products, the physical infrastructure (transportation, communication, and sanitation facilities), health, and education. High economic growth, price stability, and low unemployment resulted.

During the 1970s, disillusionment with Keynesian policies increased. Economic growth declined, consumer prices escalated, and unemployment reached high levels. Dedicated to monetary policies and deregulation of government control over financial institutions, political leaders supporting neoliberalism gained greater political power after 1980 (Gomory and Sylla 2013).

The United States and British governments most enthusiastically backed neoliberal financial policies that widened the income gap. Banks won greater autonomy from government regulation. Commercial and investment banks merged their activities. "Shadow banks"—hedge funds, private equity companies, venture capital funds, pension funds, money market funds, municipal bond insurance corporations, structured investment vehicles—conducted secret operations. Ineffective regulation, particularly over hedge funds handling US mortgage-backed securities, failed to curb risky investments (Friedman and Kraus 2011). As financial mergers and acquisitions expanded, competition among banks decreased. Financiers' risk-prone behavior propelled loans that borrowers could not repay. High debts ensued.

Financial elites took high risks that produced huge short-run economic rewards for them. Private banks' profits soared when they obtained low interest rates (near zero) from central banks and charged higher rates to borrowers or earned larger interest income from the purchase of long-term government bonds. Submitting inaccurate estimates of borrowing costs for the interbank loans enabled financial executives and traders to increase their profits, disguise their assets, and minimize the risks of funding loans. Before 2014, private banks and the British Bankers' Association set the London Interbank Offered Rate (Libor). This benchmark reflected estimated averages of the short-term interest rates on loans that banks made to one another. Social networks among financiers heading multinational financial institutions coordinated their activities that rigged the Libor, Euribor, and Tibor, the Japanese rate. Bankers and traders gained high profits from this manipulation. Influencing borrowing costs throughout the world, these interbank lending charges indirectly affected the interest rates for savings accounts, adjustable-rate mortgages, pensions, credit card fees, student loans, commercial loans, over-the-counter derivatives, futures contracts, and credit default swaps throughout the global economy.

To minimize risks, municipal, county, and regional government agencies negotiated interest-rate swaps with the largest multinational banks, such as HSBC, Barclays, UBS, Société Générale, Deutsche Bank, and JPMorgan Chase. A form of derivative, these swaps tried to insure (hedge) borrowers against losses from volatile changes in worldwide interest and currency changes. For example, a municipal transit commission would contract to swap a floating for a fixed interest rate. The commission paid a fixed rate to the bank, which paid a floating rate to the commission. When the floating rate pegged to .65 percent of Libor declined during the 2008 global financial crisis, bank payments to municipal governments decreased. Yet they still owed the banks a fixed rate of 5.6 percent. High debt charges meant reduced expenditures for schools, transit agencies, police departments, and other city services. Major costs occurred to poorer local citizens, who paid higher fees and taxes but received fewer government benefits. Hedge funds, private equity funds, and multinational banks secured the largest gains. These global financial transactions, mainly derivative contracts, totaled over five hundred trillion dollars in 2012. Benefits went primarily to multinational traders, brokers, and investment bankers (Bondgraham 2012; de la Merced 2012; Jenkins, Gapper, and Masters 2012; Lanchester 2013a; J. Thompson 2012).

Financiers and brokers earned high fees, commissions, salaries, bonuses, fringe benefits, stock options, and severance pay. Compensation received by US and British chief financial officers exceeded the pay for Western European and Japanese executives. Speculative investments occurred in commodities (oil, minerals, food), stock markets, real estate, and foreign currencies. Investors borrowed funds from low-interest-rate countries and lent funds to societies that paid higher interest. Managers of hedge funds and private equity funds gained more monetary returns than did investors (Bivens and Mishel 2013; Conyon, Core, and Guay 2011, 429–32; Shaxson 2013; Stiglitz 2012, 21, 238–64). As Keynes (1973c, 157–63) warned, speculators faced not only risks of loan defaults but uncertainty about future profits from their investments.

Risk management rested on an uncertain, speculative foundation that brought the greatest income losses to debtors, especially poor people and small businesses. Resembling language used by the Circumlocution Office, esoteric terms—collateralized debt obligations, collateralized loan obligations, credit default swaps, floating-for-fixed interest rate swaps, credit derivatives, asset-based securities—described financial measures that provided insurance against debts arising from unpaid loans. Securitization processes bundled mortgages, auto loans, and credit-card debts into diversified pools with different tranches (the French term for "slices"). The tranches provided insurance against defaults. Using the latest computer techniques, mathematical wizards devised complex algebraic formulae that supposedly predicted future returns on investments. Rational calculation became difficult because statisticians who advised investors lacked accurate, reliable information about the value of assets, whether real estate holdings, bonds, or other securities. Allied with financial institutions, multinational credit-rating agencies—Moody's, Standard and Poor's, Fitch—evaluated the risks of these loans. Lacking accurate information about future returns, they had an incentive to overvalue securities and earn higher fees (Lanchester 2010, 111–32; Milne 2009; Tanzi 2011, 311–19).

Although the pursuit of rational self-interest temporarily produced high economic benefits for financiers, the financiers' impact on society proved more costly. Chief financial officers, hedge fund traders, insurance executives, senior accountants, top-level lawyers, stockbrokers, mortgage brokers, and real estate developers earned lucrative rewards. Eventually the real estate–stock market boom crashed during 2007–2008. When borrowers failed to repay their loans, financial institutions, along with consumers, homeowners, businesses, and governments, incurred immense debts. Risk-averse attitudes emerged. Pessimism replaced optimism. Needing more cash reserves, banks stopped lending money, especially to consumers and small businesses. The credit crunch also deterred loans to governments and other banks. Less-affluent individuals endured severe losses from the economic collapse. They no longer borrowed or spent money. Faced with declining demand, private businesses ceased making productive capital investments such as equipment, the physical infrastructure, and educational facilities. When government officials declined to increase expenditures, the income gap widened. Unemployment rose. Stagnant or reduced wages hurt most employees. Both the poorest tenth of the national populations as well as middle-income persons suffered. From 1960 to 2010, the group that received the largest income rises included the richest 1 percent of national populations. Financial executives reaped the greatest income gains (Alvaredo et al. 2013; Campbell 2011; Cassidy 2009, 221–346; Giles 2011; Gorton 2013, 182–99; Guillén and Suárez 2010; Harris and Sammartino 2011, 1–19; Ingham 2008, 65–203; Kaplan and Rauh 2010; Krugman 2009, 2012; Lansley 2011; MacKenzie 2013; Peck 2011; Posner 2009, 2010; Tridico 2012a; Wolf 2010; Zandi 2008).

Where financial elites could mobilize resources behind programs that strengthened their influence over the policy agenda, greater income inequality emerged. Particularly in the United States and Britain, the largest banks gained support from dominant political parties and corporations. Wall Street and the City of London possessed the resources for influencing financial policy. Authority derived from their right to provide credit, finance debt, and thereby enhance market effectiveness. Between 1980 and 2007, US financial profits as a share of total corporate profits doubled from 18 percent to 40 percent (Castells 2011, 189; Keyder 2011, 163; Lin and Tomaskovic-Devey 2013; Wade 2011a, 17). Not only profits but administrative skills, general information, and technical expertise fortified financial managers' power. Whereas lenders (bankers, insurance executives, mortgage brokers) had extensive information, neither borrowers nor regulators could understand the technical details about derivatives, collateralized debt obligations, and triple-A tranches. Chief financial officers developed cohesive social networks. Most attended elite universities, associated with one another at prestigious social clubs, and formed joint memberships on boards of directors.

Shared values that reinforced the cohesion of financial networks legitimatized the drive toward income inequality. Hierarchy took precedence over equality. Financiers' communications assumed that egalitarian outcomes would mitigate the innovation, flexibility, and efficiency needed for economic success in a volatile market that brought insecurity even to lower-ranking employees. Viewing themselves as the best and the brightest, chief financial officers ruled as experts. Their main goal involved achieving short-term high stock prices—a prime measure of success. Individual freedom meant the right to manage financial institutions without tight controls by government regulators. A pragmatic emphasis on individual achievement, expertise, and success justified high compensation. Perceptions of the financial corporation as a virtuous entrepreneurial person mitigated efforts to challenge strict regulation. Strong personal efficacy motivated financiers to take risks and thereby earn high rewards. Yet the fatalistic veneration of the global market as an abstract entity that no government actions could control led financiers to resist policies that lessened their domination over the market (Ho 2009; Leigh 2009; Morgan 2009).

Against the power mobilized by the financial elite, government regulators faced barriers enforcing restraints, especially on shadow banks. Dispersed regulatory institutions hindered effective supervision. Exchange of personnel between key banks and government offices strengthened cohesion between the two. Rather than separated, the public and private sectors merged their activities. Each became dependent on the other for economic success. Financial institutions gained tax credits, subsidies, and loan guarantees when high debts arose, as happened from 1980 to 2010. Policymakers needed a healthy financial sector that would finance debt, lend money, facilitate economic transactions, and make investments for stimulating economic growth. Under Keynesian policies, financial institutions before 1980 cooperated with governments to perform these tasks. With the rise of neoliberalism, banks placed higher priority on trading money rather than on investing in physical capital, public infrastructure, education, health, and other social services. This policy development produced fewer benefits for low-income persons who suffered losses when the recession produced higher unemployment, bankruptcies, and defaults on loans (Blackburn 2011; Skocpol and Jacobs 2012; Tabb 2012).

After the 2008 debt crisis, the government tried to implement tighter regulations over financial institutions. They had to maintain a higher ratio of assets over liabilities so that the risks of unpaid loans would be lessened. Greater pressures emerged for looser connections between retail banks, which make loans to customers, and investment banks that focus on riskier, speculative investments. In 2013 the Financial Conduct Authority of Britain required the British Bankers' Association to abandon its supervision of the Libor. Beginning in 2014, the London office of the New York Stock Exchange Euronext based interbank lending rates not only on estimates of short-run interest rates among multinational banks but also on actual loans. Increased transparency in financial operations, especially by shadow banks, became a frequent demand for curtailing the secret trading of derivatives. Several political leaders on the European continent sought stricter government controls over bankers' salaries and bonuses as well as higher taxes on chief financial officers. Revenue measures also included a financial transaction tax, restrictions on channeling funds to tax havens, and mandatory international exchange of information about ways that governments tax investment income (Admati and Hellwig 2013, 81–114; 208–28; Houlder 2013; Kramer and Norris 2013; Lanchester 2013b; Masters and Stafford 2013; Popper 2013).

Despite efforts to regulate private financial institutions, they retained significant influence over income distribution policies. With their extensive resources, corporate directors avoided, weakened, or eventually eliminated regulations that reduced their control. Although legislators wrote laws about financial transactions, regulators often followed more secretive, informal rules for implementing the laws. Governments continued to guarantee bank debts and encourage high profits so that private benefits overwhelmed publicly financed costs. The spread of globalization produced greater interconnections among financial institutions throughout the world. Banks in one country maintained subsidiaries in other nations. Interbank loans from the United States, Canada, and Western Europe supplied credit not only to highly industrialized countries but also to developing countries in Central and Eastern Europe, Latin America, Asia, and Africa. Export nations such as China, Japan, Taiwan, Brazil, Germany, and Saudi Arabia used their surplus reserves to buy US bonds, which helped finance the national fiscal deficit. Advanced computer programs enabled international financiers to trade derivatives, equities, and foreign currencies in nanoseconds. Despite the rapid market transactions, the technologically advanced system impeded the flexibility needed to manage unexpected, volatile situations, as happened with the collapse of the stock and housing markets in 2008. Private financial institutions, governments, and especially individuals incurred high debts. Recession magnified the income gap in most industrial nations (Braithwaite, Masters, and Grant 2011; Busch 2009, 245–55; Gourevitch 2013; Guillén and Suárez 2010; Hill 2010, 107–13; Lanchester 2010, 211–12; Murphy and Jenkins 2011; Sinn 2010; Wade 2011b; Wilson and Wiesmann 2011; Wolff 2012, 25–26, 68–78).

To cope with the booms and busts of the business cycle, Keynes recommended countercyclical programs. During the boom period, governments should enact stricter regulations on risky financial actions, ensure that banks hold larger assets, and tighten credit through slightly higher interest rates. When the bust emerged, Keynes wanted policymakers to pursue the opposite strategy. As he stated in early 1937, "The boom, not the slump, is the right time for austerity at the Treasury" (Keynes 1982a, 390). According to him, governments should reduce interest rates, decrease banks' assets, and raise expenditures, especially for capital investment. He assumed that these policies would stimulate aggregate demand, give consumers more money to spend, increase economic growth, enlarge national income, and curtail unemployment (Keynes 1973c, 94–95, 320–25; 1980b, 319–20, 352–57; 1982a, 308).

Faced with recessionary conditions during the early twenty-first century, many neoliberal policymakers implemented cyclical strategies that exacerbated income disparities. Central bankers, private financiers, and creditors (bondholders), not Keynesian officials, exerted dominant influence. Faced with deficits, US state government leaders raised regressive sales taxes but curtailed expenditures for education, health care, unemployment compensation, public employees' salaries, and assistance to children as well as to sick, disabled, elderly, and poor people. At the national level, the Republican Party led the movement to reduce government social services, decrease taxes paid by the wealthy, and restrict union power over workers, especially public-sector employees.

Irish, Icelandic, Greek, Cypriot, Portuguese, Spanish, and Italian officials came under pressure from several financial institutions. The German Bundesbank, European Commission, European Central Bank headquartered in Frankfurt, International Monetary Fund, and private financial institutions required that these governments implement cyclical austerity measures in order to receive loans for reducing deficits. The cyclical policies increased value-added taxes but reduced public-sector jobs, wages for public employees, minimum wages of private workers, unemployment compensation, pensions for the retired, and government spending on education and health care. Creditors insisted that debt-plagued governments pay high interest rates to secure needed loans. These cyclical policies decreased aggregate demand. Unemployment soared. Growth rates plunged. Greater income inequality resulted. When austerity policies limited collective bargaining rights for unions, employers gained greater flexibility to hire and fire workers (Albo and Evans 2010; Blanchflower 2011; Blyth 2013, 21–93,178–244; Fontana and Sawyer 2011; Kontogiannis 2010; Krugman 2012, xi, 51–90, 166–207; Mallet, Barber, and Mulligan 2010; Panayotakis 2013; Pérez Caldentey and Vernengo 2010).

LABOR-MARKET POLICIES

From the close of World War II through the early 1970s, most governments in developed nations formulated Keynesian labor-market policies that focused on narrowing income disparities. Unions allied with labor and social democratic parties. Nationwide, coordinated collective bargaining occurred. Unions sought moderate wage demands in exchange for generous fringe benefits, such as pensions and health care. Corporate executives cooperated with union and government leaders to increase demand and reduce the widespread unemployment that had plagued workers during the 1930s. Public policies encouraged domestic production and the growth of permanent, full-time jobs in the manufacturing sector. State expenditures for capital investment promoted manufacture of autos, steel, chemicals, textiles, and the public infrastructure. Unemployed workers secured high unemployment compensation that gave them income until a new manufacturing job arose. All these policies furthered income equality, particularly among male workers (Gomory and Sylla 2013; Scheve and Stasavage 2009; Traxler and Brandl 2011).

Deteriorating economic conditions during the 1970s weakened the Keynesian approach and strengthened the neoliberal perspective toward labor-market policies. Rather than placing priority on expanding aggregate demand, neoliberal officials stressed the need to promote a more skilled labor force, entrepreneurial motivations, and a flexible labor market. For employers, flexibility meant the right to hire, fire, and manage workers. For employees, flexibility caused greater job insecurity.

When unemployment rose, unions lost political power. As membership declined, it grew more diverse. Union cohesion weakened. Older male workers with permanent, full-time jobs competed with younger, female, immigrant workers who held part-time, temporary positions, especially in the private service sector. Waiters, janitors, orderlies, domestic servants, clerks, and retail salespersons earned low wages. Whereas the "outsiders" preferred egalitarian policies that expanded their income, the more highly paid "insiders" sought wages based on seniority and technical skills. Engineers and chemical workers in large export businesses rejected actions that would equalize their incomes with wages earned by routine private service employees in small-sized domestic firms. Public employees demanded greater wage equality than did individuals who gained higher wages in private manufacturing corporations and business services. Not only interest conflicts but value cleavages fragmented union solidarity. Many less-educated workers upheld traditional values, such as the importance of God in personal life and children's need to learn obedience and religious faith from their parents. These religious beliefs took precedence over working-class identifications needed to mobilize support behind leftist unions and political parties. In contrast, secular modernists affirmed more inclusive, less hierarchical values that favored egalitarian policies of left-wing organizations (Baker 2005, 74–85, 197; Gerlach and Meyer 2010; Häusermann 2010; Lee, Kim, and Shim 2011).

Neoliberalism led to the increased influence of corporations over the policy process after 1980. Adopting a more adversarial stance toward unions, corporations became less willing to cooperate with labor leaders about the protection of workers' rights. Government expenditures for capital investment fell. The service sector gained dominance over manufacturing. Enhanced global competition motivated employers to reduce labor costs. Private corporations reduced company pensions and health insurance. Governments showed greater reluctance to expand the provision of public social services. Neoliberal policymakers emphasized workers' personal responsibility to acquire social benefits by gaining an education, learning new skills, and searching for new jobs if unemployed. Many jobs spread to developing nations where corporate managers faced weaker unions, fewer government regulations, and a lower-paid labor force (Barbieri 2009; Bernardi and Garrido 2008; Glyn 2009; Kalleberg 2006, 2009; Lansley 2011, 60–85; Neckerman and Torche 2007; Toshiaki 2010; Tridico 2012a).

During the early twenty-first century, political leaders formulated the most egalitarian labor policies in nations less influenced by neoliberal principles. Particularly where corporations faced pressures from strong labor unions and allied left-wing parties, the prospects for income equality rose. High opportunities for collective bargaining combined with inclusive union membership. When union members included over 70 percent of the labor force and collective bargaining agreements applied to four-fifths of workers, the lowest-paid employees gained more income. Strong unions won a high minimum wage. Under centralized, coordinated collective bargaining, greater equality emerged than if employers and union leaders negotiated at the industry or enterprise level (Hayter and Weinberg 2011).

Scandinavian workers enjoyed greater income equality because their labor-market policies facilitated inclusive unions and collective bargaining arrangements that promoted workers' rights. Even if unions' power has declined since the 1970s, they still played a key role over the policy agenda. In 2007 Danish, Swedish, and Finnish union membership exceeded 70 percent of the labor force. Collective bargaining rights applied to nearly all employees. Although collective bargaining became more decentralized to specific industries and enterprises, union leaders still coordinated agreements with employers. Union leaders bargained with management about wages, fringe benefits, safety standards, and working conditions. Despite their extensive resources, corporations faced countervailing powers that limited their discretion. Unlike US and British executives, Scandinavian corporate managers agreed to a narrower salary gap with workers, who often held seats on company boards.

Coalitions with social democratic, labor, and green parties gave Scandinavian unions the opportunities to pressure public policymakers for generous, inclusive benefits. Providing income security against old age, sickness, disability, and job losses, these benefits included pensions, health service, child-care facilities, paid parental leave, public elder care, unemployment compensation, and inclusive public education that extended to upper secondary and university levels. Such policies encouraged women to become paid employees. As a result, Scandinavian societies experienced more gender income equality than most other industrialized societies. Generous expenditures for active labor-market policies as a share of national income enabled Scandinavians to cope with unemployment that arose from increased global competition. Workers facing layoffs gained training in new general skills, subsidized private-sector jobs, funds for relocation, access to employment services, and opportunities to work as public employees. Scandinavian societies in 2010 had more public employees as a proportion of the total labor force than did other OECD industrialized countries (Andersen et al. 2007; Anxo and Niklasson 2008; Gustafsson 2008; Häusermann, Picot, and Geering 2013; Hayter and Weinberg 2011, 139–41; Leamer 2010; Lee, Kim, and Shim 2011, 112; OECD 2011d, 59; 2012a, 146; Pontusson 2011; Roemer 2009; Tanzi 2011, 267–98).

Labor-market policies attained less egalitarian outcomes in Southern Europe. Greek, Italian, Spanish, and Portuguese officials implemented job security programs that protected permanent, full-time male workers. Youths, women, rural residents, and immigrants suffered from this policy. Governments failed to establish paid parental leaves and public child-care centers that would help mothers who worked for pay. Grandmothers cared for their children. Compared with Scandinavia, a larger proportion of civilians operated small family businesses where self-employed persons earned low wages, secured few fringe benefits, and avoided tax payments. Elderly persons received less generous public and private pensions. Even young university graduates lacked job opportunities; many emigrated to countries outside Southern Europe. Unemployment compensation provided only limited income, especially to those working in unregulated, informal markets. Southern European governments implemented fewer active labor-market policies than did Scandinavian officials. Union coalitions with governing socialist parties remained weak. Collective bargaining never achieved the coordinated pattern experienced by Scandinavians, Belgians, Dutch, Austrians, and Germans (Addabbo, Aziz, and Reardon 2011; Bernardi and Garrido 2008; Danopoulos and Znidaric 2007; Gough and Adami 2012; Hopkin and Blyth 2012; OECD 2013c, 136–37).

In the United States, union leaders wielded limited policy influence. Employment protection laws gave employers the right to hire and fire workers. Union membership in 2011 totaled only 12 percent of the labor force: 37 percent in the public sector and far lower (under 10 percent) in the private service sector—finance, insurance, real estate, trade, restaurants, hotels, motels, resorts (ProQuest 2012, 444). As wages stagnated but labor productivity rose, workers' share of the national income declined. Corporations paid low wages to newly hired and part-time employees. Declining unionization rates since the mid-1970s meant less wage equality among workers, higher compensation for corporate executives, and a greater salary gap between them and private employees. During the early twenty-first century, the poorest third of the labor force, especially African and Hispanic Americans, suffered the most income losses from declining wages. Collective bargaining agreements covered few workers except for public employees in education, nursing, transportation, construction, and utilities. Neither public child-care facilities nor paid parental leaves supplied extensive resources to women employees. No generous, universal, comprehensive social-service benefits increased the disposable income of low-paid workers of both sexes. Although US federal income taxes helped narrow the income gap, from 1980 through 2010 the tax rates became less progressive. Whereas corporations and the wealthiest 1 percent paid lower taxes as a share of their assets, regressive payroll, sales, and property taxes rose for poorer Americans. Limited union influence over the policy process deterred the approval of egalitarian programs (Bacarro 2008; Barratt 2009, 15, 49; Bartlett 2012, 21–142; Boeri and van Ours 2008; Checchi and García-Peñalosa 2008; Esping-Andersen 2007b; Greenhouse 2013; Hill 2010, 72–184; Lin and Tomaskovic-Devey 2013; Noah 2012, 125–43; F. Norris 2013; OECD 2012a, 144–45; Reich 2012, 103; Rosenfeld and Kleykamp 2012; Schlozman, Verba, and Brady 2012, 87–94, 325–31; Visser and Checchi 2009; Wilensky 2012, 155–90; Yun 2010).

Not just in the United States but in other mainly English-speaking countries like Britain, Australia, and Canada, weak ties linked unions with left-wing parties. Neoliberal values encouraged the private provision of social services. Under Prime Minister Blair in Britain, New Labour rejected a close union alliance. Low membership, which included 29 percent of the 2007 labor force, hindered unions' influence. The party became more dependent on business donations and less reliant on union funds. It encouraged a partnership between employers and union leaders. Workfare measures required claimants to demonstrate their personal responsibility to search for a job when seeking the right to receive public assistance if unemployed. When the Australian Labor Party held power from 1983 to 1996, it initiated neoliberal programs. Lower wages and more part-time, temporary jobs resulted. Despite the Labor alliance with the Australian Council of Trade Unions, membership in unions declined. Unemployment rose. The financial service sector grew more powerful. After the Labor Party regained power in the 2007 election, business groups continued to influence economic policies. Although unions helped the Labor Party to win an electoral victory, party leaders loosened their ties with unions. Hence, they could not effectively press for policies that would curtail income inequalities, especially between urban and rural areas (Brody 2010; Cahill 2008; Faucher-King and Le Galès 2010,

26–35, 90–93; Kang 2012, 134–37; Kuttner 2011; Muir and Peetz 2010; OECD 2013c, 212–13; Sachs 2011, 146–50; Soskice 2010; Steger and Roy 2010, 21–75; Wilkinson 2007; Zehavi 2012).

CONCLUSION

Egalitarian public policies derived from the power relationships among government institutions, political parties, unions, and corporations. The highest income equality emerged in societies with an activist government committed to reducing the risks of illness, disability, old age, and unemployment. Government agencies coordinated their activities. As the scope of public power grew, more people received generous, comprehensive, inclusive social services.

Where neoliberalism dominated the political agenda, lesser income equality emerged. Governments concentrated on defending the nation, ensuring domestic order, protecting private property rights, guaranteeing stable contracts, increasing exports, and expanding productivity. The supply of inclusive, comprehensive, generous social services assumed a lower priority. Along with deregulation, privatization of state-owned enterprises became widespread. Whereas public agencies used to provide many social services, private corporations undertook major responsibilities. Unlike government agencies, they paid less-equal wages. Corporate elites received lucrative fees, bonuses, commissions, and salaries. Privatized oligopolies charged high prices for their services. After the 2007–2008 financial crisis erupted, however, interest rates charged by financiers as well as their salaries and bonuses fell under greater regulation. Government ministries, regulatory agencies, and international institutions (International Monetary Fund, World Bank, World Trade Organization, European Union, regional development banks) enhanced their authority over private financial institutions.

Faced with dispersed power, conservative financial elites opposed to income equality often gained opportunities to hinder the implementation of egalitarian programs. Particularly in the United States and Britain, the historic centers of neoliberalism, probusiness political parties dominated the policy process. From 1979 to 2008 both British Conservative and Labour governments backed financial deregulation. A similar commitment to business deregulation took place in the United States after 1976. Under both Democratic and Republican administrations, the largest corporations, especially banks, maintained close access to government department heads, civil servants, and legislators. The Republican Party particularly approved policies that eliminated nearly all business regulations, reduced taxes on capital gains, and lowered the top marginal rates of personal income taxes (Hacker and Pierson 2010; Volscho and Kelly 2012).

Even if neoliberal promarket views gained greater appeal among European political parties after 1980, social democrats implemented egalitarian policies for social services when they dominated the government cabinet, allied with other leftist parties, mobilized a high voting turnout among the working class, and gathered support from coordinated unions. Particularly in Scandinavia, the proportional representation electoral system raised voter turnout that enabled small left-wing parties to join the governing cabinet. When an alliance linked social democrats with the left-wing socialists or greens, coalition leaders enacted generous, inclusive social-service expenditures financed by fiscal surpluses. These policies won electoral backing from women, poor people, union members, and many middle-income persons who supported social democratic policies that blended equal respect and expanded economic opportunities for upward mobility with an attachment to individual freedom, achievement, and responsibility (Finseraas and Vernby 2011; Häusermann, Picot, and Geering 2013; Nelson 2013).

In continental European countries such as Austria, Belgium, the Netherlands, and Germany, labor and socialist parties exerted less government power. Christian Democrats often allied with Social Democrats to govern the society. Probusiness liberal parties also formed coalitions with the Christian Democrats. Instead of implementing universal benefits, government officials tailored policies to specific occupations. Lower income equality emerged than in Scandinavia (Beramendi and Cusack 2009; Brady 2009; Hakhverdian 2009; Iversen 2009; Jensen 2008).

Political parties had the strongest influence on policy performance when leftist parties committed to higher wage increases for workers and to culturally modern lifestyles governed a nation. Cultural values such as gender equality, female empowerment, and paid jobs for women coalesced with support for secularism, minority rights, multiculturalism, and civil liberties. These economic and cultural preferences appealed to youths and women voters. If the left-wing party gained a fairly large plurality in the legislature and held most cabinet positions, it increased expenditures for social services such as child-care benefits as a share of the GDP. Right-wing parties that preferred private corporate autonomy and traditional religious values based on a male-dominated family opposed such government-financed spending and backed lower corporate taxes. Yet from 1980 onward, as global competition became more widespread, partisan differences over tax and spending policies declined (Hieda 2013; Osterloh and Debus 2012).

Despite the divergent issues separating left-wing from right-wing parties, a disjunction often emerged between their rhetorical goals and actual policies implemented by governing parties. The incentive to win more electoral votes and thereby gain government power took priority over ideological commitments in party platforms. Unlike party activists, most voters placed lower priority on a coherent, consistent ideology. Motivated by the pragmatic desire to win office, parties needed not only to retain their activist base but to attract a broader constituency. Coalition formation with factions within the same party or with other political parties often generated policy compromises.

Political parties formed only one organization in the policy process that influenced income distribution. They shared power with other institutions: civil services, regional governments, professional associations, labor unions, and private business corporations. In the cabinet, the finance minister usually promoted less egalitarian policies than did labor or health ministers. Senior civil servants, central bankers, and top staff associates of the prime minister or president made the crucial decisions. Stressing expertise, they adopted a nonideological orientation toward fiscal programs. Faced with increased global competition, multinational corporations showed little inclination to support programs that redistributed income toward the poor. Hence, even though leftist political parties upheld egalitarian policies, they could not easily mobilize allies that sought to narrow the income gap. Pressured by financial institutions to reduce deficits, even incumbent social democratic and labor parties enacted austerity programs (Adams and Ezrow 2009; Andrain 1980, 221–23; Bermeo and Pontusson 2012; Bolzendahl 2011; Dahlström 2009; Jensen 2010; Larsen and Andersen 2009; Streeck 2011, 2012a, 2012b).

Resource mobilization theory explains the more effective power exercised by corporations than by unions during the early twenty-first century. Unlike unions, large businesses held more extensive resources: money, professional staff, technical information, and access to the mass media. Their primary role in a capitalist market economy gave them the authority to employ workers, dismiss them, and invest capital, especially under neoliberal regimes that mandated few job protections and relied on private corporations to undertake capital investments. Even in countries where policymakers showed greater enthusiasm for Keynesian programs, corporations enjoyed close access to the government. They supplied expertise, personnel, and contributions. Expertise represented a key resource for achieving business preferences. When corporate managers stimulated attention to a specific problem, highlighted a particular policy option, and used their expertise to advocate that solution, they demonstrated their mobilization capabilities. In exchange for corporate support, the government granted businesses the right to help shape public policies. Lobbyists pressured legislators, administrators, and regulators for tax credits, contracts, licenses, and subsidies (Baumgartner et al. 2009; Crouch 2011; Culpepper 2011; Woll 2007).

Besides the amount of resources, the cohesion and allies of private corporations strengthened their influence over the policy process. Compared with union members, executives heading large corporations had fewer, more homogeneous interests that increased their solidarity. If corporate lobbyists developed a unified, clearly defined policy priority about regulations, tax credits, business subsidies, and collective bargaining rights, they could more effectively mobilize their resources for desired policy achievements. Allies also proved crucial for business executives to attain their policy objectives. They needed to form coalitions with sympathetic government officials, political party leaders, other corporate leaders, and heads of professional associations. Civil servants, cabinet officials, and staffs within the president's or prime minister's office became the most significant allies. Particularly in federal systems such as those of the United States and Germany, the judiciary often allied with corporations (Ganghof 2008; Greenwald 2011, 268–74; Hartmann 2010, 130–283; Sinn 2010, 161–64; Suárez and Kolodny 2011).

Unlike corporations, smaller enterprises maintained less extensive influence over national policy formation. They possessed fewer resources such as funds, staff, expertise, mass media access, and organizational skills. Heterogeneous interests hindered small firms' attempts to achieve their policy preferences. Different ideological values and regional interests reduced their cohesion. Tied to local domestic markets, small enterprises faced difficulties coping with competition on the global capitalist market. Multinational corporations dominated the export trade. More mobile than either unions or smaller firms, the corporate giants particularly benefited from globalization. The multinationals invested overseas where high profits, government subsidies, tax exemptions, and weak union power curtailed economic equality, particularly in the diverse political systems throughout Central and Eastern Europe, Asia, and Latin America (Traxler 2010).

Chapter Three

The Politics of Development and Income Distribution Policies

Although they lived in different centuries and countries, Charles Dickens and the Chilean playwright Juan Radrigán shared a similar structural background that influenced their ideas about income distribution. At a young age both began working as manual laborers in low-paid factory jobs. The two authors rejected oppressive government bureaucracies. Whereas Dickens condemned the Tory establishment in mid-nineteenth-century England, Radrigán denounced the military dictatorship of Augusto Pinochet, who ruled Chile from 1973 through early 1990. Rather than blaming specific individuals for poverty, homelessness, and oppression, Dickens and especially Radrigán assumed that personal inequalities mainly stemmed from systemic class disparities that linked wealthy capitalists to powerful government officials. Even if neither one became actively involved in political life, their writings stimulated greater understanding about the ways that government policies shaped income inequalities (Puga 2008).

First staged in 1981, Radrigán's major play *Hechos consumados* (*Finished from the Start*) depicts three main characters who illustrate contradictory values in recent Chilean history. The play takes place on an empty lot just outside Santiago where three marginals carry on a dialogue about the causes of poverty, inequality, and social injustice. Emilio, a homeless former textile worker, embodies the democratic socialist values that President Salvador Allende tried to implement during his brief tenure (1970–1973) before the military staged a coup that overthrew him on September 11, 1973. Emilio most fervently upholds egalitarian values. For him, equality involves living in dignity, sharing resources, and suffering no humiliation from those who view themselves as better than others. Workers need more class solidarity and justice to overcome their poverty: "The only bread that cures all hungers is justice" (Radrigán 2008, 155).

Emilio sees Chileans living under an unjust military dictatorship where hierarchical values dominate political and economic activities. He takes a skeptical view of all bureaucratic authority, whether wielded in government institutions, factories, or everyday lives. Dominating the class system, "unseen" bosses oppress the workers, fire them from their jobs, and evict people from their homes. Known mainly to innocent victims, "secret" police cause dissidents to disappear from public view before torture and execution by the Pinochet regime. Facing subjugation, Emilio feels little hope of bringing social justice to society. According to him, neither personal nor political efficacy offers solutions to one's economic misery. God may listen to prayers, but the believer never receives any answers. Socialists confront immense difficulties in trying to change the political and capitalist systems under Pinochet's bureaucratic-authoritarian rule. Challenging the status quo and disobeying orders bring death. Miguel, a security guard who views the empty lot as private property, kills Emilio when he refuses to move two steps in the lot (Radrigán 2008, 171, 177, 182, 186).

In the dialectical discourse, Miguel exemplifies the bureaucratic-authoritarian, neoliberal values of the military dictatorship. A textile worker, Miguel affirms elitist, hierarchical values. Deferring to the omniscient boss, he accepts the need for order, security, and dependence on the unseen boss for assistance to help his sick wife. Whereas Emilio regards people as colleagues, Miguel polarizes the Chilean population into winners versus losers. Everyone must know his place in a hierarchical stratification system. Losers—the homeless, unemployed, criminals—are "trash." Winners deserve respect as productive workers in a machine culture. Accepting the neoliberal individualist perspective defined by the unseen boss, Miguel proclaims his responsibility to work for a living, protect his job, and retain his house (Radrigán 2008, 187). According to him, unemployment comes from voluntary choices. Blending fatalism and personal efficacy, Miguel assumes that if poor people neither complain against the capitalist boss nor disobey his commands, they may eventually secure modest improvements in the system (Radrigán 2008, 174, 185, 187).

Among the three major characters, Marta illustrates the reconciliation stance toward life. Prefiguring the center-left coalition that won the 1989 national election, she synthesizes the contradictory values of Miguel and Emilio. Making an abortive attempt to attain harmony between them, Marta takes the least fatalistic view. Emilio calls her "the president of the International Committee for Hope" (Radrigán 2008, 179). As a Catholic, she has faith in life and in the possibility of change if people treat each other with love. As an ecologist, she perceives poverty as a desert and abundance as a garden. For her, practicing love resembles planting flowers. Just as a garden needs water, seeds, and fertilizer for flowers to bloom, so personal relationships need compassion, empathy, and respect for each other. Under loving conditions, Chileans can maintain harmony with all, overcome abusive hierarchs, and live with dignity as egalitarian citizens (Radrigán 2008, 163, 177). Led by Christian Democratic and Socialist presidents, the Concertación government that held presidential office from 1990 to 2010 expressed similar aspirations about enacting reconciliation policies that would limit the extensive income gap plaguing Pinochet's bureaucratic-authoritarian regime.

TYPES OF POLITICAL SYSTEMS AND ECONOMIC INEQUALITY

Since World War I, nations have shown three distinct types of political systems: elitist mobilization, bureaucratic-authoritarian, and reconciliation. These models provide basic features by which social scientists can compare actual societies, especially their values, power structures, and individual behaviors. No exact correspondence prevailed between each model and a specific country's income distribution (Apter 1971).

Exemplified by the Soviet Union and Maoist China, elitist mobilization systems pursued policies for rapid industrialization under state management. Hierarchical values assumed that subordinates would show deference to the party-state officials governing their societies. Communications asserting political efficacy mobilized followers behind the Communists' party vision of socialist development. Although the leaders upheld the need to lessen income disparities, they hardly regarded political or cultural equality as important. For Stalin and Mao, the cult of the personal leader superseded collegial governance. They ruled the people through coercive, arbitrary power. Based on socialism and nationalism, collective solidarity took priority over citizens' personal interests.

The Communist Party mobilized government institutions, unions, and social groups to fulfill the leaders' ideological cause. It coordinated government activities, centralized the policy process, repressed dissent, and curbed social groups' autonomy to shape political decisions. Party-state bureaucrats wielded an extensive scope of power: defense, internal order, economic management, and the provision of extensive social services. Neither small domestic enterprises nor multinational corporations helped further industrialization. Tied to the Communist Party, labor unions mobilized the working class behind rapid industrialized development. Controlled by the party, they possessed some important responsibilities in the local state-owned enterprise, such as allocating health-care, pension, child-care, housing, and recreational benefits.

Party-state bureaucrats fused moral with material incentives to mobilize the populace. A moral vision based on enhanced socialist equality legitimated short-term sacrifices. Materially, leaders sought to transform their economies from a rural agricultural base into an urban, industrial society. In the process, factory workers gained more material benefits than did farmers. Rapid growth rates occurred during the early stages of industrialization. After 1970, information-processing technology became more important. Party-state restrictions on free communications hindered rational calculations for meeting complex situations. Shortages of consumer goods weakened support for the regime. The programmatic ideology no longer motivated party-state leaders to create a transformed egalitarian society (Andrain 1994, 69–88, 117–26).

Despite their failure to realize extensive economic equality, policymakers in the Soviet Union and the People's Republic of China did pursue programs that produced a narrower income gap than under the previous regimes. Government agencies, not private stockholders, financed capital investment. Profits earned by state-owned enterprises (SOEs) returned to the government or state-owned enterprise rather than to wealthy private investors. Policies abolished capital gains, dividends, and rents on private property such as land. Government wage boards lessened wage disparities. Besides devoting high expenditures to capital investment and armaments, policymakers granted generous social services to citizens. People gained state pensions, family allowances, public health care, educational opportunities, and subsidized public transportation, housing, and food from SOEs. Under state socialism, society underwent many changes: industrialization, urbanization, mass education, and expanded opportunities for social mobility as farmers moved from the rural areas into urban factory work. Public policies minimized unemployment. Low interest rates, budget surpluses, administered prices, and wage controls reduced inflationary pressures.

Even with these benefits, public policies hardly produced the egalitarian conditions promised by ideologues. Party-state elites gained educational and health-care perquisites: access to superior schools, tutors, and high-quality health services. State enterprise directors, scientists, engineers, athletes, military officials, high-level civil servants, and especially top party bureaucrats secured new apartments, free travel, vacations, and imported consumer goods. Unskilled workers and the rural poor had limited access to such benefits. Wage differences also pervaded the economy. Rapid fulfillment of industrial quotas took precedence over wage equality. Technocrats and skilled workers in heavy industry earned higher pay than did less-skilled individuals who labored in textile industries, service occupations, and farming. Although rapid industrialization occurred, the main benefits from economic development went to urban residents, not the rural population. After the deaths of Stalin in 1953 and Mao Zedong in 1976, the elitist mobilization system began to disintegrate. A bureaucratic-authoritarian style of governance became dominant (Andrain 1994, 76–79, 186; Andrain and Smith 2006,

26; Maddison 2007a, 62–99; Milanovic 2011, 53–60; Whyte 2010b, 149–50).

Aiming to achieve rapid industrialization, bureaucratic-authoritarian systems followed a program of developmental capitalism under which state bureaucrats allied with private corporate capitalists. During the late 1970s, leaders of the Communist Party in China adopted key features of neoliberalism. So did Russian government officials when the Soviet Union collapsed in early 1991. Latin American dictators also combined state control with neoliberal policies that exacerbated income differences. These regimes included the military dictatorships of Brazil (1964–1985), Chile (1973–1990), Uruguay (1973–1984), and Argentina (1976–1983). By contrast, the bureaucratic-authoritarian military officials who governed South Korea from 1961 through 1993 stressed land redistribution, inclusive education, and labor-intensive growth. Hence, they achieved greater income equality than in Latin America.

Reconciliation systems showed wide variations across Central Europe, Asia, and Latin America. In these pluralist regimes, income distribution stemmed from different power relationships among government institutions, competitive political parties, private corporations, and unions. They all held some degree of autonomy from tight state control. Besides these structures, political leaders' value priorities influenced economic policies, especially the commitment to neoliberal principles. If procedural consensus strengthened cooperative ties and accommodating tactics among the policy participants, they could more easily negotiate disputes.

The following sections explore the politics of development in bureaucratic-authoritarian and reconciliation systems. How did policy priorities of key leaders change over time? What power relationships shaped specific economic decisions? To what extent did fiscal, monetary, ownership, regulation, and labor-market programs affect income distribution?

DEVELOPMENTAL CAPITALISM UNDER BUREAUCRATIC-AUTHORITARIAN SYSTEMS

Like the elitist mobilization system, bureaucratic-authoritarian regimes aimed to secure rapid industrial development, but they granted greater autonomy to private entrepreneurs. Policymakers focused little attention on the need to redistribute income benefiting the poor. Political elitism took priority over mass political participation. Government officials stressed deference to bureaucratic authority, which upheld order, security, and defense against state enemies. Strong collectivism reinforced solidarity behind a venerated nation-state. Bureaucratic experts who guided the nation downplayed fatalistic resignation to the economic status quo. Instead, personal efficacy invigorated the drive toward capitalist industrialization.

Powerful government institutions—armed forces, police, security agencies, civil service—directed the policy process. They centralized power, coordinated policymaking, repressed state critics, and allowed social groups limited independence. The regime either banned labor unions or allowed them limited autonomy. Controlled by the state, they enjoyed few rights to strike, oppose wage inequalities, or bargain collectively with employers about working conditions. Private corporations, however, gained greater rights, such as government subsidies, tax credits, and access to public policymakers for joint collaboration about effective ways to engineer rapid economic growth.

Whereas elitist mobilization systems legitimated economic policies by a comprehensive, systematic ideology, such as Marxism-Leninism or Mao Zedong Thought, bureaucratic-authoritarian leaders relied on a more ad hoc, pragmatic set of principles. Rather than becoming fused, moral and material incentives became separated. Pursuit of national glory formed the primary moral incentive. Material benefits that accrued from market-based industrialization motivated individual action. Rational calculations underlay the drive for state-financed capital investment that linked government bureaucrats—experts, professionals, technocrats—with private domestic as well as multinational corporations. Although this strategy produced high growth, especially in East Asia, the concentrated state and corporate power often led to inflexibility, extensive corruption, and greater income inequality as the pressures for global competition intensified. China, Russia, and military dictatorships in Latin America illustrated the trend toward unequal economic outcomes.

After Mao's death, China moved from an elitist mobilization system to a more bureaucratic-authoritarian regime that decreased income equality. When party-state elites allied with wealthy private executives, the class system became more complex. Urban-rural, regional, occupational, gender, and ethnic differences escalated. Whereas in 1980 the gini coefficient was around .33, by 2012 it had increased to .49 or even higher if the gini covered unreported income (Hung 2011, 221; OECD 2011f, 65; Rabinovitch 2013; Wong 2013). Cleavages separated richer coastal regions from poorer western inland provinces. The income gap also split urban residents from village dwellers. The registration system curtailing movement to the cities harmed rural migrants who lacked access to public health care and high-quality education for their children (Dickson 2008, 21, 218; Di Martino 2011; Lin et al. 2010; OECD 2010b, 130; Song, Storesletten, and Zilibotti 2011, 204–5). Groups who gained the fewest benefits from the rapid growth rates comprised not only migrants to the cities but also farmers, women, and minority ethnic groups (e.g., Tibetans, Mongolians, Uyghurs). Unskilled laborers, private service workers, and small-scale entrepreneurs who conducted their businesses in the unofficial economy also suffered relative deprivation. Wealthier groups included coastal residents, permanent urban workers, men, Han Chinese, and several elites: senior party leaders, top government officials, real estate developers, bankers, and managers of large private corporations. Some neoliberal features—privatization, a flexible labor market, foreign investment, foreign trade, user fees, and fiscal decentralization to local governments—helped generate these inequalities (Foster and McChesney 2012; James Galbraith 2012, 235–49; Jie and Walker 2013; Loyalka 2012; So 2010).

Fiscal policies exacerbated the inegalitarian trends. After the Maoist mobilization system disintegrated, government expenditures for public education, health care, pensions, elder care, and housing subsidies declined. Even though rural household income increased from 1979 to 1988, during the next decade the Chinese Communist Party (CCP) elite granted fewer benefits, such as inexpensive credit, to small farmers. Until the early 2000s, they had to finance their own health-care costs and pay expensive school fees. Limited pensions and unemployment assistance hurt the rural poor and migrant laborers seeking work in the cities. As under Mao's leadership, permanent urban residents, particularly those working in the public sector, gained the most benefits: educational opportunities, health care, housing, unemployment compensation. Regressive taxes scarcely strengthened movement toward income equality. Although personal income taxes remained fairly low, value-added taxes, punitive taxes on farmers, and high tax evasion by the wealthy enlarged income disparities.

Monetary policies rewarded private corporations and the rich elite. Formal government regulations restricted interest rates, reserve requirement ratios, and lending practices, but informal institutions evaded these restrictions. The Chinese Banking Regulatory Commission could not control numerous shadow banks: trust, finance, and leasing companies. Whereas state banks financed state-owned enterprises, shadow banks granted loans at higher interest rates to private businesses, which paid less-equal wages than SOEs. Investments in shadow banks enabled wealthy individuals to gain generous returns. Extensive borrowing by trust companies financed the construction of shopping malls, apartments, and huge office buildings. Often owned by municipal government bureaucrats, these shadow banks increased the money supply throughout the Chinese economy. Charged high interest rates by private lenders, poorer people failed to benefit from the loosely regulated money market. State banks, which paid low interest rates for savings deposits, gave limited credit to small enterprises. Wealthy elites relied on personal networks, ties with Hong Kong financial institutions, and shadow banks to receive lucrative returns from their financial investments (Barboza 2013; Rabinovitch 2012; Sender 2011).

Ownership, regulatory, and labor-market programs increased the power of large private corporations over labor unions. An alliance of private enterprises with party-state institutions intensified income polarization. No sharp distinction separated public from private organizations. The CCP controlled the government, guided economic development, and supervised the activities of private enterprises, whose managers benefited from close links with the party-state elite. Rational calculations led the CCP to recruit young, highly educated business executives from large corporations. In exchange for political support, the CCP government gave these "red capitalists" subsidies, loans, tax credits, expenditures for capital investment, protection against competition, and access to the policy process. Elite networks among the new entrepreneurs cemented the personal connections needed to gain more money (Chen and Dickson 2010, 18–67, 105–63; Osburg 2013, 1–36, 183–91). CCP cadres who used to head state-owned enterprises became managers of privatized firms, which minimized health-care, education, and housing assistance to employees. Independent unions had little power over wages, working conditions, and enterprise management. Monitored by the CCP, the All-China Federation of Trade Unions (ACFTU) gave workers' demands for higher wages and more healthful working conditions only limited support. It stressed the need to manage and mediate labor conflicts. Pledged to maintain labor discipline, stimulate economic development, and preserve social harmony, the ACFTU allied with enterprise managers and local party-state leaders to preserve hierarchical management. The CCP restricted opportunities for alternative unions to organize several different enterprises. Part-time, temporary jobs rose (Pringle 2011; Pringle and Clarke 2011, 38–44, 56–96).

Rapid industrial growth and productive efficiency took priority over wage equality. Whereas gross capital formation as a share of GDP rose from 35 percent in 2000 to nearly 50 percent in 2011, during that period consumption expenditures declined by 15 percent (IMF 2012a, 82, 85). Low wages helped produce high trade surpluses. Export manufacturers secured high profits for sales on the world market. Along with bankers, exporters used their profits to speculate in urban real estate and the stock market. Their economic rewards increased. Local government officials expropriated poor farmers' land, paid them a low price, and then sold the land to urban real estate developers who established commercial enterprises such as luxurious apartments, shopping malls, and sports complexes (Peston and Knight 2012, 263–97).

Disturbed by rising inequality that threatened political disorder, top CCP leaders after 2005 promoted more egalitarian labor policies. Expanded health-care subsidies went to the farmers who received vocational education. Private firms that hired unemployed workers gained loans and tax credits. The minimum wage increased. Government subsidies financed apartments for low-income urban residents, especially for migrant workers, who gained greater freedom to move from their villages, work in the cities, and earn more money. Unions enhanced their influence over SOEs and local governments. Particularly when supported by the enterprise's CCP committee, unionized employees in SOEs and in joint ventures between Chinese and foreign investors won higher compensation. Spurred by local union activists, the ACFTU recruited young migrant workers as members, especially in private domestic firms and multinational corporations. It focused on retraining unemployed workers, finding them jobs, and formulating labor laws that encouraged workers to seek legal settlements for their grievances. Despite these improvements, the differentiated class structure caused by rapid economic growth failed to curtail the inequalities linked to occupational differences. Managers, not rank-and-file workers, secured the primary benefits (Anderlini 2011; Davis and Wang 2009; Dickson 2008; Frazier 2010; Galbraith, Hsu, and Zhang 2009; Huang 2008, 2011; Hurst and Sorace 2011; Lee and Liu 2011; Lin et al. 2008, 2010; OECD 2013b, 18–21, 88–93; Schucher 2009; So 2007a, 2007b, 2010; Walder and Hu 2009; Wang 2008; Whyte 2010b, 11–32; Zhou 2008).

The bureaucratic-authoritarian regime that replaced the Soviet Union in early 1991 implemented policies that widened the income gap after the elitist mobilization system collapsed. From 1992 to 2007, the gini coefficient in the Russian Federation soared from .27 to .48 (OECD 2010b, 130; Sukiassyan 2007, 46–47). When capital investment rates decreased after the state socialist period ended, lower growth resulted. Unemployment rose as workers lost their jobs in SOEs that manufactured industrial goods. Central government planners no longer determined wage rates. The growth of private-sector employment raised wage differences. Private-enterprise managers and financiers, particularly those linked to multinational corporations, became the wealthy elite. Many had previously functioned as Communist Party officials heading state-owned enterprises. Now they managed privatized enterprises purchased at a low price from the state. The decline of formal-sector jobs led to greater self-employment in the unofficial, informal economy, where high income disparities prevailed. Low minimum wages hardly protected these workers from high inflation rates during the 1990s. Unpaid or delayed wages hurt employees in both state corporations and smaller private businesses. Managers adopted a callous attitude toward rights of workers, who feared unemployment. Autonomous unions wielded little authority over management decisions or public policymaking. Union density declined, especially in the eastern and rural regions. Neither government officials nor managers enforced labor laws, especially over collective bargaining. Strongest in the state sector—health, education, coal mining—unions had little influence over wages and employment conditions, particularly in the private commercial sector. Bureaucrats dominated both public and private sectors. State officials and private entrepreneurs formed a close alliance. For them, increased production and labor discipline took priority over higher wages, job security, labor retraining, and generous unemployment compensation (Christensen 2013, 180–83; OECD 2011e).

Government bureaucrats as well as private oligopolies, conglomerates, and criminal syndicates opposed egalitarian wages and social-service programs. State regulators had limited control over economic conditions. In the mixed-market economy, private energy companies and financial institutions possessed some autonomy from direct government control. Public officials consulted with private business executives who offered advice on economic policies. Pervasive bribes and payoffs illustrated the corrupt interactions between government and private bureaucrats whose actions brought few material rewards to poorer Russians. Unlike the People's Republic of China (PRC), the Russian Federation lacked a powerful political party. Even the governing party, United Russia, focused on managing elections and shaping legislators' preferences, not on coordinating the policy process. Dominated by the federal president and regional governors, it retained little independence from the executive branch. Police and security agencies inherited from the Soviet era mainly influenced government decision making, controlled by President Vladimir Putin, who tried to arbitrate conflicts among contending factions that allied government officials with private business oligarchs. Security forces repressed labor leaders, journalists, media personnel, students, educated urban youths, gay rights advocates, and other dissidents who sought a more democratic, less stratified system.

Fiscal policies exacerbated income inequalities. Even if the market-based neoliberal "shock therapy" curtailed inflation by the end of the 1990s, low government expenditures for education, health care, disability, child care, social assistance, and housing magnified income disparities. Regional and municipal governments often lacked sufficient money to finance social services that employees used to receive from their SOE. A proportional (flat) personal income tax, low taxes on corporate profits, and high value-added taxes reinforced income polarization.

Not only in China but also in Russia, similar groups benefited and lost from the bureaucratic-authoritarian policies. Losers included unskilled blue-collar workers, people with less formal education, low-ranking employees in private commercial services, migrants from rural areas to the cities, and unemployed individuals. They lacked access to benefits that unions used to provide workers in state-owned enterprises. Poor farmers as well as elderly persons in rural areas endured the lowest incomes. Employees in health, education, and small retail sales also gained few economic rewards from their labor. By contrast, the winners comprised highly educated youths and senior personnel employed by large private corporations headquartered in such cities as St. Petersburg and Moscow. These favored groups comprised financiers, oil-gas executives, commodities traders, factory directors, and heads of construction industries. Allied with government bureaucrats, the corporate oligarchs used informal networks to win monetary privileges, especially short-term profits. Senior civil servants, top security officials, and managers of state corporations also gained economic benefits from the bureaucratic-authoritarian system. Perquisites such as high-quality health care, luxurious automobiles, country houses, and free vacations enhanced their economic well-being. Nepotism facilitated jobs for children of the bureaucratic elite. All these policy trends produced greater class differences than during the Soviet era (Andrain and Smith 2006, 37–38, 47–48; Belton and Clover 2012; S. Clarke 2007; Easter 2008; Gorshkov 2010; Kramer and Herszenhorn 2012; Ledeneva 2013, 7–27, 247–48; Makarenko 2012; Markus 2007; Popov 2012; Remington 2011; Shlapentokh 2008; Tikhonova 2011; Wegren 2007; Wood 2012).

Unlike Russian bureaucrats, South Korean officials under military rule (1961–1993) engineered higher income equality and faster growth. The state capitalist program secured an annual GDP per capita growth rate that averaged around 7 percent. Ginis ranged from .26 to .31 (Asian Development Bank 1989, 179; Kim et al. 2012, 170; Kwack and Lee 2007). Rapid growth rates derived mainly from a powerful central government that promoted industrialization. Advocating hierarchical values, it coordinated activities, suppressed opposition, allowed only limited social pluralism, and expanded its scope of responsibilities. Headed by the army, police, and Korean Central Intelligence Agency (KCIA), the central government quashed student associations, churches, and unions that demanded enhanced rights. Only when these groups refrained from challenging the bureaucratic elites did they retain limited autonomy to engage in nonpolitical activities. Of all social groups, the large private conglomerates (*chaebols*) held the strongest influence over the policy process. They gained generous government subsidies and low taxes. Yet central bureaucrats closely regulated their actions. State planners directed their investments into new industries. The alliance between the state and *chaebols* promoted the export of manufactured goods, such as textiles, chemical products, steel, and electronic products. Civil servants played the decisive role in waging the battle for rapid industrialization. By granting loans, trade rights, licenses, contracts, and protective tariffs, the bureaucratic-authoritarian elite not only controlled private businesses but helped create a new capitalist class.

Powerful government institutions assumed responsibility for directing economic development. Committed to enhancing productivity, these agencies included the Economic Planning Board, Ministry of Finance, Korean Development Institute, Trade Promotion Agency, and Ministry of Trade and Industry. State organizations formulated five-year plans, controlled prices, authorized foreign loans, approved applications for foreign investment, and monitored foreign currency exchanges. Along with low interest rates levied by state banks, high government spending on the physical infrastructure (transportation, communications, roads, sanitation facilities) stimulated capital investment. State capitalism thrived.

Rather than resulting from progressive taxes or generous government expenditures for social services, South Korea's relatively low inequality stemmed from policies toward land, education, and employment. Wealthy families that headed the *chaebols* paid low taxes. Corrupt interactions with state bureaucrats permitted tax evasion. Public spending on such services as retirement aid, health care, unemployment compensation, sickness insurance, and social assistance remained low. Families, private corporations, and local voluntary associations took the main responsibility for supplying benefits for children, the elderly, and disabled veterans. The central government concentrated on expanding primary and secondary education. As enrollment rates rose, illiteracy fell. Workers learned new skills needed for an industrialized economy. Labor-intensive manufacturing firms that exported goods helped maintain low unemployment. During the immediate postwar period, US military personnel enacted land redistribution measures that expropriated land held by the Japanese and their Korean allies. Korean family farmers received small land plots. After 1961, Korean government technocrats granted small farmers low-cost credit, inexpensive fertilizer, capital investment, marketing assistance, and extensive public education. These programs not only expanded farm productivity but enhanced equality. Policies motivated rural youths to move to the cities where new industrial factories provided jobs. All these government programs increased income equality from its level during Japanese colonial rule (1910–1945). Rapid industrial growth ensued.

The same groups that won and lost income from South Korea's "guided capitalism" resembled those in Russia and the PRC. The main beneficiaries comprised state bureaucrats, educated professionals, technocrats, families who headed private conglomerates, and full-time male workers in large factories. Losers included women, less-skilled workers, part-time, temporary employees, and subsistence farmers. Corporate executives and coercive government bureaucrats (the KCIA, police) repressed autonomous unions, which had few members and collective bargaining rights. Based in the company, not an industry, union organizations faced constraints on their right to protest low wages, long working hours, industrial accidents, and an unhealthful job environment. Women employees in textile and electronics factories endured even more dire conditions. Not until the emergence of a reconciliation system in the 1990s did low-income groups gain the opportunity to organize for more egalitarian economic rights (Andrain 1994, 36–41; Chang 2008; Haggard and Kaufman 2008, 114–42; Kalinowski 2009; T. Kim 2008; Kim et al. 2012; Park 2008; Teichman 2012, 26–48).

Whereas the South Korean military dictatorship pursued a state-guided program for industrial growth that increased equality, the coup that overthrew Chilean president Salvador Allende's reconciliation government on

September 11, 1973, rejected egalitarian policies. The administration of the Socialist president nationalized several privately owned enterprises and redistributed land to low-income farmers. Increased government expenditures went for social services. These policies lowered income inequality and unemployment. Yet sluggish growth, skyrocketing inflation, and enhanced equality for the poor mobilized opposition to the Unidad Popular administration. Support for the coup came from several groups: wealthy capitalists, landowners, truckers, major newspapers, courts, right-wing party leaders, Christian Democrats, and neoliberal economists. Influenced by market-oriented economists at the University of Chicago such as Arnold Harberger, Milton Friedman, and Friedrich Hayek, the "Chicago boys" sought to extirpate the "cancer of Marxism" that they saw infecting Allende's democratic socialist government. Viewing the Allende government as a totalitarian dictatorship, they rejected the Socialist president's policies that strengthened unions, expanded public ownership, established price controls, administered central planning, and backed egalitarian outcomes. According to them, Pinochet's authoritarian government would cleanse Chile from its impurities and secure freer markets, greater efficiency, lower inflation, and higher growth (Andrain 2011, 151–82, 196; Farrant, McPhail, and Berger 2012).

Under the bureaucratic-authoritarian military regime, the Pinochet dictatorship used coercive power to enforce its elitist decisions. The army, police, and surveillance agencies ("secret" police) kidnapped, tortured, and executed their opponents. Thousands of deaths occurred from late 1973 through 1977. Major victims included Socialists, Communists, leftists, union leaders, journalists, artists, professors, teachers, and other supporters of Allende's policies.

Pledged to restore low inflation, achieve high growth, and establish political order, neoliberals implemented inegalitarian policies. Poor farmers lost assets when the government redistributed land to the wealthy. Privatization of state-owned enterprises generated lower wage equality. Corporate executives earned high salaries and generous fringe benefits. Deregulation of the labor market weakened unions, abolished strikes, and quashed collective bargaining rights. When union power declined, domestic and foreign private businesses grew stronger. Deregulation of the financial market expanded foreign capital investment, dependence on foreign loans, and export competition. Increased dependence on multinational corporations for investment capital intensified income inequalities, particularly when government bureaucrats offered the corporations tax credits, subsidies, and authority to repatriate profits. The gap splitting rich from poor widened as multinational subsidiaries made contracts with smaller, nonunionized firms that paid low wages. Along with the decline of domestic manufacturing, the rise of financial-commercial private services scarcely generated greater equality. Faced with fewer government jobs and limited opportunities in the formal private service sector, workers turned to the unregulated informal economy for income. Yet these jobs supplied few social benefits or high wages.

Neoliberal programs toward social-service provision reduced government expenditures for pensions, education, and health care, privatized their administration, and imposed higher fees for both public and private services. Government subsidies increased for private providers: pension funds, healthcare agencies, and schools. Only the wealthy could afford to pay for the superior-quality private schools and health clinics. Neither poor persons nor informal workers benefited from the neoliberal priority on private provision. Instead, the most advantages went to the wealthy and some middle-income classes, mainly agribusiness executives, bankers, financiers, speculators, exporters, and conglomerate heads.

As neoliberal policies became stronger during the late 1980s, popular pressures arose for a less coercive political system that reconciled conflicts. Chilean unions, students, and other groups staged protests against the bureaucratic-authoritarian regime. Truck drivers, some merchants, military officers from the navy and air force, as well as the United States ambassador to Chile pressured General Pinochet to relinquish power. He agreed after losing the 1988 plebiscite that gave voters the right to approve or reject another eight years of his presidency. An opposition coalition—the Concertación—of the Christian Democratic Party, Party for Democracy, Socialists, and Radicals contested the December 1989 presidential election won by its candidate, Christian Democrat Patricio Aylwin. Chile returned to civilian rule. Continuing promarket neoliberal programs, reconciliation leaders expanded civil liberties, encouraged competitive elections, and took incremental steps that reduced poverty (ECLAC 2011a, 75; Ffrench-Davis 2010, 1–13, 174–208, 220; Haggard and Kaufman 2008, 61–65, 80–83; Leiva 2008, 53–62; B. Loveman 2001, 230–307; Teichman 2012, 61–72).

REFORMIST DEVELOPMENT IN RECONCILIATION SYSTEMS

Reconciliation systems have placed higher value on advancing political and cultural equality than on attaining more egalitarian results. Policymakers stressed equal opportunities, respect for diverse people, and the right to vote in competitive elections. They took a skeptical view of political authority. Extensive group pluralism enabled persons to assert their distinctive views. Rather than resign to the status quo, individuals could demonstrate the personal and political efficacy required to secure incremental reforms, which occur through negotiating divergent interests.

Political power in reconciliation systems rested on a pluralistic foundation. Government institutions exerted limited control over social groups. Policymakers' key tasks focused on accommodating the different values and interests held by independent groups. Committed to legal restraints on power, political leaders sought civilian control over coercive agencies, even though constitutional limits on the military and police became difficult to institutionalize if widespread violence threatened personal security. Particularly when developing nations industrialized, pressures arose for an increased scope of government responsibilities. Government employees, labor unionists, and workers in the formal sector struggled to receive higher government pensions, health-care facilities, and educational opportunities. Under neoliberalism, however, policymakers faced pressures to reduce expenditures for social services and decentralize their provision. They devised strategies for reconciling divergent demands from private corporations, labor unions, political parties, and foreign institutions such as the International Monetary Fund.

Unlike elitist mobilization regimes, reconciliation systems lacked a dominant party that coordinated government activities and controlled private corporate influence over the policy process. Neither leftist parties nor labor unions could easily mobilize their supporters behind a transformative, egalitarian program that reduced the income gap. Instead, private domestic firms often coalesced with multinational corporations to reject generous, comprehensive, universal policies for social-service provision. They wanted low taxes, business subsidies, and restrictions on unions' right to collectively bargain, gain higher wages, help manage the firm, and improve working conditions. Police and army often quashed strikes, union demonstrations, and occupations of business headquarters. Strongest in the public sector, union leaders achieved greater success vetoing government programs than initiating positive measures that secured more egalitarian outcomes (Andrain 1994, 43–68).

Compared with the wealthiest Northern European societies, reconciliation systems in Asia and Latin America implemented policies that produced less egalitarian outcomes. In most developing nations, poor persons in the rural and informal sectors received few benefits from social-service expenditures. Government revenue mainly came from taxes on goods and services, not personal income. Hence, the rich incurred minimal tax burdens. Labor-market programs impeded workers from forming unions and participating in collective bargaining that would help low-wage employees. Ineffective regulation facilitated extensive corruption between government officials and private businesses, including both domestic oligopolies and multinational corporations. This alliance weakened policies for income redistribution. Like the situation in industrialized societies, the greatest hardships affected mainly women, immigrants, youths under thirty years of age, rural residents, informal workers, part-time, temporary employees, the unskilled, and the unemployed (Cornia 2011; OECD 2011a, 47–82).

From 1980 to 2010, Central Europe and South Korea attained greater income equality than did most Latin American societies, India, and Turkey.

What fiscal, monetary, ownership, regulatory, and labor-market policies explained these regional differences? How did power relationships among government institutions, political parties, private corporations, and labor unions influence policy priorities in these reconciliation systems? Not only the policies inherited from previous regimes but also the comparative strength of neoliberal programs affected income distribution.

Central Europe

Among all emerging market economies, the Czech Republic, Hungary, and Poland most closely resembled Western European societies in their fiscal policies. Even if neoliberal programs allocated lower expenditures for social service since the disintegration of Communist Party governments in 1989, public spending on such services as education, health care, pensions, and social assistance to the poor as a percentage of the GDP in 2009 totaled between 23 and 28 percent—about the same share as in the Netherlands (OECD 2013c, 195, 213). Taxes had a less egalitarian impact than did social-service spending. Personal and corporate income taxes remained fairly low as a share of total tax receipts. The highest tax revenues came from value-added taxes and social security contributions. As a result of the fiscal policies, Czechs and Hungarians had income distributions that resembled the egalitarian patterns among Scandinavians, with Poles facing greater inequality (Appel 2006; OECD 2006, 60–61; OECD 2011a, 45; OECD 2012c, 104; OECD 2013c, 66–67, 195, 213, 226–27; Tridico 2012b; Zaidi 2009, 7).

Labor-market programs reflected the dominance of corporations over unions. Even though the communist parties in Czechoslovakia, Hungary, and Poland had controlled labor unions, they still performed important activities after 1989 for workers, who gained health care, housing subsidies, and recreation-vacation facilities resulting from union participation in state enterprises. Under the reconciliation system, union membership fell. Collective bargaining occurred at each firm rather than throughout the whole nation. With the privatization of state-owned enterprises, union influence declined, particularly in private firms. Managers and owners made crucial decisions without consulting workers. Unions also exerted limited influence over government officials, who enacted generous subsidies and lower taxes for private businesses, especially multinational corporations. Lower wages ensued. The minimum wage failed to match the high inflation rate during the early 1990s. Privatization hurt unskilled workers, who suffered the most from rising unemployment. Even in Poland, where the Solidarity movement mounted strong opposition against the communist regime in the 1980s, union strength decreased soon after Solidarity controlled the government from 1989 to 1991.

Committed to the neoliberal preference for a flexible labor market, no major political party offered policies that supported greater income equality for Czechs, Hungarians, and Poles. Both leftist social democrats and more right-wing promarket parties agreed on similar neoliberal programs. Private business owners, technical experts, senior employees of multinational corporations, and managers of remaining state enterprises emerged as the winners from neoliberalism. The urban-rural income gap rose as urbanites living in Prague, Budapest, and Warsaw gained more economic benefits than did rural residents (Cook 2007; EU 2012, 89–92; Förster, Jesuit, and Smeeding 2005; Ivanova 2007; Kaufman 2007; Ost 2009; Słomczyński and Janicka 2008).

Asia

The South Korean reconciliation system followed the Japanese model after 1992, when competitive elections and civilian rule grew stronger. Influenced by United States military authorities after World War II ended, both nations' government leaders enacted inclusive education and land redistribution programs. Fear of communist influence from the People's Republic of China and North Korea motivated officials to adopt some redistributive policies. Under Japanese colonial rule from 1910 to 1945, Koreans felt antagonism toward their former oppressor, yet they resolved to improve their status through hard work, innovation, economic efficiency, individual achievement, personal efficacy, national pride, and bureaucratic expertise. The central government assumed a dominant role in forging economic development, particularly by allying with large domestic conglomerates that produced manufactured exports, such as automobiles, electronic products, computers, and information-processing equipment. Overseas investment that spread to low-wage societies such as China curtailed employment opportunities for unskilled workers at home. Company unions enabled managers to make major decisions within each corporation. As the labor market became more flexible after the early 1990s, income equality declined in Japan and South Korea. By 2009–2010, the gini equaled .31 for Korea and .34 for Japan (Brinton 2011, 178–87; Kwack and Lee 2007, 6; OECD 2013a; Yun 2009, 1–2).

From 1997 to 2008, South Korea's government included a higher proportion of individuals who gained more comprehensive, generous benefits. Although spending on social services as a share of the GDP was lower than in other industrialized OECD nations, expenditures for national health insurance, public assistance, and unemployment insurance increased. Under the previous, more repressive regime, civil servants, teachers, military forces, and male factory workers in large corporations enjoyed the greatest benefits. Now the rural and urban self-employed, as well as some low-income citizens, gained coverage.

Yet after the 1997–1998 financial crisis, Korean government officials enacted policies that led to a wider income gap than during the 1985–1995 era. Fiscal measures had a minimal impact on redistributing income toward the poor. Besides extensive tax evasion by the self-employed, low taxes on personal income and capital gains hardly produced greater economic equality. Economic growth took priority over expansion of social services. Low replacement rates for pensions harmed the elderly poor, particularly women. Pressured by the IMF to reduce labor costs and enhance global competition, corporations provided fewer benefits, such as housing subsidies, school fees, and vacation facilities. As individualist values became more widespread, family solidarity weakened. Young people were no longer so willing to transfer cash assistance to their parents. When company and family assistance declined, the government supplied higher social-service benefits to more individuals. Over 70 percent of full-time workers employed by large corporations and government agencies received pensions, health insurance, and unemployment benefits. Among part-time, temporary contingent employees who worked in small private firms, under 40 percent secured these services (An and Bosworth 2013, 1–13, 97–143; Jung and Walker 2009; Kim et al. 2012, 180; Park 2011; Shin 2010, 223).

When extensive bankruptcies, unemployment, and lower revenues occurred after 1997, the trend toward neoliberal priorities generated flexible labor-market policies that reduced union power over public policymaking and corporate management. Union membership decreased from nearly 20 percent in 1990 to around 10 percent in 2008. Collective bargaining covered only one-tenth of workers (OECD 2012a, 146). Laws restricted the right of civil servants and teachers to form unions, especially to strike for better working conditions. Fragmentation weakened the union movement. The two largest union federations—Federation of Korean Trade Unions (FKTU) and Korean Confederation of Trade Unions (KCTU)—competed with each other for support. Whereas the older FKTU adopted a more probusiness, progovernment stand, the newer KCTU supported more militant tactics, such as strikes and demonstrations. Within each federation, weak national leaders contended with stronger local-branch members who struggled for greater union autonomy. Company unions of full-time permanent workers sought job security and higher wages but demonstrated little support for mobilizing the large unorganized labor force. More independent unions took responsibility for organizing the numerous contingent workers. Staging hunger strikes, street demonstrations, and sit-ins, these unions allied with social movements that campaigned for social justice, civil liberties, and human rights, not just for economic demands. Student groups, civic associations, women's networks, and the urban poor formed cross-class coalitions to support these independent unions (Kang 2012, 66–111; Lee, Chung, and Jang 2008).

Strong business opposition from large conglomerates hindered union power to achieve greater income equality. After the 1997–1998 South Korean financial crisis, the *chaebols* experienced a more pluralist business environment. Shareholders, foreign investors, and social movements—People's Solidarity for Participatory Democracy, Citizens' Coalition for Economic Justice, Council of Movement for People and Democracy—rejected direct economic management by the family dynasties. Nevertheless, the *chaebols* retained extensive resources to influence the public policy process. They dominated numerous industries: automobiles, home construction, theme parks, the media, nonbank financial institutions, local bakeries, electronics, and information processing. Chief executive officers evaded tax payments. Campaign contributions to political parties strengthened the *chaebols*' policy impact. Multinational enterprises such as Hyundai, Samsung, Lucky-Goldstar, and the Sunkyung Group invested all over the world. Maintaining close ties with the IMF, conglomerate directors opposed union power over corporate decision making. They preferred the neoliberal stress on expanded trade, foreign investment, privatization, and deregulation of labor markets. According to them, lower replacement rates for pensions as well as more short-term, low-paid contracts enhanced export competition.

Senior military officers, government technocrats, and the wealthy viewed rapid economic growth, higher export sales, and national security, not economic equality, as the primary objectives behind the Global Korea public policies. Allied with senior civil servants and technocrats, corporate executives secured low-interest loans from government banks as well as public subsidies for export industries. Deregulation of Korean financial markets facilitated loans from foreign creditors. The more flexible labor-market policies gave conglomerate managers greater authority to hire and fire employees, especially the vulnerable contingent workers obtaining low wages, few bonuses, and minimal social-service benefits (Bulard 2013; Choi 2008; Kuk 2010; Lim 2010; Park 2008; Park and Mah 2011; Teichman 2012, 132–51; Yun 2009; Zhang 2010).

As a result of the neoliberal programs, the main beneficiaries included full-time, permanent employees with senior positions in large corporations and government institutions. Women and contingent workers endured the greatest costs. Compared with men, Korean women held more part-time, temporary jobs that paid lower wages. Employed as clerks, salespersons, and private service workers, they secured limited benefits, including unemployment compensation, retirement pensions, and paid maternity leaves. Higher unemployment led to greater poverty, less job security, and more economic hardships than faced by male executives. Hierarchical values prescribed by the newer conglomerates and the older Confucian ethic reinforced gender inequality, even though younger Koreans challenged the stress on hierarchy. Because the *chaebols* hired fewer full-time, permanent employees, young university graduates lacked job opportunities. Immigrant laborers also suffered from economic inequality. They took low-wage, temporary, part-time jobs as unskilled laborers in construction, manufacturing, and private commercial services (An 2009; H.-K. Kim 2009; Oliver and Buseong 2012; H.-Y. Song 2013; J. Song 2009).

Unlike South Korean conditions, a poorer, more diverse population fragmented by caste, regional, religious, occupational, and gender cleavages hindered the formation of coalitions among different Indian occupations. Higher-income groups comprised men, upper-caste Brahmins, Hindus, university-educated persons, workers in the organized formal sector, and urban residents living in the south. Regional cleavages divided the north, dominated by conservative Brahmin elites, from the more prosperous southern regions led by more leftist secular officials. Wealthy families and clans that maintained close ties with government officials headed the largest corporations. Women, child laborers, low-caste Dalits, and Muslims experienced lower incomes. From 1991, when the neoliberal era began, until 2005, the income gap widened, especially between urban and rural residents. Poor farmers sought jobs in the city. The urban poor faced difficulties securing formal-sector jobs, educational opportunities, water, sanitation facilities, and high-quality health benefits, especially for mothers. Whereas the wealthiest 20 percent made large income gains from 1990 to 2005, the poorest 40 percent faced stagnant incomes (D. Banerjee 2007; Cain et al. 2010; Chandrasekhar and Mukhopadhyay 2010; Deaton and Drèze 2005; Deshpande, Satpathy, and Deshpande 2007; Kohli 2012, 135–211; Mastoor 2008; Sarkar and Mehta 2010).

No cohesive central government could implement programs for greater land and income equality in the diverse, pluralist Indian society. Whereas wealthier regions obtained higher government grants, central policymakers reduced social-service benefits to poorer rural residents, particularly for education and health care. Compared with South Korean and Chinese leaders, Indian government officials spent a lower proportion of the GDP on pensions, unemployment compensation, social assistance, and disability. Under the regressive tax system, only around 3 percent paid personal income taxes. Wealthy urban and landed elites evaded tax payments. Supreme Court cases approved the avoidance of capital gains taxes by foreign-owned corporations that claimed locations in offshore headquarters, such as Mauritius and the Cayman Islands. Labor policies advocated by neoliberals encouraged the growth of part-time, temporary employees in the unofficial, informal economy. As a share of the total labor force, over 90 percent worked in this sector, which, around the year 2000, produced over 60 percent of the GDP. Most informal employees—street vendors, trash pickers, rickshaw drivers, artisans, repairers, retail salespersons, poor farmers—experienced low wages, few fringe benefits, frequent dismissals, and high job insecurity. Young women migrating to the cities worked in small-scale firms that produced clothes for export sales by multinational corporations. The informal economy lacked effective tax collection, strict labor law enforcement, and supply of public social services by central and state governments. Traditional hierarchies based on caste, religion, and family patriarchy intensified social stratification (Agarwala 2008; Bhushan 2012; Chatterjee 2008; Das 2007; OECD 2011f, 69–71; Pande 2007; Piketty and Qian 2009).

Fragmented governments and political parties reflected the incohesive, pluralist nature of Indian society. In this reconciliation system, no organization had the transformative power to secure a more egalitarian income distribution. Needing to accommodate group differences, political leaders implemented gradual procedural changes that scarcely reduced rich persons' income. The decentralized federal system granted power to economic elites, such as wealthy landowners, who controlled state and local governments. Educated professionals who managed public institutions enjoyed high salaries and other perquisites. As patrons, they supplied subsidies, contracts, and tax credits to business clients in exchange for their electoral support.

The competitive party system hindered any dominant party from coordinating government activities. Coalitions of several parties usually controlled the parliaments. Both the secular Congress Party and the Hindu nationalist party BJP (Bharatiya Janata Party) after 1991 supported neoliberal programs. Globalization, decentralization, and especially privatization stymied egalitarian policies. Wealthier Indians relied on private suppliers of education, health care, transportation, electricity, water, sanitation facilities, and security guards. Poorer groups coped with unavailable, insufficient, or low-quality government services. Even the Communist Party of India (Marxist), which shared power in Kerala's Left Democratic Front government, supported tax relief for domestic and foreign capitalist investors. State policymakers expropriated land from poor farmers, gave them low prices, and awarded the land to developers who constructed shopping malls. Multinational corporations, domestic capitalists, wealthy farmers, and CPI (Marxist) leaders, not poor farmers or workers, benefited from these neoliberal policies. The ideological commitment to socialism in Kerala encouraged measures that increased literacy, lowered infant mortality, and lengthened life expectancy. Yet federal government officials made little progress toward reducing income inequalities throughout India. Indians faced greater adult illiteracy, shorter life expectancy at birth, as well as higher rates of poverty, hunger, and infant mortality than did Chinese and especially South Koreans (S. Banerjee 2011; Bardhan 2009; Dalrymple 2012; Drèze and Sen 2013, 72–80, 213–26, 292–306; Ganguly-Scrase and Scrase 2008; Kohli 2012, 192–211; OECD 2011f, 54–55, 74–77; Williams 2008, 97–99).

Flexible labor-market policies weakened union power over India's private managers and government officials. As the service sector grew more powerful, unions' influence fell. Information technology, science, finance, real estate, and private businesses employed more workers, whom unions had difficulties organizing. Opposed to unions, both government administrators and especially private managers felt little inclination to enforce labor laws. Only around 5 percent of the total labor force belonged to a union. Membership remained highest in the public sector and large urban industries, which showed greater wage equality than the nonfarm informal sector, where around 10 percent were union members. Few rural residents gained access to union benefits. With the mechanization of agriculture and the establishment of large agribusinesses, lower-caste workers, especially women, had to take more part-time, temporary jobs as low-wage farm laborers. Besides low membership, other weaknesses hindered union power. Separate unions belonged to the four major parties: Congress, BJP, Communist Party of India, and Communist Party of India (Marxist). Although allied unions demonstrated greater opposition to neoliberal measures for cutting labor costs, restraining wages, and lessening job security than did political party leaders, union heads wielded limited positive power. Instead, they could delay labor legislation, demonstrate, and strike. Antiunion decisions by the Supreme Court of India and state courts, which backed employers' preferences, limited even these tactics (D. Banerjee 2007; Gillan 2007; Hensman 2011, 86–208; Majumder 2007; Pande 2007; Parthasarathy 2012; Uba 2008).

Despite these obstacles, the Indian reconciliation system did enable a few unions to organize some informal workers at the local neighborhood level. The Communist Party unions recruited women who worked for small cigarette producers. Independent unions and nongovernmental organizations gained members among rural migrants who labored in the cities as construction workers. Committed to low-cost, flexible labor, neoliberal policymakers faced a dilemma. On the one hand, they opposed active government regulation over private businesses. On the other hand, since these firms supplied few social-service benefits, workers became more dependent on government for health care, educational scholarships, housing subsidies, marriage expenses, and funeral costs. Through hunger strikes, nonviolent demonstrations, and media publicity, unions pressured workers' welfare boards to deliver benefits funded by state governments, employers, and workers. Appeals for effective state government implementation of these benefits proclaimed the need for guaranteeing citizens' legal rights. As in a typical reconciliation system, procedural justice appeared a more feasible objective than did achievement of higher wages and enhanced job security for informal employees (Agarwala 2008).

Neoliberal policies reinforced the political power of large-scale corporate capital over smaller firms throughout India's economy. Informal entrepreneurs feared market uncertainties looming from increased globalization. With the rise of formal education among youths, small family businesses held less appeal than did jobs in finance, computer operations, and global communications. Corporate capitalists, especially those heading the Confederation of Indian Industry, supported freer trade and expanded foreign direct investment. They relied on professional management and bureaucratic expertise to manage financial institutions and information-processing centers. High personal efficacy took priority over fatalism. Through corrupt interactions with government officials and most political parties, business lobbyists won desired tax exemptions, subsidies, and contracts. Yet during the late 2000s, disenchantment with restrictive government regulations over corporations produced greater conflicts between leading industrialists and public policymakers (Crabtree 2012; OECD 2012a, 149; Sinha 2010; Yadav 2011).

Linking Asia and Western Europe, Turkey shared similarities with nations in both continents. As in many Asian countries, business groups exerted greater policy influence than did the fragmented labor union movement. Foreign multinational corporations formed joint alliances with domestic firms. Class cleavages pitted managers, professionals, and entrepreneurs against low-paid private-service employees and those working in the large informal sector. Gender, religious, and regional cleavages hindered programs for lessening income inequality, especially between cities and rural provinces. Unemployed youths often sought work in European countries. Like Western European officials, Turkish political leaders pursued neoliberal policies that privatized many SOEs, deregulated private businesses, promoted a flexible labor market, encouraged greater competition, conducted more overseas trade, and welcomed foreign direct investment (Şenses 2012). As ties with Europe expanded, competition among political parties facilitated election of governing parties led by civilians. Yet in Turkey, unlike Western Europe, secular parties lost strength during the early twenty-first century. Gaining government control in 2002, the Islamist Justice and Development Party (Adalet ve Kalkinma Partisi—AKP) reduced military power but did not enact egalitarian public policies. Instead, the AKP formulated an interpretation of Islamic capitalism that reconciled Muslim justice with rapid economic development (Ertuğrul 2012). Under the AKP government, private entrepreneurs gained greater public benefits than did labor unions or low-income Turks. Growth took precedence over income equality. By 2009, Turkey's gini equaled .41—a higher coefficient than in any Western European society (Kaya 2008; OECD 2013a, 4).

Neither expenditures nor taxes had an egalitarian impact. Social-service expenditures in 2007 comprised a smaller share of the GDP than in the more industrialized OECD nations (OECD 2013c, 213). Turks became dependent on their extended family, neighborhood, mosques, and informal networks for services. Although the elderly poor gained assistance from the public social security system, partial privatization of pensions, health insurance, unemployment compensation, and disability payments contributed to less equality. Lower-income individuals lost benefits when a public pay-as-you-go retirement system financed by taxes and social security contributions changed to a defined contribution program under which individuals invested in the volatile stock market. High administrative costs reduced payments to the elderly. Minimal child-care benefits deterred women from joining the paid labor force.

The AKP placed a low priority on gender equality. Patriarchal, hierarchical norms claimed that women and men should perform different roles. Whereas men earned money in the paid labor force, women focused on caring for their husband, parents, and children. Participating mainly as informal laborers, females gained limited wages and few government social-service benefits. A large income gap arose between men employed in the formal sector and women who held part-time, low-paying jobs or worked as unpaid laborers in family businesses. Committed to business, rather than government, provision of these services, AKP policies relied on tax reductions to private enterprises as a strategy for expanding women's employment. Regressive taxes collected from the sale of goods and services, rather than from personal or corporate income, enlarged economic inequalities (Dedeoglu 2012; Elveren 2008, 104–6; OECD 2012c, 104).

Although fragmented by regional cleavages and divergent interpretations of Islamic justice, corporations wielded greater policy influence than did labor unions. When the AKP became the dominant governing party and implemented neoliberal policies, the two largest business associations supported the government. The more secular Turkish Industrialists' and Businessmen's Association (TÜSİAD) represented large corporations, especially financial institutions, centered in Istanbul. Initially opposed to the AKP, it backed the party's program that expanded exports and upheld business interests over labor union rights. Even though founded by Muslim entrepreneurs, the Independent Industrialists and Businessmen's Association (MÜSİAD) gave priority to economic interests over religious values. Closely aligned with the AKP, it favored policies that produced high growth, low business taxes, price stability, cheap credit from Islamic banks, and government contracts for private firms. Originally against Western European trade, MÜSİAD enterprises later supported neoliberal measures for expanding exports to European, Middle Eastern, and Asian nations. Like the AKP, Islamic business associations sought to restore the regional influence of the Ottoman Empire. Rejecting socialism and state-owned enterprises, they shared the AKP's commitment to privatization, business deregulation, and a flexible labor market. Powerful networks strengthened business cohesion. Patron-client ties linked government officials with private entrepreneurs, whatever their associational membership. Control over television, radio, and newspapers heightened their policy impact. Labor unions had fewer resources to influence government policies (Buğra and Savaşkan 2012; Demiralp 2009; Emrence 2008).

Not only political changes but economic changes in the labor market hindered union efforts to redistribute income toward women and poor people. Among the three largest union confederations, two took a secular stand, and the most recently established one—Confederation of Turkish Just Workers' Union—allied with the AKP. Although asserting a more secular outlook than the AKP and showing less enthusiasm for extensive privatization of SOEs, the main opposition Republican People's Party also adopted a neoliberal stance that deterred close ties with unions. Besides the weak manufacturing and public sectors, the growth of private services and the informal economy decreased union authority. Unlike manufacturing employees, private-service, agricultural, and informal sector workers proved more difficult to organize, even though they comprised 75 percent of the 2009 labor force. Union density comprised only 6 percent of the 2010 employed labor force. Neither the government bureaucracy nor private businesses felt impelled to grant union workers more wage equality (Atasoy 2007; Barratt 2009, 49; Blind 2007; Coloma 2013; Coşar and Özman 2008; Kaya 2008; Şahin 2010; Şenses 2012, 17–18).

Latin America

Why did Latin American societies experience lower income equality than Turkey and such East Asian nations as Taiwan and South Korea? The Taiwanese and Korean policymakers implemented land reform and inclusive education programs that assisted the poor. Labor-intensive capital investment produced high growth rates that provided the revenues for funding social-service benefits, which have become more universal. Government planners focused on increasing manufactured exports whose production narrowed the wage gap among workers. In Latin America, however, Spanish and Portuguese colonialists established agricultural systems ruled by landed oligarchs who charged high rents. Small farmers, except in Costa Rica, possessed little wealth. Since the 1970s, agribusiness conglomerates mainly exported food, such as soybeans, sugar, beef, and bananas. Besides food, minerals comprised a larger share of exports than in East Asia. Historically, education policies stressed university education benefiting mainly children from wealthy parents. Even if the wealthiest Latin American governments enacted higher expenditures for social services than did Korean political leaders, most services accrued to urban formal-sector employees working for the armed forces, civil service, and manufacturing enterprises. Rural residents and workers in the informal economy gained fewer benefits (Cornia 2011; Dellepiane-Avellaneda 2010; Huber et al. 2006; Mann and Riley 2007; Teichman 2012, 2–25; Thorp 2012; Williamson 2011, 162–63, 231–34).

Despite their European heritage, developments in Latin American societies since World War II showed striking differences from developments in

Western and even Central Europe. Unlike European states, Latin American governments enacted lower social-service expenditures as a share of the GDP and levied less-progressive taxes, especially on personal and corporate income. As a result, Latin American nations experienced lower income equality. Ginis exceeded .45 in most countries (ECLAC 2011a, 75–76; OECD/ECLAC/CIAT 2012, 21–22).

Whereas Europeans' household disposable income after taxes and transfers became more equal, in Latin America fiscal policies redistributed less income to the poor from 1980 to 2000. Even though larger expenditures for education and health care produced higher wage equality, the posttax, posttransfer ginis showed only minor decreases from the coefficients for market income (Ekkehard and Escudero 2008, 53; Morgan and Kelly 2013; OECD/ECLAC 2011, 77–78). Most social-service expenditures, particularly pensions, went to the wealthiest fifth employed by government and large, urban-based private corporations. Rural and informal workers received fewer benefits, such as high-quality health care, secondary education, water, sanitation, nutrition, and access to a modern infrastructure. Policy priorities on secondary and especially university education hindered poor people's opportunities to attain upward mobility. With the rise of neoliberalism since the 1980s, targeted programs for poor people gained stronger support. High administrative costs, insufficient funds, and exclusion of the eligible poor mitigated the egalitarian impact of conditional cash transfers paid to low-income mothers whose children attended school and received care from a health clinic. The major inclusive public program for reducing poverty focused on primary education, even though its deficient quality motivated wealthy persons to send their children to private primary schools.

Regressive taxes exacerbated income inequality among Latin Americans. Most revenues came from indirect taxes, particularly the value-added tax. Fearing reduced investment by private enterprises, government officials lowered corporate income taxes after 1980. Understaffed, underfunded tax collection agencies enabled the wealthiest 20 percent to avoid paying personal income taxes. Poorer people in the unregulated informal economy also evaded tax collection. Because of the high proportion of revenues derived from general consumption, particularly the value-added tax, the richest fifth actually paid a lower share of their income in taxes than did the poorest 20 percent (Bastagli 2011; Burchardt 2010; Cárdenas and Perry 2011; Dion 2010; Ghosh 2011; Goñi, López, and Servén 2011; Hart 2010; Klasen and Nowak-Lehmann 2009; Lloyd-Sherlock 2009; McGuire 2012; Ocampo 2011; OECD/ECLAC 2011, 72–78, 221–26; OECD/ECLAC/CIAT 2012, 20–22; Tanzi 2011, 236–43; Teichman 2012, 151–65).

Privatization failed to narrow the Latin American income gap. Influenced by neoliberalism, political leaders during the 1980s privatized such public utilities as water, sanitation, gas, electricity, and telecommunications.

Wealthy corporations paid a low price for these SOEs, which often became private monopolies. They charged high fees for the services; rural residents gained limited access to utilities. No effective government regulation limited the private utilities' decisions. Privatization of such social services as education, health care, and pensions raised poor people's costs for these benefits.

Policies that established a more flexible labor market impeded movement toward egalitarian programs. When neoliberal government officials promoted greater numbers of part-time, temporary workers, the informal economy grew larger as a share of the labor force. With the growth of commercial agribusinesses selling food for export, poor farmers sought work as agricultural laborers. The diversity of the rural population—agribusiness owners, wealthy family farmers, subsistence farmers, sharecroppers, landless wage earners—weakened cohesion and policy efforts to secure land redistribution to poorer farmers. Many moved to the cities, where they worked in the informal economy, which included the self-employed, street vendors, workers in small businesses, domestic servants, and wage earners who lacked a labor contract. By the twenty-first century, this sector comprised around one-half the nonfarm labor force. Urban informal workers held temporary, part-time jobs in restaurants, hotels, retail stores, and construction sites. They received low wages, gained few social-service benefits, and depended on personal networks for assistance. Small family firms that contracted with larger industries to supply inexpensive parts also paid their workers low wages.

Concentrating on public-sector and manufacturing workers, unions often showed little enthusiasm for organizing the disorganized, heterogeneous informal employees. Instead, unions focused on gaining higher wages, job security, and more fringe benefits for their members. When employment decreased in both the manufacturing and public sectors from 1990 to 2005, union strength fell. The rise of financial institutions and other private business services reduced pressures for policymakers to approve measures that would redistribute income toward the poor (Acharya, Schneider, and Ugaz 2006; Anner 2008; Cinoli, Primi, and Pugno 2006, 89; Kay 2008; Kurtz and Brooks 2008; Patroni 2008; Petras and Veltmeyer 2007; Ramos 2010; Tokman 2011; Vos 2011).

Latin America's inegalitarian trends reflected the dominance of corporations over the policy process. Although foreign multinational corporations became more pervasive after 1980, domestic conglomerates—*los grupos*—usually wielded dominant influence. Compared with smaller, specialized firms, the conglomerates possessed greater capital resources, supply of credit, information about economic conditions, and access to policymakers, including the president and government ministers. Frequent consultations with political leaders enabled corporate executives to secure low-interest loans, contracts, licenses, restrictions on imports, and subsidies for exports. A few wealthy families often owned the conglomerates. Many *grupos* controlled diverse economic sectors: finance, manufacturing, construction, shipping, food processing, mineral production, electricity, hotels, transportation, and telecommunications. Domestic conglomerates allied with the government and multinational corporations. Globalization not only enhanced foreign direct investment in Latin America but also strengthened Latin American multinational corporations that invested overseas. Maintaining subsidiaries in other parts of the continent, the United States, Asia, and Europe, the *multilatinas* gained high profits. As the global, financial, and informal markets grew stronger, job insecurity and wage stagnation increased. Earning low wages, women, rural residents, and informal-sector workers suffered the greatest costs from corporate power. Senior executives, financiers, high-ranking government technocrats, and family heads of the multinational conglomerates, such as Mexican billionaire Carlos Slim, reaped the most economic benefits (Boito 2007; Bull 2008; Leiva 2008, 119–44, 189–214; B. Schneider 2008; Stallings and Peres 2011).

Latin American policymakers had less power than did European officials to implement an egalitarian agenda. The conflict between a president from one party and a legislature controlled by different political parties often led to policy stalemates. Fragmented, uncoordinated, and decentralized governments failed to protect poor residents from exploitation. For example, landed elites in northeastern Brazil hired private militias to repress protests by subsistence farmers. Extensive corruption based on personal-client ties impeded efficient government management throughout Latin America. Technocrats who made the crucial decisions in government ministries and private conglomerates, particularly financial institutions, deterred attempts to reduce income inequalities. Among most Latin American countries, elitist pluralism reinforced the dominance of oligopolies that skillfully used their resources to secure beneficial subsidies, tax incentives, regulations, contracts, and information from government officials.

Few political parties in Latin America possessed the resources to mobilize support for redistributive public policies that would lessen income disparities. Compared with Northern European societies, left-wing parties exerted weaker power. Socialist party leaders and union heads did not develop close ties, even when a left-wing president governed. Supported by influential business associations, rightist parties often won elections by stressing issues like fiscal stability, low inflation, national security, and crime. Their nationalist, religious, and populist slogans advocated a promarket agenda. To gain more electoral support, leftist parties felt the need to ally with centrist parties by accepting some aspects of neoliberalism, such as lower corporate income taxes, fiscal surpluses, freer trade, greater foreign investment, and a more competitive market economy (Huber, Mustillo, and Stephens 2008; Huber and Stephens 2012, 177–207, 253–63; Levitsky and Roberts 2011).

Even though Latin American ginis increased during the 1980–2000 period, after 2002 the income gap declined. Particularly in societies governed by a center-left party, such as Argentina, Brazil, Chile, and Uruguay, poorer individuals gained greater access to public social services. Presidents from the Argentinian Partido Justicialista, Chilean Socialist Party, Brazilian Workers' Party, and Uruguayan Frente Amplio (Broad Front) promoted the expansion of union rights, civil liberties, unemployment compensation, and public health care, pensions, and education. As enrollment in primary and secondary schools grew and students gained more cognitive skills, income disparities lessened. Progressive income taxes took slightly larger shares of the GDP. Higher growth rates, increased tax revenues, and lower interest rates financed larger, more inclusive social-service benefits. The minimum wage increased. Less-skilled workers in labor-intensive export industries gained higher wages as commodity prices boomed on the world market. Latin American governments became less dependent on foreign financial institutions, such as the World Bank and IMF. Committed to gradual change, leftist parties helped reduce poverty and income disparities. Despite these achievements, the ginis remained higher than in Europe and East Asia (Birdsall, Lustig, and McCleod 2012; Buchanan 2008; Flores-Macías 2012, 173–93; Gasparini and Lustig 2011; Goñi, López, and Servén 2011; Gower, Pearce, and Raworth 2012; Hart 2010; Levy and Schady 2013; Lustig, Lopez-Calva, and Ortiz-Juarez 2013; Lustig, Pessino, and Scott 2013; McCleod and Lustig 2011; OECD/ECLAC 2011, 68–78; Santiso and Zoido 2011; Schneider 2012).

CONCLUSION

Political power relationships among governments, political parties, labor unions, and corporations influenced the impact of public policies on income distribution. High coordination among government agencies strengthened the power of officials committed to an egalitarian agenda. They wielded a high scope of power over economic management and provision of social services. In reconciliation systems, accommodating pluralism encouraged the sharing of power among several groups, including labor unions, business associations, women's organizations, and citizens' networks. If group leaders shared similar egalitarian values, fewer policy stalemates occurred. Government leaders could enact generous, comprehensive, and inclusive expenditures for social services as well as progressive personal and corporate income taxes (Ocampo 2011).

In elitist mobilization systems such as Maoist China and the Soviet Union under Stalinist rule, extensive coercion by government agencies denied private corporations the right to participate in the policy process. They lacked the power to hinder Communist Party leaders' programs for narrowing income differences based on private ownership of capital. Neither multinational corporations nor intergovernmental institutions such as the International Monetary Fund and the World Bank influenced the policies preferred by elitist mobilization officials.

A few elite groups dominated bureaucratic-authoritarian regimes that rejected egalitarian policies for income distribution. Widespread popular participation remained limited, especially by labor unions, leftist political parties, and social movements. Rather than supplying inclusive, comprehensive, generous social services, governments concentrated on rewarding private corporations with tax credits, subsidies, licenses, contracts, and influence over public policymaking. Unions and small businesses lacked sufficient power to frame the policy agenda. Highlighting the need for national security, Latin American and Asian military officers ruling bureaucratic-authoritarian systems repressed opposition. Under such conditions, leaders who sought a reconciliation system faced constraints on their opportunities to establish a regime change that expanded civil liberties, popular participation, and income equality.

Reconciliation systems promoting egalitarian programs supported countervailing power among political parties, unions, and private businesses. Political parties competed for electoral support. Policy achievements increased when leftist leaders developed political skills to negotiate agreements among different parties and factions within the same party. Conflicts that divided business organizations expanded opportunities for left-wing parties and allied unions to attain their egalitarian policy preferences. If cohesive labor unions linked to a leftist party organized a large share of the labor force, successful prospects for income redistribution rose. Yet unlike Scandinavian societies, in most developing nations leftist parties and cohesive unions had limited power over government administrators. With the decline of the manufacturing sector and the rise of private services, particularly financial institutions, corporate influence became more pervasive. Multinational corporations enhanced their importance under neoliberalism. Information technology, foreign trade, overseas investment, and immigration heightened global interdependence. Global pressures interacted with national power relationships to affect policies toward income distribution (Alemán 2008; Flores-Macías 2012, 60–93; Glenn 2009; Noble 2013; Sandbrook et al. 2007, 1–62; Thomas 2013).

Chapter Four

Policies and Income Distribution under Global Capitalism

From 1863 through 1871, the Russian novelist Fyodor Dostoevsky became obsessed with gambling. Pressures from an unscrupulous publisher caused high debts. Fearing imprisonment for failure to pay his creditors, Dostoevsky chose gambling as a way to acquire needed money. Unfortunately for him, he lost all his money, even his pawned watch. Despite his compulsion to secure short-term benefits, roulette yielded long-run costs, both to him and to his wife Anna (J. Frank 2010, 537–39; Pevear 2005).

The novella *The Gambler* reflected Dostoevsky's personal experiences with gambling. Linking personal behavior to national cultural values, it portrayed the ambivalences and contradictions that motivated the major character Alexei Ivanovich. A young university-educated nobleman, he worked as a tutor for a Russian general who showed him little deference. For Alexei, money represented not an end in itself but a sign of success, which brought self-respect, social status, and power over other people. Dostoevsky (2005, 323) believed that gambling illustrated the contradictory values that prevailed among Russians. Personal efficacy conflicted with fatalism. Plagued by doubts, Alexei needed to triumph over fate and achieve self-control. Yet he could not stop gambling after a few wins. His irrational behavior led to short-term gains but long-term losses. Individualism contradicted collective values. The desire for immediate personal rewards ignored concern for the public good.

Stereotypical beliefs overcame regard for individual qualities of people from other nations. The novel took place in a German city that Dostoevsky named Roulettenberg. In this multinational setting, several European nationalities gambled at the casino. Alexei stereotyped them with distinctive cultural values: the calculating French "riffraff," hierarchical Germans, crooked Poles, pragmatic English, and outrageous Russians who "gamble futilely."

According to Dostoevsky, gambling brought despair to the individual and the Russian nation. Conducted by a banker, roulette reflected the irrational speculation that thrived on bets to win a rich payoff on the wheel of fortune. Alexei claimed: "Roulette is just made for Russians. . . . We are . . . very prone to such methods as, for instance, roulette, where one can get rich suddenly, in two hours, without any work. . . . But since we also gamble futilely, without working at it, we lose!" (Dostoevsky 2005, 196–97). Addiction to this type of reckless bravado hardly produced long-term benefits for the Russian nation.

Seventy years after Dostoevsky portrayed the irrational effects of gambling, John Maynard Keynes compared global financial speculation to gambling at a casino. Quick rewards preceded eventual losses, higher unemployment, and greater income inequality. According to him, "The game of professional investment is intolerably boring and over-exacting to anyone who is entirely exempt from the gambling instinct. . . . When the capital development of a country becomes a by-product of the activities of a casino, the job is likely to be ill-done" (Keynes 1973c, 157, 159). Recalling the post–World War I political instability and the 1930s depression, Keynes sought to avoid these negative outcomes after World War II. Keynes functioned as the major British representative from the UK Treasury at the Bretton Woods UN Monetary and Financial Conference that took place in New Hampshire during July 1944. There he strove to establish multilateral financial institutions that would operate for the global public good, not for the limited, special interests of a particular nation or dominant economic group. He viewed the International Monetary Fund and the World Bank born at Bretton Woods as children: "Master Fund" and "Miss Bank." From his perspective, they should wear Joseph's coat of many colors, operate in an ecumenical way, belong to the whole world, and pursue the general world good. Keynes wanted experts who guided the IMF and Bank to act with courage, energy, decisiveness, patience, discretion, and wisdom. Committed to lessening income inequality, he opposed high salaries for the executive directors running the IMF and Bank. Supporting cooperation between the United Kingdom and the United States, he rejected US officials' dominance of the two international financial institutions (Keynes 1980c, 188–95, 215–19).

Neither the IMF nor the World Bank heeded the warnings made by Keynes from 1944 to his death in 1946. Despite his objections to using cyclical policies to curtail high unemployment, the IMF and Bank directors failed to recommend countercyclical programs when low growth struck a nation. The emerging children created in 1944 had become strict parents after 1980. With their austerity programs, they imposed fiscal discipline on governments that appealed for loans to finance deficits. When accepted by policymakers, such programs raised consumption taxes, lowered expenditures for social services, reduced pensions, decreased public-sector wages, cut minimum wages of private employees, and enacted tighter regulation over labor unions. These policy recommendations hardly reduced unemployment or enhanced income equality. Low-income, unskilled workers, particularly those employed in temporary, part-time jobs, suffered the greatest losses. Speculative financial investments in bonds, derivatives, equities, and mortgage-backed securities brought short-run rewards for financiers. Many societies, however, experienced long-term negative effects, such as poverty, income inequality, high debts, and lower growth. The winners from global capitalism comprised foreign investors, export manufacturers, international financiers, multinational retailers (Walmart, Carrefour, Tesco), and numerous professionals: consultants, lawyers, accountants, lobbyists, engineers, scientists, and information technologists. They gained bonuses, dividends, higher salaries, stock options, and lucrative fringe benefits.

Domestic finance ministers, central bankers, and neoliberal, promarket economists, along with executives from multinational corporations, exerted the strongest influence over international financial institutions. Representatives from Britain, France, Germany, Japan, and especially the United States dominated their decisions. As the world's most powerful capitalist economy after World War II, the US Treasury Department and Federal Reserve Bank played the key role managing global financial risks. The US dollar served as the major international reserve currency that facilitated global exchanges. Other nations adopted the interest rates set by the Fed. With its vast economic resources and world transactions, the US government held the most shares in both the IMF and World Bank, headquartered in Washington, DC. An American official with close links to both government and multinational corporations headed the World Bank. Until the twenty-first century, few developing nations, whatever their income or growth rates, could persuade the Bank and particularly the IMF to adopt policies that would lessen income inequality. Interacting with domestic economic policies, globalization had a more harmful impact on income distribution in less-developed countries than Northern European industrialized societies (Carabelli and Cedrini 2010; Keynes 1973c, 152–64; Panitch and Gindin 2012, 67–107, 247–370; A. Roberts 2010; Roubini and Mihm 2010, 115–57, 238–301; Skidelsky 2009, 184–86; Stiglitz 2010, 184–237; Stiglitz and UN Commission 2010; Tonkiss 2006, 3–84, 157–73).

DIMENSIONS OF GLOBALIZATION

Although globalization produced a high degree of integration throughout the world, its three dimensions—cultural, economic, political—revealed imbalances and conflicts that affected income distribution. Culturally, the global media of communication transmitted contradictory values and information. Whereas some media upheld a Keynesian perspective, others advocated neoliberalism. Economically, the imbalance between trade surpluses in some nations like Germany and China and deficits in other societies increased financial instability. Overseas investment, especially financial speculation, brought cycles of boom and bust. Migrant laborers immigrating to wealthier countries usually endured lower wages, less healthful working conditions, and higher unemployment than did national citizens. Politically, the distribution of power in the global arena involved more conflict than cohesion. National officials mainly controlled fiscal policy, immigration, foreign trade, and openness to foreign investment. Neither regional nor global institutions had the power to enact the taxation and spending programs that would narrow the income gap. Yet even the most powerful nation-states could not impose their will on domestic policies toward income distribution (Centeno and Cohen 2010, 11–37).

Role of the Media

Multinational private oligopolies not only selected information to highlight in the mass media but framed values, rules, and normative expectations over radio, television, newspapers, magazines, and the Internet. These media gave limited attention to such complex issues as the causes of income distribution. The most popular private television programs and newspapers highlighted mass entertainment, sports, sexual conduct, personal political scandals, gossip, and celebrity behavior. Information about business conditions, stock markets, and technological innovations took precedence over labor rights, workers' solidarity, and income inequality.

Media broadcasts reached people all over the world. The BBC, Al Jazeera, and CNN channels broadcast news to millions. Particularly in urban centers, the Internet communicated myriad messages about politics, economics, entertainment, and personal life. It made available conflicting information from different sources. Different ideological values interpreted the same situation from opposed perspectives. Despite this diversity, the media owned by multinational corporations placed the greatest emphasis on entrepreneurial values linked to neoliberalism, such as competition, efficiency, and personal economic success. Fusing entertainment with publishing divisions, the News Corporation and allied Fox Group produced multiple types of media: TV networks (Fox), newspapers (*Wall Street Journal*, *Sunday Times* of London), film studios (Twentieth Century Fox), the Internet, and broadband services. These media reached over three-fourths of the world's population. Editorials in News Corporation newspapers opposed egalitarian public policies, high corporate taxes, labor union rights, and government regulation of business, especially communications networks (Arsenault and Castells 2008; Muthyala 2008; Wade 2012, 31–39).

Even if the Internet offered more information outlets than did News Corporation and Fox Group, individuals who most frequently used websites comprised urban youths with a college education, not low-income people. Maintaining strong personal efficacy, active users participated in social networks. The Internet hence could potentially expand the political power of groups, especially youths, formerly excluded from access to the policy process. Mobile phones, Facebook, Twitter, YouTube, Tumblr, and Google facilitated new electronic contacts based on shared interests and values. Not only elitists but individuals committed to economic equality gained the opportunity to win greater global support in such arenas as the blogosphere and Internet cafés (Castells 2012, 1–19, 218–37; Chen and Wellman 2005; Shanto Iyengar 2011, 114–24; Schlozman, Verba, and Brady 2012, 483–533).

Trade and Foreign Investment

From 1950 through 1973, the global capitalist economy followed the major recommendations of Keynes. The General Agreement on Tariffs and Trade specified the rules for international trade. It encouraged fixed but adjustable currency exchange rates. National governments regulated their economies and placed restrictions on capital outflows. Domestic capital investment took priority over foreign direct investment. The state played a leading role financing capital investment for schools, health centers, and the infrastructure (transportation, communication, sanitation facilities). Private national businesses concentrated on expanding the manufacturing sector. Such international institutions as the IMF and the World Bank promoted postwar economic reconstruction. Loans to domestic enterprises and governments helped produce high growth rates. Governments, businesses, and labor unions cooperated behind the effort to secure high employment and price stability. These institutions accepted basic Keynesian principles that upheld the need for government to lower joblessness and provide social services (Rodrik 2011, 69–76, 95–101; Wade 2009).

During the 1970s Keynesian policy influence waned. When countries experienced rising unemployment, higher inflation, increased oil prices, and union demands for wage hikes, neoliberal preferences gained greater support among elites. The United States faced growing competition from manufacturing corporations in Western Europe, Japan, South Korea, and Taiwan. To curtail trade deficits and expand US exports, the Nixon administration in 1971 stopped linking the US dollar to gold. Floating exchange rates facilitated world currency transactions that involved speculative activities. Risky investments grew (Block 2012a; Kregel 2009; Roubini and Mihm 2010, 256–67). Established in 1995, the World Trade Organization formulated rules promoting freer trade and regulating trade disputes among nations. Neoliberal policymakers stressed the importance of market exchanges as the effective way to expand productive efficiency. Government officials not only curtailed their power over trade and foreign capital flows but also lowered protective tariffs and import quotas.

After 1980 corporate executives gave priority to financial investments in stocks, bonds, foreign currencies, real estate, oil, and food. Located mainly in the United States, Britain, Germany, France, Switzerland, the Netherlands, Japan, and China, multinational banks began investing their money all over the world. Although the World Bank and IMF promoted financial investment, neither international nor national governing institutions had the authority to regulate global investments. A private regulatory organization—the International Accounting Standards Board—formulated rules for financial standards. Dominated by technical experts, the IASB operated in a secret, hierarchical way that avoided any supervision by government officials. Multinational financial institutions, especially ones in the United States, wielded the greatest influence over this private regulation. National government fragmentation collided with private global economic integration. Financial investment became more volatile (Boyer 2012; Büthe and Mattli 2011, 5–17, 71–79, 215–26; Ekkehard and Escudero 2008; James Galbraith 2007; Tanzi 2011, 309–11). Lower income equality resulted.

Financial crises escalated from 1980 through 2010. Whereas only one banking crisis (Brazil in 1963) occurred between 1950 and 1973, afterwards financial institutions in most countries experienced one or more of the following crises: uncollectible loans, insolvency, bank runs, bankruptcies, liquidations, and defaults on foreign debts (Reinhart and Rogoff 2009, 8–10, 344–92). Financial speculation caused many bank crises. Like Keynes, Miguel Centeno and Joseph Cohen (2010, 87–88) equated financial speculation with gambling: "Over-leveraged investment or short-term, high-stakes compensation schemes have brought us to the point where finance . . . acts more like a casino in which players roll for massive payoffs, no matter how much (or whose) wealth is at stake." Although risk-prone behavior brought immediate payoffs for financiers, over the longer period, the odds of winning economic rewards declined. Excessive borrowing financed risky investments. Debts ensued when borrowers could no longer repay loans. Credit collapsed. Recessions throughout the world brought the greatest harm to low-income debtors.

Trade policies that stressed expansion of exports produced more equality in South Korea and Taiwan than in China or Latin American societies. China, South Korea, and Taiwan concentrated on exporting manufactured goods. Their governments and corporations channeled high profits, export earnings, and foreign dollar reserves into domestic capital investment. Rapid growth spurred income equality among Koreans and Taiwanese. Unlike Asian policymakers, Latin American officials from 1950 to 2000 allocated fewer funds from trade surpluses for the construction of the physical infrastructure, public schools, health centers, and quality housing. Instead, most construction involved hotels, shopping malls, and luxury homes used by the wealthy. Neither the urban poor nor small farmers gained benefits from export-led growth. Nevertheless, after 2002 higher income from trade surpluses provided policymakers with expanded revenues to finance many social-service programs and infrastructure projects. Hence, during the first decade of the twenty-first century, income inequality fell in many Latin American countries.

National governments in North America, Japan, and Western Europe often subsidized their agricultural exports but imposed tariffs, quotas, and protective tariffs on food imported from less-developed societies. This policy harmed poor farmers more than agribusiness conglomerates. Trade policies granted subsidies to agribusinesses (OECD 2012a, 159). They sold their food exports at low prices to developing countries where governments lowered tariffs. As a result, domestic food production by small farmers declined. Multinational agribusiness corporations, such as Cargill, Archer Daniels Midland, Bunge, DuPont, and Monsanto, made high profits. Especially in developing nations like Mexico, small farmers lost land, moved to cities, worked as low-wage laborers in the informal domestic economy, and found insecure jobs in the United States.

When Chinese corporations increased exports of clothing, toys, electronic goods, and power equipment but paid workers meager wages, global price competition ensued. Although consumers paid lower prices for imports, workers both in industrialized and particularly in developing nations faced income losses. A wage gap separated more-skilled employees (engineers, computer technicians, accountants, lawyers, managers) from less-skilled workers who performed routine, standardized activities (Alpert, Hockett, and Roubini 2011; Chase 2008; Clark 2011; Cornia 2011; Epifani and Gancia 2008; Holt-Giménez and Patel 2009; Kiely 2007; Kollmeyer 2009; Meschi and Vivarelli 2009; Petras and Veltmeyer 2009, 3–30, 201–37).

Foreign direct investment (FDI) that increased outsourcing and subcontracting of jobs widened income differences. Under the globalized economy, production no longer occurred in only one place. Instead, workers often assembled parts of an automobile, television set, or computer in several different countries. Offshoring transferred service jobs from industrialized nations to societies like India and the Philippines, where government officials offered tax credits, low labor costs, and government subsidies for FDI. Young, educated, urban residents processed applications, prepared payrolls, coded software, drafted contracts, read x-rays, and took customer phone calls. Although paid higher wages than most employees in domestic firms, multinational corporation (MNC) managers treated phone operators, clerks, debt collectors, accountants, and lawyers as subordinates, whatever their titles as "customer care executives." The multinationals subcontracted employment to smaller firms that offered few fringe benefits and curtailed union rights to collective bargaining. Women working in export-processing zones endured the greatest harm from policies promoting FDI among developing nations (Jensen 2011; Nadeem 2011).

More volatile than FDI, financial investments raised income inequalities during the past thirty years. Particularly from 1980 to 2000, developing nations in Latin America, Asia, and Central and Eastern Europe faced the most severe hardships from capital flight. A boom-and-bust cycle ensued. Speculative financial investments produced a boom in real estate, stocks, corporate bonds, foreign currencies, fuel, and food. To finance debts, governments, domestic financial institutions, corporations, and households borrowed more money, especially from global financial markets. Neoliberal policies promoted the growth of worldwide private financial capital flows, which rapidly changed. After the initial expansion, a bust eventually followed the boom. Domestic investment declined. Interest rates rose. Foreign banks provided more loans to large domestic industries than to smaller family businesses. People in poor rural areas faced difficulties securing access to cheap credit from domestic banks or local moneylenders. Policymakers followed a cyclical strategy of "shock therapy." Regressive consumption taxes hurt poor consumers. Higher interest rates, lower wages for civil servants, and decreased expenditures for public social services reduced inflation. These austerity policies, however, raised unemployment and income inequalities. When governments restricted union rights, the share of national income going to labor declined, but capital's share rose (Charlton 2008; Griffith-Jones 2009; Kristal 2010; Krugman 2009, 30–118; Ndikumana 2009; Reinhart and Rogoff 2009, 242–47, 344–47; Stallings 2007; Stiglitz 2012, 58–64, 138–42; Tanzi 2011, 311–15; UNCTAD 2012, 79–112; Wolf 2010, 193–214).

Labor Migration

The financial crises that caused high joblessness and wage inequalities led to severe hardships for immigrants. After World War II, reconstruction programs encouraged workers from outside Western Europe to seek employment in that region. Keynesian policies imposed few restrictions on labor migration. When faced with recession after 1975, European government officials limited freedom of immigrants seeking jobs. Like people born in Europe, the following groups of immigrants faced the lowest wages: women, youths under twenty-five, and less-educated laborers who held temporary, part-time jobs as construction workers, cleaners, nannies, hotel workers, and restaurant employees. Turks, Moroccans, Algerians, sub-Saharan Africans, Asians, Roma (Gypsies), Poles, and Romanians confronted the greatest discrimination. Male immigrants who had a university education, knew the dominant national language, and held long-term positions as a professional or manager earned higher annual salaries. Despite a person's having extensive formal education, individual achievement scarcely eliminated salaries based on ethnicity, national origin, or Islamic religion. Even in fairly egalitarian societies like Norway and the Netherlands, immigrants who had the same high formal education as native Europeans attained lower earnings and occupational status. Gender, ethnic, and regional divisions reinforced class cleavages. Nevertheless, the second and third generations of immigrants gained the opportunity to pursue higher education. When they became professionals, managers, and business owners, ethnic ties weakened, but class cleavages grew stronger among immigrants who originally came from outside Europe (Bauder 2011; Brekke and Mastekaasa 2008; Kogan 2006; Sainsbury 2006; Snel, Burgers, and Leerkes 2007).

Like European states, the United States government restricted immigrants seeking employment in the United States. Whether documented or undocumented, workers from Mexico and Central America experienced the greatest hardships. Obliged to work for low wages in part-time, temporary positions, many lacked the opportunity to form unions, secure social-service benefits, gain an education, and get job training. Although the national government formulated immigration policy, it allocated few federal funds for implementation. Instead, state governments implemented and funded the programs. Despite the obstacles, Asian immigrants and their descendants from China, Korea, and India in 2010 attained the highest formal education, largest median family income, and lowest poverty. When labor mobility from overseas regions expanded, wage inequality barely increased (Card 2009; Franz 2007; ProQuest 2012, 39–41, 469–72, 479).

Chinese immigrants to Japan fared less well than in the United States. Although the 2009 Japanese civilian labor force comprised under 1 percent of immigrants, a low birthrate and aging population encouraged public policymakers to recruit foreign workers (ProQuest 2012, 868, 886). Backed by private corporations, a government training program recruited young Chinese women to work for small subcontracting firms that supplied parts to multinational Japanese corporations like Toyota and Mazda. Despite promises of high pay, these trainees suffered low wages, unhealthful working conditions, long hours, high debts, and meager fringe benefits. They gained hardly any rights to collective bargaining. National government programs failed to benefit the migrant workers (Nakamoto 2010; Tabuchi 2010).

POWER OF NATION-STATES IN THE WORLD ECONOMY

Nation-states influenced the impact of globalization on income distribution. Government policies affected labor conditions, media communications, foreign capital flows, tariffs, export subsidies, interest rates, and currency exchanges. No world institution could effectively regulate most economic transactions among different countries. Instead, national officials usually enforced bilateral investment treaties and regional trade agreements. National governments with sufficient power supported coups in less-developed countries, occupied them with military bases, provided arms, enacted trade embargoes, and imposed financial sanctions.

Since the nineteenth century, neither European colonialism nor US military interventions brought more equality to less-developed nations. Western European governments colonized societies in the Caribbean, Latin America, Asia, Africa, and the Middle East. Forced labor, slavery, and plantation agriculture implemented by colonial powers laid the foundations for inequality. Particularly when a colonized country faced low economic development and repression of ethnic groups, that legacy continued to influence income distribution after a society gained political independence (Mahoney 2010, 222–28, 259–70).

In Latin America and the Caribbean, the United States government pursued policies that exacerbated income inequality. It allied with military officers, wealthy landowners, and business elites to remove from power elected leaders who upheld egalitarian policies: land redistribution, state ownership of private industries, expanded union rights, and higher wages. After World War II, US officials backed coups that installed bureaucratic-authoritarian regimes in several Latin American and Caribbean nations, including Guatemala (1954), Brazil (1964), Argentina (1966), Chile (1973), Grenada (1983), Haiti (1991, 2004), and Honduras (2009). For example, the Honduras military coup benefited multinational corporations producing bananas, minerals, hydroelectric power, automobile parts, and electrical equipment for sale overseas. Honduran military and police officers not only increased their repression against dissidents but became owners of state-owned enterprises and profited from participation in drug-trafficking. Poor farmers, unionists, taxi drivers, and indigenous peoples lost the most income from the US-backed coup. Whereas poverty rose, the richest tenth secured the highest income gains (Dent 1999, 28–30, 65–66, 78–82, 185–88, 201–5, 229–31; D. Frank 2012; Korzeniewicz and Moran 2009, 23–59; B. Loveman 2010, 253–313, 387–404; Weisbrot 2013).

US defense policies widened the income gap in many developing nations. American federal officials in 2010 allocated a higher share of the GDP to military expenditures than did any other government leaders except those who headed Middle Eastern societies like Saudi Arabia, Oman, United Arab

Emirates, Israel, and Jordan. US prosecution of wars rewarded defense contractors, warlords, and local wealthy elites. Yet Iraqis, Afghans, Pakistanis, Somalis, Libyans, Yemenis, and wounded NATO soldiers suffered greater losses from the wars. Higher income inequality emerged when the Pentagon focused on the development of capital-intensive armaments, such as supersonic aircraft, surface-to-air missiles, Reaper drone aircraft, and laser-guided bombs. Operation of these high-tech weapons required a highly educated military, which decreased prospects for upward mobility by less-skilled individuals. Cyberwarfare worsened health conditions for people under attack. Private US defense contractors—Lockheed Martin, Boeing, Northrop Grumman, General Dynamics, United Technologies, Honeywell, General Electric, Hewlett-Packard—secured high profits from the sale of armaments, which went mainly to developing nations in the Middle East and Asia (Kentor, Jorgenson, and Kick 2012; Lutz 2009; SIPRI 2012, 202–9, 248–55, 266; Stiglitz and Bilmes 2008). In the policy conflict between guns and butter, guns won the battle. Hungry people lost.

Despite the extensive power wielded by wealthy governments over global income distribution, no nation-state could mobilize total control over resource allocation. Globalization hardly represented a unified phenomenon; instead, it rested on multilateral foundations. Complex interactions of independence, dependence, and interdependence linked the central government with several domestic structures. These included social groups, political parties, and subnational governments. Other nation-states, regional alliances such as the European Union, and international institutions like the IMF also challenged the autonomy of specific governments to control income distribution. Although industrialized countries achieved greater independence than did lower-income developing nations, even the wealthiest core societies—the United States, Germany, Britain, France, Japan—remained dependent on foreign trade, financial investment, and capital flows.

As the world became more pluralistic, differentiated, and filled with contradictions, the degree of income equality within a society depended on sociopolitical networks that transcended national territorial borders. Networks in government agencies, corporations, nongovernmental organizations, and other states, as well as regional and international institutions, made crucial decisions about income distribution. Not only coercion but consensus, negotiation, and persuasive communications mediated the power relationships among all these structures. No consistent policy followed from the interactions. Conflicting priorities among diverse organizations led to uncertain outcomes, such as the degree to which egalitarian policymakers fulfilled their objectives. Imperfect information, peer group conformity, and the difficulty of accurately estimating future consequences restricted rational choices about goal attainment.

Since World War II, governments in the United States and Western Europe have wielded the greatest power to influence income distribution, but their control waned during the late twentieth and early twenty-first century. As victorious allies in 1945, the US and British governments spearheaded the establishment of international institutions like the IMF, World Bank, and United Nations. National elites agreed on global policies to secure low unemployment, reconstruct societies from wartime damage, achieve rapid growth through state finances, and maintain price stability. These Keynesian priorities succeeded from 1950 through 1973, when the United States government achieved its greatest dominance.

The world became more diversified, both domestically and overseas, after 1980. Although divided among competing nations, the European Union challenged US supremacy. Japan as well as South Korea, India, and especially China became key centers of Asian development. Their governments promoted overseas trade, foreign direct investment, and financial investments all over the world. Through the China Development Bank and the China Export-Import Bank, Chinese leaders made loans not only to industrialized societies but also to other Asian countries, Latin America, the Middle East, and Africa. During 2010 more financial loans originated from China than from the World Bank. Headquartered in China, Singapore, Norway, Russia, Australia, South Korea, and several Middle Eastern countries, sovereign wealth funds controlled oil and investment corporations. They invested their extensive foreign reserves in the United States, other industrialized economies, and prosperous developing nations. State-owned enterprises remained strong in China, Russia, and Brazil. Like powerful domestic private corporations, they placed a low priority on achieving greater economic equality. The US Treasury Department, Federal Reserve Bank, and supportive private financial institutions on Wall Street rejected egalitarian outcomes. The IMF, World Bank, and World Trade Organization also pursued neoliberal policies that increased income inequality (Agnew 2009; Bernstein, Lerner, and Schoar 2013; Dunn 2009a, 2009b; Dyer, Pilling, and Sender 2011; Harvey 2005, 2007; Hay 2008; Lundestad 2012; Mastanduno 2009; Sarai 2009).

THE POWER OF INTERNATIONAL FINANCIAL INSTITUTIONS

Influenced mainly by the United States and Britain, the International Monetary Fund and World Bank began operations at the close of World War II. John Maynard Keynes, who represented the Bank of England, and Harry Dexter White, the assistant secretary of the US Treasury Department, formulated the articles of agreement for the two international financial institutions (IFIs). Supporting lower tariffs, Keynes and White advocated government controls over private foreign capital flows as a strategy to prevent speculative financial investment. Keynes wanted a new international currency—the bancor ("bank gold")—to become the world currency. During 1941–1942 he tried to convince US Treasury officials to locate the Bank in London. He protested the 1946 decision that established the headquarters of both IFIs in Washington, DC, rather than in New York, the center of the United Nations. Keynes also doubted the US Treasury choice about pegging the global exchange rate to the US dollar. Although British influence over the IFIs has waned since the 1940s, economists trained in Britain and the United States continued to work as senior staff members for the IMF and World Bank. Finance ministries, central banks, and private financial organizations from the United States, Britain, and Western Europe exerted the greatest policy influence over the two institutions. Technical experts supported policies emphasizing price stability. Measures to achieve low inflation took precedence over more expansionary policies that Keynes and White believed necessary for rapid growth and full employment (Babb 2007; Boughton 1998; Chwieroth 2010, 61–137; P. Clarke 2009, 88–95; Keynes 1980a, 72–80, 92, 134, 185–86; 1980c, 211–12).

After most nations experienced high inflation during the 1970s, the IMF and World Bank required that countries with large trade deficits adopt neoliberal structural adjustment programs (SAPs) as conditions for receiving loans. These programs led to unequal economic outcomes. Regressive taxes on consumer goods disadvantaged poor individuals. So did reduced government expenditures for pensions, education, and health care. When state-owned enterprises became privatized and sold to domestic oligopolies or foreign private owners, prices for utilities, water, and electricity often rose. Restrictions on public-sector unions limited workers' wages and their right to collective bargaining. Higher interest rates hurt consumers and smaller businesses. All these cyclical policies did reduce inflation; however, private corporations, both domestic and multinational, gained the most rewards from the SAPs. After the 2008 world financial crisis, IMF structural adjustment programs spread to countries in Southern Europe, including Greece, Italy, Portugal, and Spain. These societies faced high trade deficits as a share of GDP (OECD 2013c, 90–91). Neoliberal austerity policies lowered growth, raised unemployment, and widened income disparities.

In many developing nations, governments resisted the austerity conditions imposed by the IMF. As unemployment increased and citizens lost income, IMF legitimacy declined. Critics rejected its competence to promote policies for managing the financial crises and establishing fair procedures. Based on a nation's financial contributions, the weighted voting rules on the IMF executive board gave the United States, Britain, Canada, France, Germany, and Japan decisive influence over decisions about loans. However large their populations and need for credits, developing nations lacked equal representation on the executive board. Governments throughout Latin America, Asia, and the Middle East expanded their foreign reserve earnings, sought more loans from private foreign markets, and no longer depended on the IMF. Many countries relied on foreign investments from China, but Chinese enterprises paid low wages to part-time subcontractor workers and denied them the right to form a union. When Chinese government representatives gained increased voting rights in the World Bank, they claimed that the Bank should operate as an "apolitical" institution, not focus mainly on income equality (Beeson and Broome 2008; Faiola 2010; Glenn 2008; Joyce 2009a, 2009b; Paloni 2009; Stiglitz 2008; Wade 2013; Weisbrot and Montecino 2010).

The Bank's executive directors and senior staff economists viewed private markets as the best way to ensure efficiency, rapid growth, and poverty alleviation. Using complex econometric models, technical experts backed elitist rule by financiers who operated in hierarchical networks. Private financial institutions bought Bank bonds on global markets and supplied key material resources to the Bank. Executive directors wanted countries seeking loans to rely on private multinational banks from the United States and Europe. Coercive tactics occurred when donor nations like the United States refused to grant loans if borrowing countries refused to accept the conditions for credit. Pressured by the US Nixon administration, the World Bank withheld loans from Chile during the early 1970s when President Salvador Allende implemented egalitarian socialist policies that restricted domestic and foreign capitalist decisions.

Affirming the virtues of private corporate actions, Bank directors pressured their senior economists to accept the neoliberal priority on private entrepreneurs, investors, and creditors as the major sources of economic well-being. Economists who deviated from the dominant neoliberal paradigm encountered pressure from the US Treasury Department. In 2000 the Bank president fired Joseph Stiglitz, a Keynesian who challenged the neoliberal assumption that competitive markets reduce poverty through rapid growth.

Despite the power of private financial institutions, the Bank's emphasis on research about poverty and income distribution did enable egalitarian advocates to gain information about the possible causes of inequality and tentative solutions. Each year the Bank published numerous books, research papers, and journals that contained extensive statistical data. Policy advocates could use this information in their efforts to empower the poor, expand educational opportunities, increase health-care facilities, and develop a country's infrastructure. Even if the Bank directors regarded poverty alleviation as more important than enhanced income equality, the statistical knowledge justified the appeals of those who wanted Bank loans to finance egalitarian projects (Gilbert and Vines 2009; Oatley et al. 2013; Wade 2010; Weaver 2008).

Of the three major international financial institutions, the World Trade Organization had the least authority, staff, money, and independence to affect income distribution. Unlike the IMF, World Bank, and regional institutions such as the OECD, the WTO secretariat comprised only a limited number of staff members. They published few research documents. Reliant on national governments to enforce its global trade standards, the WTO faced difficulties implementing rules aimed to reconcile multinational trade disputes by its Dispute Settlement Body. Bilateral and regional trade agreements became common. Multinational corporations and governments from the most developed nations exerted the greatest influence over procedures for settling trade disputes. Low-income producers in developing nations gained fewer benefits.

WTO activities hardly facilitated an egalitarian approach toward global trade. Multinational corporations backed the transformation of the General Agreement on Tariffs and Trade (1947–1995) into the WTO. They encouraged trade agreements that would not only stimulate exports by the multinationals but also protect their foreign investments. Ecological associations could not persuade WTO directors to institute global trade rules ensuring a greener environment. Labor unions lacked the power to gain WTO support for their rights to collective bargaining, minimum wages, healthful working conditions, and control over dismissals. The protection of corporate profits that emerged from free trade took priority over universal standards promoting greater income equality for workers (Blackhurst 2009; Rodrik 2011, 76–83, 190–200; Steger and Shpilkovskaya 2010; Stevis and Boswell 2008, 16–43).

THE POWER OF MULTINATIONAL CORPORATIONS AND GLOBAL UNION ORGANIZATIONS

Multinational corporations exerted greater power over public policies than did labor unions. Although competition among multinationals and between MNCs and domestic enterprises split corporate solidarity, MNCs achieved more unity than labor unions, which faced opposition from rival unions and businesses. High geographical mobility and complex functional interdependence strengthened MNC power because the multinationals performed diverse activities throughout the world. These activities included employment, capital investment, finance, and provision of private social services, such as pensions, health care, and training. Multinational elites often maintained strong ties to the global community that exceeded national allegiances. By contrast, workers who joined unions had less mobility. They remained oriented to the nation, even to subnational areas. In Northern Europe, unions developed a regional European identity and implemented government-financed programs for health care, pensions, and unemployment insurance. Active labor-market policies for retraining workers lessened job insecurities that resulted from overseas investments by European corporations (Pontusson 2011). Particularly in less-developed countries, unions concentrated on job security and higher wages mainly for workers in the public sector and private formal economy.

Powerful networks based on shared values strengthened the power of multinational corporations over the policy agenda. Wealthy family owners, corporate managers, and intellectuals, especially neoliberal economists, operated through social networks: company boards, clubs, forums, professional conferences, schools, gated residences. These elite networks coordinated MNC decisions. Regional ties cemented solidarity, especially in Northwestern Europe and North America, where directors from different nations served on corporate boards. Within several global organizations, networks linked elites across countries. The most important included the International Chamber of Commerce, International Organization of Employers, World Economic Forum (WEF), Institute of International Bankers, Institute of International Finance, and European Round Table of Industrialists. These networks emphasized successful achievement in a modern, cosmopolitan, urban culture. In this global culture, highly educated managers, administrators, professionals, and entrepreneurs affirmed the need for hierarchical control, role differentiation, and specialization. They gave little attention to the meager incomes of uneducated individuals, landless farmers, domestic-service workers, and employees in the informal economy (Carroll 2009, 2010; Freeland 2012, 229–75).

Multinationals mobilized extensive economic resources behind activities that sought greater influence over government policymakers. Lobbies pressured finance ministries, regulatory agencies, central banks, parliaments, courts, and international organizations like the IMF, World Bank, and WTO. Personnel from MNCs took positions in these institutions. Campaign contributions went to elected officials such as legislators, presidents, and prime ministers. MNC directors sought lower taxes on corporate income but higher consumption taxes if government deficits rose. They framed the policy agenda so that economic growth and low inflation took priority over egalitarian redistribution measures. Multinational executives wanted institutions to implement informal rules that would enhance corporate welfare. Such rules facilitated foreign trade, overseas investment, private property rights, stable contracts, and minimal national government or global regulations over business activities. Committed to corporate autonomy, MNCs still wanted government to provide state assistance—subsidies, tax credits, licenses, contracts—reinforcing their interests. They resisted rules that gave global institutions the power to enforce workers' rights to form unions, bargain collectively, and influence corporate investment decisions. Promoting a flexible labor market became a primary way for expanding part-time, temporary workers who gained lower wages and fewer fringe benefits than did full-time employees. When neoliberal priorities grew stronger after 1980, the manufacturing sector expanded among developing nations that had lower labor costs. In the industrialized OECD countries, workers who used to manufacture textiles, steel, and automobiles lost their jobs.

Aiming to maximize benefits but minimize costs, multinational corporations used both consensus and coercion as they exercised political power. Consensual power occurred when MNC directors negotiated with government officials, labor leaders, and staff employed by international organizations. Persuasion encouraged MNC alliances with supportive government agencies, political parties, and domestic private enterprises. When faced with opposition, MNC executives could threaten sanctions or withdraw capital, hire no more workers, stage lockouts, and deny credit to poorer individuals. These coercive tactics widened a society's income gap.

Communications by multinational corporations affirmed the basic cultural values that gave priority to neoliberal assumptions. Through media messages transmitted by research papers, journals, newspapers, radio, television, and the Internet, MNCs upheld the values of hierarchy, elitism, personal efficacy, and a blend of individualism with collectivism. The focus on hierarchical authority and corporate secrecy deterred circulation of information that would damage multinationals' reputation. Deference to the expertise of corporate executives and technocrats hindered egalitarian programs. Discourse urged MNC managers to demonstrate personal efficacy through innovation, flexibility, efficiency, and achievement of high profits. Corporate executives used these profits to recruit international lawyers, computer programmers, and accountants who underreported assets, exaggerated liabilities, and avoided tax payments. Income disparities widened.

Multinational communications fused individualist with collectivist values. Discourse praised the skilled entrepreneur who attained greater monetary rewards but blamed those who failed to work hard, take risks, and achieve success. A collectivist message emerged when the media equated self-interests of the corporate elite and multinational enterprise with the good of the nation, region, and world. The particular interests of General Motors, General Dynamics, General Electric, and General Foods became linked to the common good. Denouncing the notion of casino banking, a Barclays' chief executive, John Varley (2010), claimed that the successful business model represented by his global bank strengthened the best interests of British stakeholders. For financiers like him, these interests scarcely included stronger unions (Bonanno and Constance 2008, 1–15, 241–65; Davis and Cobb 2010; Freeland 2012, 38–87, 141–87, 237–56; Kotz and McDonough 2010; Pfeffer 2010; Stevis and Boswell 2008, 114–41; Tabb 2010).

Despite their limited policy influence, global labor organizations used their resources to campaign for narrowing the income gap that brought high profits to MNCs. Unlike the multinationals, which functioned through only a few global associations, unions relied on numerous world organizations. The most important comprised the International Trade Union Confederation, Council of Global Unions, World Works Council, Education International, Public Services International, and International Metalworkers' Federation. These global labor organizations (GLOs) advocated the most egalitarian programs in Northern Europe, Brazil, South Africa, and South Korea. Unions in the United States, Britain, China, India, Japan, and Indonesia, however, gave less support to international cooperation for income redistribution. With fewer resources to mobilize than smaller-sized, more centralized MNCs, global labor organizations lacked the political power that would convince government officials to adopt egalitarian policies.

Yet GLO representation at meetings of the OECD, World Bank, and particularly the International Labor Organization (ILO) facilitated opportunities for consultation, coalition formation, and the sharing of information. Based in Western Europe, the Union Network International, Business and Wood Workers International, International Metalworkers' Federation, and European Works Council, along with national unions, negotiated with multinational corporations. International framework agreements upheld global labor standards and expanded workers' rights proclaimed by the ILO. Agreements signed with Volkswagen and Norwegian Statoil strengthened union influence over Northern European policymakers. Even if GLO communications lacked the extensive coverage transmitted by MNCs, the publications issued by the ILO, Global Union Research Network, and Global Labor University specified information that justified the need to institutionalize more egalitarian values in the global capitalist system. Working-class solidarity, collective political efficacy, and opposition to corporate hierarchy mobilized supporters behind global labor cooperation. Their demands for income equality focused on increased rights for women, unskilled laborers, small subsistence farmers, indigenous peoples, undocumented immigrants, and itinerant workers employed by subcontractor firms (Mosley 2011; Spilerman 2009; Stevis and Boswell 2008).

CONCLUSION

Global imbalances produced higher income inequality throughout the world. When aggregate demand declined because of high debts, an oversupply of manufactured goods resulted. Multinational banks offered limited credit to consumers and smaller businesses that needed loans. Whereas countries like Germany, Japan, China, and Saudi Arabia accumulated trade surpluses,

Southern European societies during 2004–2011 faced huge trade deficits. To cope with these deficits, their governments sought loans from the International Monetary Fund, European Commission, and European Central Bank (ECB), which required austerity policies in exchange for financial assistance to banks. Reducing debts and deterring inflation took priority over lowering unemployment and narrowing the income gap. Under pressure to decrease labor costs, many multinational corporations moved from countries with higher wages to less-developed economies with political stability, generous tax credits, an educated labor force, loose government regulations, weak unions, and low wages.

Greater interdependence within the capitalist global economy caused less equality within a nation. More prosperous regions sought enhanced autonomy from poorer areas. For example, among Western European societies, Catalonian, Flemish, and northern Italian leaders opposed sharing their taxable income with less prosperous residents in southern Spain, Wallonia, and southern Italy (Aglietta 2012; Bermeo and Pontusson 2012). Movements arose for independence from central government control.

Regional inequalities also threatened the viability of the European Union. Even if governments in the eurozone shared a common currency, they lacked the right to devalue their currencies. Northern European nations, especially Germany, prospered from trade surpluses. Their residents secured inexpensive credit. Allied with financial institutions that supplied loans to Southern European banks, German officials sought to control funds allocated by the European Central Bank. They supported austerity policies for "fiscal discipline," which meant hierarchical control over dependent European countries. Ireland, Greece, Cyprus, Spain, Portugal, and Italy came under financial pressures to expand exports, reduce wages, and achieve a more balanced budget. They paid high interest rates charged by German, French, and Dutch banks. Unemployment rates soared. Hence, the income gap widened between Northern and Southern Europe (Beck 2013, 45–65; Boyer 2012; Hein 2011; IMF 2012b, 207; Jenkins and Masters 2011; Jenkins, Masters, and Braithwaite 2011; Krugman 2012, 150–87; Peston and Knight 2012, 202–62, 209–91; Steen 2013; Wolf 2012). Although bankers sought to centralize fiscal policy in European institutions, especially the ECB, many national leaders resisted regional centralization. They wanted to control the ECB supervisory agencies or retain national control over both fiscal and monetary policy. Public opinion rejected EU decisions that increased austerity.

Globalization attracted widespread opposition in most societies. Public opinion, political parties, and social movements criticized its impacts on income distribution. Demanding greater protectionism, nationalists claimed that freer trade, expanded overseas investment, and foreign labor migration ruined the economic well-being of individuals who lost jobs, income, and status. Right-wing populist parties took a xenophobic stand against immigrant workers. Many leftist parties rejected the neoliberal preference for fiscal austerity. Protests arose from skilled manufacturing workers and service employees when multinational corporations transferred jobs from industrialized countries to China, India, Mexico, and Brazil. Small and medium-sized businesses producing goods for the domestic market rejected lower tariffs that facilitated cheaper imports. The worldwide Vía Campesina as well as several global labor organizations represented the policy claims of poorer farmers, fishers, and workers. They campaigned for governments to give greater priority to a green environment, domestic food production by small farmers, and rights for women, indigenous peoples, and low-income groups.

Protests advocating greater income equality occurred at meetings of the IMF, World Bank, World Trade Organization, and World Economic Forum. According to protesters, these international financial institutions enacted programs harming low-income groups. Private market gains generated public losses when structural adjustment programs caused governments to reduce public expenditures for social services, curtail health regulations, raise consumption taxes, and institute more part-time, temporary jobs. Environmental associations charged that global intergovernmental agencies downplayed the ecological aspects of development. Rapid growth that produced widespread pollution caused poor persons to suffer the most damage (D. Cohen 2012, 145–71; Holt-Giménez and Patel 2009, 84–86, 104–6; Sheng 2009, 403–8; Weaver 2008, 183–85).

Unlike the neoliberals who preferred bureaucratic leadership by technocrats, activists founded the World Social Forum (WSF) in 2001 to counterbalance the hierarchical authority upheld by the World Economic Forum. Resisting neoliberalism and the capitalist global economy, WSF protesters advocated larger expenditures for public education, health care, and retirement benefits. The WSF sought higher tax payments by MNCs as well as more progressive taxes, such as a tax on international financial transactions originally recommended by economist James Tobin. Resistance mounted against the global power exercised by industrialized nation-states, multinational corporations, and international financial institutions. The WSF believed that the IMF, World Bank, and WTO should implement egalitarian programs, such as lower interest rates for developing nations, more favorable trade agreements, and reduced debts owed the IFIs.

An inclusive orientation toward global solidarity paralleled the WSF stress on equality. Although valuing national, ethnic, and religious differences, activists formed local, national, regional, and world forums that transcended more particularistic identities. Forums encouraged individuals to view themselves as citizens of humanity, not just of nation-states.

Political education in these forums promoted higher political efficacy. Through networks like the Boston Social Forum and European Social Forum, members discussed political issues, disseminated information, and shared plans for influencing the policy process at diverse geographic levels. As a result, they raised their awareness of the complex ways that social groups interact with government agencies. Forums communicated discourses about effective tactics for enhancing global cooperation. To those who perceived no alternative to global capitalism, a key WSF motto proclaimed: "Another world is possible."

WSF activists concentrated on developing nonviolent, flexible, pragmatic tactics for realizing their egalitarian goals. They contacted government officials, signed petitions, and held conferences. Artistic performances communicated cultural values and policy preferences affirmed by the WSF. Demonstrations at meetings of the IMF, World Bank, WTO, and WEF publicized their opposition to neoliberal priorities. The 1999 protests at the Seattle WTO meeting of financial leaders provoked extensive media coverage when reporters recounted stories about the "battle of Seattle."

Opportunities created by WSF activists enabled them to mobilize resources behind their global mission. Composed mainly of highly educated professionals who had the income to travel overseas, they established coalitions among students, university professors, feminists, ecologists, leftist clerics, indigenous peoples, antiwar activists, farmers, and unionists—groups that supported egalitarian domestic protests. Allies also came from several international organizations, including the International Forum on Globalization, Vía Campesina, Amnesty International, Greenpeace International, and Funders Network on Transforming the Global Economy. Leaders from these associations became global brokers who negotiated agreements among diverse social groups. Heterogeneous networks led campaigns for general goals like human rights, social justice, and equality. Activists communicated information through modern digital technology such as mobile phones, tablets, and the Internet. By publicizing the more dramatic movements, the mass media spread messages about WSF policy preferences. The number of participants in WSF activities increased.

Despite these opportunities, several obstacles impeded WSF influence over government policymakers, multinational executives, and international financiers who favored a neoliberal agenda. Police repression restricted protest demonstrations at meetings of the World Bank, IMF, and WTO. Because the WSF comprised so many diverse groups, factional conflicts weakened its cohesion. Some network leaders placed priority on social spontaneity by self-managed autonomous communities led by the Assembly of Social Movements. Other activists, however, preferred forming coalitions with influential organizations such as leftist political parties heading governments that backed comprehensive social services. Different policy perspectives emerged between activists who rejected capitalism and those who sought a more humane, regulated, reformed capitalism upheld by Keynes.

Individuals from Brazil, France, and the United States led the original WSF conferences during the early 2000s. Later meetings spread to Asia and Africa, where protesters sought greater control over WSF activities.

The WSF never mobilized the comprehensive resources held by neoliberal organizations. It lacked access to the finances, technical expertise, media coverage, and assets of multinational corporations, international financial institutions, and powerful governments like the United States. The WSF's major achievement involved spreading a global consciousness among young, university-educated, left-wing activists who led domestic protests for greater income equality (Byrd and Jasny 2010; Della Porta 2009a, 2009b; Gautney 2009; Ponniah 2011; Reese et al. 2011; Santos 2006; Scerri 2013; Smith 2008, 2009; Smith and Wiest 2012, 1–17, 163–82; Starr, Fernandez, and Scholl 2011).

Chapter Five

Protest Movements against Economic Inequality

The French novel *Germinal* depicted a strike that pitted coal workers against capitalist mine owners. Émile Zola (1840–1902) wrote the novel in 1884 after he investigated a coal mining strike at the Anzin mining company in northeastern France. He descended into the mine, interviewed workers, observed their dwellings, attended union meetings, and visited local bars. From this background, Zola told the story of injustice that motivated the decision to strike from March 21 to April 19 in Germinal, which French revolutionaries had named the seventh month of the new calendar. The novel's title reflected the revolutionary potential that Zola perceived in the numerous strikes facing France.

During the early 1880s, the French experienced turbulent conditions, including a severe depression. A disequilibrium occurred between overproduction and underconsumption. Industrialization had just begun at a time of emerging globalization. French companies faced competition from other national enterprises as well as from corporations in England, Germany, Belgium, and the United States. As the economic world became more integrated, conditions in other countries affected the French situation. Mergers multiplied. Speculative investments increased. To raise profits and overcome greater competition, capitalist managers lowered labor costs. Wages declined. Unemployment rose. When working conditions worsened, the Anzin coal miners staged a strike to protest their dire situation. After Zola died in 1902, coal miners who marched behind the Paris funeral procession chanted "Germinal! Germinal!" (Hemmings 1991; Lethbridge 1993; Zakarian 1972).

Tracing the loves and deaths of its protagonists, *Germinal* vividly depicted the goals, tactics, and outcomes of the strike. The specific demands focused on specific issues of economic justice: higher wages, shorter hours, healthier working conditions, enhanced human dignity. These goals stemmed from more general cultural values: equality, collective solidarity, group efficacy, and rejection of hierarchical management. Étienne Lantier, the socialist union organizer and leading character in the novel, voiced the major demands. According to him, equality meant popular control over the government, enhanced participation in political decision making, more equal wages, and the treatment of all persons as human beings who deserved dignity. Enhancing collective solidarity, a successful strike aimed to give workers control over factory management, machinery, and tools. As workers gained access to a technical education, their individual independence would rise. Families would become free and equal communities. Lulled into apathy, resignation, and acquiescence, workers had long submitted to capitalists' hierarchical authority. Étienne hoped that his mobilization activities would enlighten the workers, expand their political efficacy, and motivate them to join the strike against the Montsou capitalist management, which placed its highest priority on earning more money—"*mon sou*" (Zola 2007, 152, 258–59). As conditions changed throughout the strike, Étienne's ideas about tactics changed. Eventually he came to prefer a Marxist approach that upheld class conflict mobilized by unions and a socialist political party. With his commitment to education, he stressed the need for tactics that would raise workers' consciousness behind the secular protest movement.

Although preferring secular tactics toward socialist revolution, Étienne used religious imagery to mobilize the miners. He saw himself as a "fighting missionary for the revolution," an "apostle bringing the gospel of truth" (Zola 1954, 273, 495). Organizing the strike, mobilizing behind the socialist cause, and proclaiming economic justice evoked a spiritual ecstasy. As the miners listened to Étienne, "a religious ecstasy uplifted them with the hopeful fervor of the Church's first Christians waiting for the coming reign of justice. Many obscure phrases baffled them. They hardly understood the technical, abstract arguments. But even the obscure abstractions raised their expectations, so that the hope for justice seemed like a dazzling field of dreams. What dreams! To be masters, to suffer no longer, to enjoy life at last!" (Zola 1979, 286–87). All these religious symbols strengthened emotional commitment to the strike and enlightened the workers about the feasible prospects for transforming the capitalist system.

Unfortunately for the coal miners, the strike failed to accomplish its objectives. Disaster resulted. Although some capitalists favored a cautious, risk-averse approach toward investments and others preferred to take speculative risks, they showed cohesion about the need to repress union actions. Workers, however, remained fragmented over conflicting values and interests. As conditions changed, comrades became antagonists. Slogans polarized Belgian scabs against French strikers. Conflict with the capitalists degenerated into struggles among the working class. Different socialist leaders could not agree on the best tactics for gaining a positive outcome from the strike. Idealistic rhetoric clashed with feasible, realistic means of goal attainment. Besides this factionalism, the union lacked the monetary resources in its mutual reserve fund to continue the two-month strike. Repression by the capitalists undermined union activities. The French police and army killed fourteen strikers, including two children and three women. Many other miners suffered wounds and imprisonment. Workers needed wages to buy food. After the strike collapsed, they submitted to the capitalists' conditions for work: lower wages, higher fines, longer hours, unhealthful conditions. Miners continued to suffer anemia, bronchitis, rheumatism, lung disease, asthma, and silicosis caused by coal dust (Zola 1954, 148, 279, 488–89). At least in the short run, the strike protest neither germinated new life for the miners nor achieved a more egalitarian society.

Although published in 1885, *Germinal* contains fertile insights about the causes, processes, and outcomes of contemporary protest movements. Political protests still revolve around conflicts. Global capitalism stimulates movements protesting economic inequality. Polarized values split advocates from adversaries. Each contending group tries to reinforce unity among its supporters while it divides the opposition. Tactics stem not only from cognitive understandings of rational ways toward goal attainment but also from emotional commitments based on religious imagery. The "have-nots" struggle against the "have-lots." Protesters awaken the apathetic, recruit active participants, persuade allies to join the movement, and strive to demobilize opponents. When factionalism weakens solidarity and political repression increases, optimistic expectations about a favorable outcome wane. As *Germinal* depicted, mobilizers lose momentum.

As we explore protest movements all over the world, resource mobilization theory elucidates the complex interactions among their goals, tactics, and outcomes. Three questions deserve consideration. First, why do people participate in protests? What individual motives and structural conditions explain their participation? Second, how do the movement's goals and tactics affect their influence over the policy process? Third, why do some protests achieve greater success than others in attaining egalitarian public policies?

RESOURCE MOBILIZATION AND POLITICAL PROTESTS

According to resource mobilization theory, protest movements will most likely attain their objectives when opportunities outweigh constraints. The interaction between the movement and the external political environment becomes crucial for a successful outcome, such as obtaining more egalitarian public policies. Not only structural conditions but cultural values and individual actions affect resource mobilization. Cultural values shape the movement's goals. Protest leaders need to frame key objectives that resonate among the audience, whether potential followers, activist supporters, or allies outside the movement. Opportunities expand when values affirm political efficacy, reject deference to established authority, and merge personal identity with a strong identification toward the collective movement. Values interpret the meaning of complex political reality so that the movement can gain support from diverse adherents. Through political education, they learn to perceive these values as important guidelines to their experiences. If followers feel resigned to the status quo, accept the hierarchical authority upheld by established elites, and remain individually atomized, values constrain egalitarian political action.

Leadership and political structures play a key role formulating, interpreting, and communicating protesters' goals. In highly unequal societies, a "Robin Hood" figure often rallies followers around redistribution of income for the poor. Particularly in a reconciliation political system, effective protest movements combine visionary leaders with more pragmatic entrepreneurs. Whereas the visionaries mobilize supporters behind a transformative idealistic cause, pragmatists negotiate with group allies and government officials for the incremental achievement of protest objectives. Pragmatic *bricoleurs*—jacks-of-all-trades—devise innovative tasks that transform routine incidents into extraordinary events. Graphic stories channel individual grievances into collective protests targeting the perceived causes of injustice. Slogans, posters, songs, and graffiti challenge the legitimate authority of ruling elites. Parades, demonstrations, festivals, and ritual ceremonies reiterate the protest movement's basic values. Reinterpretations of traditional values transmit new meaning to changing conditions. Without innovative leaders, protest organizations face obstacles in the struggle to coordinate activities, promote collective solidarity, and unify activists against opponents (Apter 2006; Johnston 2009).

Pierre Bourdieu's concept of social capital clarifies the way that protest leaders mobilize resources. He distinguishes among three crucial types: economic, political, and cultural. Economic capital refers to control over money, finances, property rights, wealth, usable time, and plants, equipment, and machinery. Political capital emerges when individuals use coercive and consensual strategies to form alliances with diverse groups, weaken opponents, and increase support for translating policy preferences into binding public decisions. This mobilization involves reliance on cultural capital, such as statistical information, legal authority, and the titles, degrees, and educational achievements that confer high status as well as enhance a protest leader's legitimacy. By forming social networks, a movement strengthens its cohesion against opposing groups. Success in mobilizing support depends on the amount of capital and on leaders' skills in translating one type of capital into the other kinds. This task requires linking objective material conditions—

power relations, economic interactions—with subjective will. Effective mobilizers combine several types of struggle: class conflicts, cultural cleavages over legitimacy, and political competition to influence public policy performance. Through this mobilization that pits marginals against dominant elites, Bourdieu hopes that a more egalitarian, inclusive, and participatory system will emerge. Yet he doubts an immediate transformation in the bureaucratic state and the neoliberal capitalist economy (Bourdieu 1986, 1998a, 1998b).

Constraints emerge when organizations take a hostile stand against the protest movement. Particularly when facing a leftist egalitarian movement, right-wing leaders may mobilize an opposition. Rejecting income equality, they oppose any disruptive tactics that endanger political order. In a bureaucratic-authoritarian or mobilization system, government institutions that consistently impose repression over a lengthy period dissuade protesters from mobilizing. Severe risks generate fear that deters participation. Yet moderate coercion applied inconsistently over time stimulates a perception that the police, military, and security agencies enforce indiscriminate, arbitrary, illegitimate coercion. Under this condition, anger against government repression may increase protesters' activities, especially when leaders stay united and maintain close network ties with their followers. If the movement gains support only from weak parliamentary parties or encounters opposition from powerful political parties that wield government power, that constraint immobilizes its adherents. Corporate hostility and divided labor unions also weaken the movement, as does the failure to secure support from other social movements. When the mass media censor protesters' activities, communicate hostile images, and publicize negative information about their tactics, public attitudes may grow less favorable. Fewer participants mobilize behind the movement. Lacking access to virtual electronic networks, activists cannot communicate their shared policy preferences and tactics over numerous sources on the Internet.

Seeking to influence government policy, a protest movement must choose the most effective tactics for fulfilling such goals as greater economic equality. Consensual tactics like contacting government officials, filing court cases, and signing petitions try to accommodate conflicts through orderly procedures. Greater disorder erupts from more adversarial, nonviolent tactics: marches, demonstrations, boycotts, strikes, sit-ins, road blockades, factory occupations, and personal confrontations with political leaders. Protest leaders least often resort to violent tactics such as riots and political assassinations (Opp and Kittel 2010; Piven 2008; Platt 2008; Siegel 2009, 2011; Tarrow 2011; Verhulst and Walgrave 2009; Walder 2009).

A movement's policy success depends less on visionary goals than on effective tactics. Some protesters never regard effective goal attainment as their primary purpose. According to them, protests that highlight moral outrage against perceived injustice represent an end, not merely a means. Whatever the outcome, the ethical cause justifies their activism. Even if such ideological commitments as the hope for a redeemed society or anger against unfair treatment motivate political participation, a protest movement must not only devise tactics that attack reprehensible injustice but also formulate comprehensible tactics that will lead to egalitarian change. Extensive information about potential supporters, opponents, and government officials enables protesters to estimate the consequences of using specific tactics, whether orderly or more disruptive. If protesters communicate clear, shared interests that involve concrete benefits like higher wages, safer working conditions, more land, cheaper credit, and increased educational opportunities, their influence over the policy agenda grows. Protest activists can also influence specific policy options considered by government officials. To finance public health-care expenditures, should higher corporate income taxes take priority over larger social security contributions?

Winning approval of desired policies presents difficulties for protesters. They often have limited power over laws, executive decrees, administrative orders, regulations, and judicial rulings. These decisions are implemented by numerous agencies: local governments, civil services, regulatory agencies, courts, political parties, corporations, labor unions, nongovernmental associations. Particularly in reconciliation systems or even large-scale bureaucratic-authoritarian systems like China, administrative organizations function in decentralized, uncoordinated, complex ways. Hence, protesters can exercise only limited influence on policy implementation (Kolb 2007, 25–31, 279–81).

Resource mobilization theory helps explain the ways that protests throughout the world tackle the issue of income inequality. By comparing several societies, we can better understand the effectiveness of different movements. What goals and especially tactics explain the outcomes on public policies? The following sections compare Chinese with Indian movements and explore protests in three Latin American societies: Argentina, Brazil, and Mexico. Besides probing Western European left-wing and right-wing protesters, the theory highlights the differences between the rightist Tea Party movement and the more leftist Occupy movement in the United States.

PROTESTS IN CHINA AND INDIA

China and India share several similarities. Decentralization disperses political power among the central, regional, and local governments in these populous, geographically large societies. Heterogeneous interests and values hinder protest solidarity. Divisions split cities from rural villages, coastal from inland areas, wealthier from poorer regions. Capitalists, both foreign and domestic, unite with government officials to wield power over labor unions.

Concerned to stimulate rapid economic growth, the Chinese and Indian governments from the early 1990s onward adopted neoliberal policies that promoted privatization, foreign capital investment, freer trade, low public expenditures for social services, and limited rights for unions. When rapid growth occurred, greater income inequality increased. Despite their meager resources, poor people mobilized to protest perceived economic injustice. They sought concrete benefits—access to land, jobs, higher wages, improved working conditions, pensions, health care, educational opportunities, housing subsidies, lower interest rates. More abstract ideological demands assumed lesser importance.

However important these similarities, China and India differed in their policies toward protests. As a reconciliation system, India showed greater social pluralism. Nongovernmental associations retained the freedom to organize, mobilize activists, and try to influence public policies. Competitive political parties rotated in executive office. Coalitions among different parties formed national and regional governments. Although government officials imposed coercion against protesters, less repression occurred than in China, a bureaucratic-authoritarian system. Exerting dominant power, the Chinese Communist Party (CCP) granted social groups little independence to organize against the government. Unions had slight opportunity to press their claims on policymakers or enterprise managers. Allied with party-state elites, "red capitalists" rejected worker protests. Censorship, public humiliation, police surveillance, arrests, detention, imprisonment, executions, and other coercive strategies deterred public protests. Nevertheless, Chinese farmers, urban factory workers, and middle-income city residents protested against inegalitarian policies. As in India, the success of these protests depended on the way that goals and tactics expanded structural opportunities while reducing constraints.

Recent Chinese protests revolved around diverse goals that reflected the desire for more egalitarian public programs, especially expanded material benefits. Small farmers struggled to retain their leased land that local party-government officials expropriated for industrial development by private capitalists, real estate developers, and construction managers. Farmers' protests also sought inexpensive public health care and education for themselves and their children. Older factory workers who lost their state jobs in northeastern China wanted higher severance pay, unemployment allowances, and housing subsidies as well as larger pensions when they reached retirement age. Afflicted with lead poisoning, village factory workers who manufactured lead-acid batteries denounced polluted conditions. Rural migrant laborers who secured urban jobs along the industrializing urban coast struck for higher wages, more fringe benefits (health care, pensions, housing subsidies), shorter hours, safer working conditions, fewer fines, and better treatment by managers and supervisors. The right to form independent unions and to strike represented another key demand directed against foreign multinational corporations from Japan and Taiwan, such as Honda, the auto manufacturer, and Foxconn, the electronics company which produced parts for Apple, Dell, Sony, Microsoft, and Hewlett-Packard. Middle-income urban residents demonstrated against CCP city government elites who expropriated their homes for the construction of shopping malls, industrial parks, and luxury mansions by private real estate developers. Drivers owning small trucking firms protested high diesel prices, fines, taxes, and port fees charged by government agencies in Shanghai and Beijing. Several cities faced protests by taxi drivers who resented high fuel prices, stagnant wages, and minimal access to public social services. Ecologists campaigned against the air and water pollution caused by rapid industrial growth.

Chinese urban and rural protesters used similar tactics. The most accommodating tactics comprised collective petitions, lawsuits, informal mediations, and contacts with local government leaders, particularly urban street and rural township officials. Local civil servants, CCP heads, and enterprise managers often bargained with protest leaders for higher wages, jobs, promotions, and land. Improved public services for water pipes, electricity, garbage collection, schools, and health care also represented key demands. If the party-state elite ignored or denied these consensual requests, then protesters turned toward more disruptive tactics, such as marches, demonstrations, and traffic blockades. Extensive disruption that spread beyond the locality often provoked government coercion against the protesters, especially intellectuals, human-rights lawyers, journalists, and religious dissidents (Lee and Zhang 2013).

A powerful coalition among local government officials, CCP elites, and private entrepreneurs resisted egalitarian reforms. Local courts and labor bureaus declined to enforce laws formulated by the national government. Controlled by CCP leaders, the official All-China Federation of Trade Unions (ACFTU) usually sided with management, not the workers, when protests arose. Divisions fragmented working-class solidarity. Receiving higher pay and more generous public fringe benefits, permanent urban residents employed by state-owned enterprises felt little unity with rural migrants working in the cities for private manufacturers or commercial service firms.

Despite these constraints, Chinese protesters did attain policy benefits if they found allies, developed local networks, and gained information from modern technology like the Internet. Several journalists, lawyers, educators, and intellectuals became sympathetic allies. Seeking to retain support from the central government, even a few local CCP cadres backed the protesters when thousands of participants stimulated media publicity. On rare occasions, the village CCP elected a protest leader as party secretary. Concerned that disruptive protests would endanger regime legitimacy, central and provincial authorities occasionally granted protesters' demands that focused on specific local issues or reflected nationalist opposition to practices by foreign corporations, such as those from Japan and Taiwan. Under these conditions, protesters gained lower agricultural taxes, larger grain subsidies, greater rural infrastructure, higher minimum wages in the cities, and expanded access to public schools and health-care facilities throughout China. Aware that rapid economic growth fomented rapid social change, the CCP tried to avoid political disorder. Declining birth rates and an aging population caused labor shortages, particularly along the industrializing coast. Hence, the CCP pressured MNCs like Foxconn to raise migrant laborers' wages and improve working conditions. Some municipal government officials encouraged greater collective bargaining rights, including the right of workers to elect their union representatives, participate in management, and negotiate salaries. Rather than allying with enterprise managers, the ACFTU began giving greater support to migrant laborers. Striking truck drivers convinced the Shanghai Transport and Port Authority to decrease fees. Shanghai taxi drivers won concessions from the city government, which increased their fuel subsidies.

Even if opposition to social pluralism hindered independent group action, Chinese protesters did form nongovernmental organizations that evaded tight CCP control. Examples included charities, property owners' associations, and environmental organizations. They formed networks based on shared interests and values, such as the need for more economic equality, public social services, legal justice, human dignity, and transparent government. Ecologists campaigned against pollution. When the city bureaucracy requisitioned residents' private homes for real estate development, networked organizations protested their shared losses. Middle-income property owners sought legal protection against greedy apartment developers. Unemployed bank tellers in Beijing filed petitions against financial executives and staged sit-ins at branch offices of state-owned banks. Village farmers who lost land resented unjust treatment by local party-state elites. Older workers who lived in northeastern China and lost their jobs recalled the Maoist rhetoric that stressed mass action against labor exploitation. Collective political efficacy rose.

To facilitate political stability amid rapid economic change, beginning in the 1990s the CCP central government formulated labor laws that required employers to sign contracts with workers. When neither local governments nor private enterprises implemented these regulations, protesters denounced corrupt treatment that denied them humane, just working conditions. According to them, failure to enforce these laws violated their legal rights as citizens. Rural migrants working for multinational corporations in southern China lived in dormitories next to the factory; hence, they could easily form local networks that led strikes against Honda and Foxconn. Nongovernmental organizations such as migrant women's clubs, cultural communication centers, and centers for industrial health supplied legal advice, stressed ways to influence municipal officials, and educated migrant workers about adaptation to urban lifestyles.

Whether in villages, small towns, or cities, most Chinese protesters had access to modern information technology. Through Internet cafés, mobile phones, e-mail messages, and big-character posters, they mobilized networks supporting protests. Even though government censorship blocked information exchange, innovative hackers devised effective ways to communicate plans for protesting government policies that fostered official corruption, economic inequality, arbitrary justice, and inhumane treatment (Andreas 2010; Barboza 2011a, 2011b; Barboza and Tabuchi 2010; Bradsher 2010; Cai, 2010; Foster and McChesney 2012, 21–24; Friedman and Lee 2010; Froissart 2009; Hille 2013; Jacobs 2010, 2012; Kim and Voorhees 2011; Lee 2010; Lee and Liu 2011; Lee, Nielsen, and Alderson 2007; Li and O'Brien 2010; Lum 2011; Rocca 2009).

Operating mainly at decentralized government levels, Indian protesters sought similar goals as those pursued in China. Typical demands included access to more land, subsidized food, employment opportunities, education, health care, and housing subsidies. Yet unlike the Chinese situation, no single powerful party or central government dominated the policy process. Private entrepreneurs and especially foreign investors gained greater freedom over economic management. Although freer trade policies lowered consumer prices for imported food, they ruined small-scale farmers who lacked the resources to compete with multinational corporations. Prices for agricultural inputs, such as seeds, fertilizer, water, tractors, electrical power, and transportation, increased costs to farmers. Unable to secure inexpensive credit from banks or microfinancial agencies, they incurred high debts. Faced with high costs but few benefits, farmers condemned regional governments and multinational corporations. Protesters occupied the Bangalore headquarters of Cargill, the MNC that charged high prices for seeds needed by small farmers. Other movements denounced state governments' expropriation of land for development of steel mills, bauxite mines, power plants, and irrigation projects, mainly by private corporations. The neoliberal focus on rapid industrialization, privatization, and reduction of public social services brought few benefits to small independent farmers, agricultural wage laborers, and fishers. They suffered from industrial pollution, ill health, and poverty. Many committed suicide by drinking pesticide intended to raise agricultural productivity.

Numerous constraints hindered the use of effective tactics for realizing protesters' intentions. Like the Chinese, Indians filed lawsuits, mounted demonstrations, staged hunger strikes, and occupied buildings. Violent attacks occurred, especially in poorer northeastern regions. Yet group diversity deterred collective solidarity. Several cleavages impeded movement cohesion: upper versus lower caste, tribal (indigenous) peoples versus other ethnicities, Hindus versus Muslims, men versus women, urbanites versus villagers, richer versus poorer occupational classes. Capitalist class differentiation weakened collective solidarity. Groups that recently became poor participated at higher levels than low-income individuals who remained poor for more than six years. Because most urban residents worked in the informal economy, union leaders could not easily organize them. Business executives, wealthy agribusinessmen, and medium-income landowners resisted egalitarian demands. Police repressed violent protests and even intimidated more peaceful demonstrations, particularly in the poorer northeastern regions. Patron-client interactions hindered egalitarian policies for education and health. Corrupt government officials who made payoffs to their influential clients hurt low-income people.

Yet protesters in a few Indian states exploited opportunities that facilitated policy gains. Allies, social networks, and access to information strengthened collective solidarity, political efficacy, egalitarianism, and opposition to paternalistic, hierarchical authority. The Kerala state achieved the greatest policy successes. More than most other state residents, Keralans obtained higher government expenditures for education, pensions, and health care. Small businesses received inexpensive credit. Even though agricultural wage laborers gained fewer benefits, state governments redistributed land to poor farmers. Key group allies, especially political parties, provided support to protesters. The Communist Party of India (Marxist) formed the Left Democratic Front coalition that governed Kerala for lengthy periods. Religious and caste divisions remained weaker than in other states. The Kerala population included around 20 percent Christians and 20 percent Muslims but only 60 percent Hindus. Not only the Communist Party but the Congress Party stressed class ties over ethnic-religious identifications. Protesters formed inclusive social networks that bridged differences among diverse communities. With high literacy rates, Keralan protesters consumed information from several sources: books, magazines, newspapers, pamphlets, Internet media. Extensive public libraries made information widely available. Hence, protesters could communicate their demands, recruit supporters, rally activists, and organize plans for mobilization (Drèze and Sen 2013, 74–80; Krishna 2009; Lamont 2011a; Mannathukkaren 2011; Mohanty 2010; Moolakkattu 2007; Nadeem 2011, 192–220; Pai 2010; Sahoo 2010; Swain 2010; Williams 2008, 1–62, 89–104, 119–56).

PROTEST MOVEMENTS IN LATIN AMERICAN SOCIETIES

Like Indian farm movements, the Mexican Zapatistas and the Brazilian Movement of Landless Rural Workers (Movimento dos Trabalhadores Rurais Sem Terra—MST) struggled to realize a more egalitarian society. Opposing domestic and multinational agribusinesses strengthened by neoliberal policies, these protesters sought greater access to land, especially land expropriated for industrial development by the MNCs. According to the protesters, government officials should raise agricultural subsidies to small farmers and grant them inexpensive credit so that they could produce food for domestic consumers rather than foreigners. These two movements also supported higher social-service expenditures for education, health care, housing, and the infrastructure: water, sewage treatment, roads.

To attain these goals, the Zapatistas and the MST used similar tactics. These included land invasions, demonstrations, marches, work stoppages, and occupations of such government buildings as public banks. Negotiations with national and regional government officials pressured policymakers. Local networks mobilized support for the movements. In the Chiapas state, the Ejército Zapatista de Liberación Nacional (EZLN) established good-government councils and autonomous rebel municipalities that transmitted egalitarian values. Political education stressed such cultural values as collective political efficacy and rejection of paternalistic, hierarchical authority. Collective solidarity integrated identities based on ethnicity (Mayan Indian traditions) and Mexican national citizenship. Local organizations provided opportunities for women, youths, and low-income people to participate in political decisions that considered education, health care, land management, women's rights, and justice. In Brazil the MST occupied public land and privately held land viewed by government leaders as unused or unproductive. Roadside camps alongside the invaded land created strong networks that strengthened political efficacy, social solidarity, and commitment to socioeconomic equality.

Of these two farm movements, the Zapatistas realized fewer policy achievements than did the MST. The EZLN faced greater structural constraints. Federal government officials refused to enforce land redistribution laws. National soldiers, local police, and paramilitary bands organized by landowners repressed the Zapatistas. They never gained support from the two major political parties—the Partido Revolucionario Institucional and the Partido Acción Nacional. EZLN leaders even declined to ally with the left-wing Partido de la Revolución Democrática. Divisions among indigenous groups further weakened Zapatistas' power. Whereas many young Indians backed the rebel movement, others joined militias organized by commercial landowners. Lacking government or party allies, the EZLN did attract support from Catholic liberation theologians, environmentalists, human-rights advocates, and leftist intellectuals like Zapatista leader *subcomandante* Marcos. He wrote letters to newspapers that publicized the rebel cause. The Vía Campesina, a global social movement campaigning for enhanced rights for small farmers, also supported the Zapatistas. Through their autonomous local communities, they established cooperatives, health clinics, public libraries, and potable water. These egalitarian programs helped small farmers and artisans.

Yet the EZLN never achieved sufficient power to challenge the neoliberal paradigm. During the 1990s when the Mexican government privatized land formerly held as communal *ejidos*, poor Indians lost access to their land. Favoring the export of oil from Chiapas and the development of hydroelectric power projects, public policymakers placed little emphasis on self-sufficient food production for domestic consumption. The Zapatistas began their rebellion in 1994, the year that Mexican, Canadian, and US government officials ratified the North American Free Trade Agreement. It promoted inexpensive food imports from the United States and export production by agribusiness corporations. Poor farmers who used to grow crops like corn and coffee gained few benefits from these neoliberal policy priorities (Collins 2010; Cortez Ruiz 2010; de la Torre 2008; Dent 2008, 76–79; Monsiváis 1997, 129–47; Morton 2007; Rao 2010, 150–72; W. Robinson 2008, 167–225; Stahler-Sholk 2007).

Like the EZLN, the MST faced numerous structural constraints. The army, provincial police, and paramilitary rural commands, especially in the northeastern Amazon region, imposed severe repression on land occupiers. Regional, ethnic, and class cleavages fragmented leftists' collective solidarity. Divisions among agricultural wage laborers, small family producers, sharecroppers, and renters split the rural population. Whereas the national Ministry of Agrarian Development supported land redistribution to poor farmers, the Ministry of Finance pursued neoliberal policies that favored freer trade, privatization of public enterprises, more foreign capital investment, and financial deregulation. Under neoliberal programs adopted by the Workers' Party (Partido dos Trabalhadores—PT), multinational agribusiness corporations gained a powerful influence over rural development. Backed by the World Bank, they engineered the industrial development of the Amazon region. Small farmers lost their land. Cargill, Monsanto, and Bunge corporations purchased land, exported food, and financed the capitalist production of cattle, soybeans, corn, herbicides, pesticides, and timber. Although government officials granted subsidies and tax credits to the agribusinesses, small farmers had less access to low-interest loans. They incurred high debts.

Nevertheless, structural opportunities facilitated some policy gains at the local level. Unlike the Zapatistas, the MST developed more influential allies with government institutions, political parties, and other social movements. Under President Luiz Inácio Lula da Silva, who held office from 2003 to

2010 and headed the Workers' Party, government repression declined. Even if still illegal, land invasions became accepted as legitimate tactics by local decision makers in the Institute for Colonization and Agrarian Reform. Lacking finances and staffs, Institute officials negotiated with MST leaders about land management and government funds for subsidized food, public education, and health clinics. By 2005, around 10 percent of the total farm population had gained access to small plots of redistributed land (Ondetti 2008, 228–35). Numerous allies helped the MST achieve its goals. Supportive groups included Catholic liberation theologians, Lutheran clerics, lay activists, urban unions, left-wing intellectuals, environmentalists, Vía Campesina, World Social Forum, and especially the Workers' Party. They communicated information that rallied activists behind the protesters' policy goals. Although the Workers' Party financed many MST operations, its activists wanted independence from direct party control and remained disenchanted with the PT's failure to implement more extensive land redistribution policies.

After the PT became a national government party, a pragmatic orientation motivated its central leaders to curtail protests; however, political participation in many city councils from 1988 to 2008 produced greater equality. Beginning in Porto Alegre and extending to several other cities, the Workers' Party instituted participatory budget practices that expanded public employment, elementary education, health-care services, day-care facilities, bus transportation, and access to housing. Cash grants went to the elderly and young mothers. Small businesses and cooperatives secured inexpensive credit. To finance these egalitarian benefits, city councils levied progressive taxes and tried to ensure that wealthier persons paid their taxes. Such policies brought more positive outcomes to low-income residents in the urbanized, industrialized south than in the poorer northeast, where the PT confronted greater opposition from the agribusiness elites. Although government policies failed to narrow the regional income gap, they did secure concrete benefits that reduced the poverty rate. By encouraging access to urban officials, municipal housing councils helped poor families in the *favelas* gain paved streets, electricity, and legal title to their homes. Administered partly by city governments, the Bolsa Família program gave cash assistance to low-income mothers whose children attended primary school and secured preventive health care. This conditional cash transfer policy benefited many individuals, especially in the informal sector (Barrionuevo 2011; Carvalho Filho and Mendonça 2007; Cleary 2007, 69–85; Donaghy 2011; Fernandes 2009; Goldfrank 2011, 38–40, 60–83, 165–218; Goldfrank and Schrank 2009; Hunter 2010, 146–56, 202–3; 2011, 306–20; Karriem 2009; Loera 2010; Martínez-Torres and Rosset 2010; Ondetti 2008; Rénique 2009; Stédile 2007; Wolford 2010).

Despite these policy achievements, governments dominated by the Workers' Party faced widespread protests beginning in 2013. As urbanization, the electronic media, and prosperity increased, expectations for policy performance rose. Students, youths, city residents, union workers, and many middle-income people became frustrated with the extensive government corruption, unjust courts, higher fares for public buses and subways, traffic congestion, deteriorating public education and health services, and extreme economic inequalities that marginalized the poor *favelas* from adjacent luxurious condominiums for rich Brazilians. Protesters denounced the lavish government spending on 2014 World Cup and 2016 Olympic stadiums but lower expenditures for high-quality public health care and education. Numerous cities faced mass protests. Expressing political alienation and dominance of the consumer society, protesters relied on advertising slogans to broadcast their discontent. Such slogans as "*O gigante acordou*" (The Giant Woke Up) and "*Vem ora rya vem*!" (Come to the Street, Come!) originated from commercials by the Fiat car company and Johnnie Walker whisky—both manufactured by multinational corporations. Even though PT political leaders at the municipal, regional, and national levels tried to meet some of these protesters' demands, demonstrators viewed the proposals as insufficient. The military police tried to deter further protests by using tear gas, rubber bullets, and pepper spray against dissidents (Barbara 2013; Carrión 2013; Gaspari 2013; Hilton 2013; Leahy 2013; Pearson 2013; Romero 2013a, 2013b; Stephens 2013).

A more urbanized society than Brazil, Argentina experienced several factory occupations that opposed neoliberal austerity policies demanded by the International Monetary Fund for repayment of loans. During the late 1990s, deregulation, privatization, high interest rates, and lower expenditures for social services increased unemployment rates, income inequality, and the share of informal workers. As a result, youths, women, and workers staged protests. They demanded greater domestic industrialization, public employment, jobless compensation, and access to public health-care centers and educational opportunities. Tactics to realize these objectives involved petitions to provincial legislatures and negotiations with local city officials, as well as marches, demonstrations, and occupations of bankrupt or abandoned factories. Women played a key role in neighborhood associations, which upheld gender equality, collective solidarity, political efficacy, and resistance to hierarchical male authority. Factory committees and workers' assemblies organized activists.

Fragmentation hindered leftist solidarity among Argentinian workers. The Peronist Partido Justicialista (PJ), a nonideological party based on patron-client ties, had numerous factions. Whereas the factory occupiers sought a populist democracy with widespread participation from below, the Peronistas preferred a more hierarchical system dependent on strong personal leadership. Brokers acted as patrons mediating between government officials and local clients, such as factory workers. Despite workers' preference for local autonomy and independence from party control, they relied on the government for financing subsidies, unemployment grants, education, and health care. The worker-managed factories never reconciled this contradiction. Further constraints emerged from powerful groups preferring elitist policies. Private corporations, both domestic and multinational, opposed worker-managed factories. Right-wing middle-income persons resented government expenditures for egalitarian benefits, especially those received by the "undeserving" militants who led factory takeovers. From the rightist perspective, disruptive factory seizures threatened social order, violated private property rights, and caused low growth rates.

However great the obstacles, workers' assemblies and factory councils did achieve a few policy successes at the local level. They relied on several allies, particularly the Front for Victory PJ faction led by presidents Néstor Kirchner (2003–2007) and (from 2007) Cristina Fernández de Kirchner. Their policies favored the urban poor. Other allies included PJ legislators, lawyers, leftist intellectuals, teachers, students, and social workers. Journalists provided information about mobilization activities. A coalition formed between local government institutions and workers' assemblies. The Buenos Aires city council declared abandoned factories a public good, hence open to worker cooperatives. Whereas government officials supplied funds and technical assistance, workers' assemblies managed production. Their decisions attained fairly equal incomes. Lacking hierarchical management, worker cooperatives avoided high salaries, bonuses, commissions, travel expenses, and lucrative profits. Neighborhood assemblies enhanced opportunities for local political participation. Through these networks at work and residences, members gained a political education that emphasized egalitarian, efficacious values. Factory occupations thereby helped workers gain policy influence over national, regional, and especially local governments. Worker-managed cooperatives not only provided jobs for the formerly unemployed but established cultural centers and leadership training centers. More public schools, hospitals, and houses became available for workers' families. In the highly pluralist Argentine society riven by social conflicts, these benefits stemmed from populist mobilization (Castorina 2007; Dinerstein 2007; Frey and Crivelli 2011; Garay 2007; Jiménez-Huerta 2008; Lavaca Collective 2007, 14–44, 210–24; Meyer and Chaves 2009).

MOBILIZATION OF PROTESTS IN WESTERN EUROPE AND THE UNITED STATES

Throughout Western Europe and the United States, protests from the ideological left and right mobilized against the establishment. Claiming to represent "the people," leftists and right-wingers challenged dominant institutions, especially bureaucratic institutions and governing political parties blamed for failing to resolve current economic problems. Although neither movement comprised members who held identical policy preferences toward income distribution, each one shared similar cultural values framing policy goals. How did left socialist movements differ from rightist anti-immigrant groups?

Western Europe

Left-wing Western European protesters stressed a comprehensive approach toward equality. They opposed neoliberal austerity policies that privatize social services, increase regressive taxes, deregulate financial institutions, and reduce union rights, especially for public employees. Rather than asserting the dominance of the private market over the public sector, left-wing movements advocated higher government expenditures for social services: health care, day care, elder care, education, inexpensive housing, retirement benefits. They assumed that these public services would narrow the income gap that splits rich from poor. Opposed to the neoliberal emphasis on a flexible labor market that encourages part-time, temporary jobs, left-wing protesters wanted more full-time positions that paid high wages, granted generous fringe benefits, and gave unions an active role in management. From the leftist perspective, economic institutions should not become obsessed with short-term profit accumulation for a few capitalists but encourage the structural conditions that further the well-being of all persons, however low their social status. Not only economic equality but gender and ethnic equality assumed high importance. Immigrant and women workers deserved more-equal pay, treatment, and respect. Political equality involved expanding participation in political life and government treatment of all persons with greater fairness. For example, the Spanish *indignadas/indignados* movement mobilized political participation through several associations: neighborhood assemblies, cooperatives, roundtables, forums, and commissions that handled communications, health, education, housing, judicial issues, and political matters. Opposed to hierarchical leaders, these populist associations aimed to reconcile communal well-being with individual demands for social justice (Álvarez 2012; Castells 2012, 110–55; Valenzuela 2012).

Leftist movements fused collectivism with individualism. Keynes based his favorable assessment about personal protests on respect for individual differences: "To such fanatics of the individual judgment as many of us are born to be, this right of personal protests is an essential and unsurrenderable privilege" (Keynes 1982b, 77). With their high formal education and membership in numerous voluntary associations, leftist leaders supported divergent lifestyles, legal abortions, and homosexual rights. Viewing individuals not as isolated atoms but as social beings, they affirmed a collective solidarity based on mutual cooperation. Rather than excluding immigrants, the nation should become an inclusive entity open to all, not just native Europeans. Even if leftists supported a multicultural society, many downplayed the primacy of ethnic-religious loyalties. They proclaimed a secular concept of working-class solidarity that included not just factory workers but all employees who work for pay.

Support for inclusive values coincided with leftist opposition to hierarchical authority. Instead of deferring to oligopolistic corporations, arbitrary centralized governments, and the European Commission, individuals should reject bureaucratic authority. Left socialist movements condemned the Communist Party of the Soviet Union that dominated an authoritarian state. They also stressed their differences with social democratic parties run by technicians who adopted major neoliberal policy preferences. For these left socialists, political life needed to promote greater popular participation from below. Not only in political life but in the family, neighborhood, workplace, and local community, individuals should gain the opportunity to make decisions affecting their lives. Widespread popular participation must instill a new cultural hegemony linked to persuasion, not state coercion. Striving to raise people's consciousness through political education, contemporary left socialists wanted participants to merge identities toward the locality, nation, and world.

Political participation and education led by left socialists helped increase political efficacy. As involvement rose in voluntary associations, participants discussed important issues, communicated their discontent toward policy performance, and shared information in local networks. Members became more receptive to values about gender equality, civil liberties, tolerance of diverse lifestyles, and widespread participation in political decision making. Personal fatalism waned. When political education about economic injustices expanded, participants expected that political efficacy would motivate individuals to mobilize behind nonviolent protests for greater income equality (Barr 2009; Dalton, van Sickle, and Weldon 2010; Freire 2008; Klandermans, van der Toorn, and van Stekelenburg 2008; Welzel and Deutsch 2012). Inspired by Stéphane Hessel, who joined the French Resistance movement against the Nazi occupation during World War II, left-wing activists broadcast his conclusion from *Time for Outrage: Indignez-vous!*: "TO CREATE IS TO RESIST. TO RESIST IS TO CREATE" (Hessel 2011, 29). This injunction generated collective political action.

To rally support for these cultural values, left-wing protesters relied on several tactics. Some activists campaigned to elect socialist left parties, such as the Izquierda Unida (United Left, Spain), Socialist Left Party (Norway), Syriza (Coalition of the Radical Left, Greece), and Progressive Party of the Working People (Cyprus). Marches and demonstrations conveyed egalitarian slogans. Students chanted: "We stand against the cuts, in solidarity with all the poor, elderly, disabled, and working people affected." Unemployed workers shouted: "No more inequality—give us real jobs. We want real democracy, not just freedom for bankers." Unions staged strikes, mounted work stoppages, and occupied factories. Students sat in university buildings. The homeless squatted in abandoned houses. Protesting austere living standards, Greeks who called themselves "Desperate Housewives" and "The Forty Thieves without Ali Baba" stole food from supermarkets and distributed it to poor street people. Mobilized by the Andalucian Workers' Union, landless farm workers in Andalucía occupied estates of absentee Spanish elites, built homes, and raided supermarkets. During the twenty-first century, the more disruptive tactics usually involved little violence except when the police forbade protesters from marching in restricted areas or evicted them from occupied buildings. A few anarchists expressed their anger through armed struggle (Martínez 2007; Minder 2012; Minder and Castle 2010; Pautz and Kominou 2013; Psimitis 2011).

The socialist left movements faced several obstacles when they protested the austerity policies sweeping across European societies. Difficulties of resource mobilization hindered protesters from gaining power over government officials who curtailed egalitarian public programs. No collective solidarity emerged. Fragmentation divided the unemployed, poor people, factory workers, and students. Rather than joining a protest, many individuals with less formal education refrained from protest participation because of divergent values, interests, and policy preferences. Although public opinion favored government provision of social services, a majority of Europeans opposed expanding rights for immigrants. During recent national legislative elections except in Greece and Cyprus, under 15 percent of the popular vote went to a left socialist party. Adopting key ideas from the neoliberal agenda, most social democratic parties showed little enthusiasm for left socialist participation in a national coalition government. As markets became more commodified, private consumption took priority over reliance on the public sector for social services. Domestic and multinational corporations resisted egalitarian priorities. Left-wing protesters did attract allies from students, trade unionists, ecologists, feminists, peace activists, and some professionals like teachers, civil servants, journalists, and lawyers. These highly educated urban residents had access to extensive information from the Internet, Facebook, and mobile phones. Yet modern digital technology failed to communicate a shared political outlook that heightened social solidarity. As inclusiveness expanded, leftist mobilizers could not easily reach a consensus among their diverse supporters, who sought greater local autonomy. Leaders never effectively reconciled the contradiction between high popular participation from below and centralized direction by an activist government from above. Unlike right-wing populists, who secured greater cohesion around hostility to immigrants, left-wing populists achieved less solidarity around their egalitarian agenda (Karapin 2007, 238–48; Krishnan and Thomas 2007; Lahusen 2013; Streeck 2012a, 2012b).

Opposition to immigrants and foreigners shaped right-wing populists' approach toward the four cultural values. Collective solidarity based on identical values took precedence over support for individual diversity. Rejecting multiculturalism, they viewed "the people" as a homogeneous entity threatened by enemies, especially immigrants, foreigners, ethnic minorities, leftists, Marxists, globalists, gays, Jews, and Muslims. Roma, Turks, Iranians, Africans, Pakistanis, and Eastern Europeans became stigmatized for endangering personal security, health care, public education, employment prospects, and living standards. Upholding an exclusivist nationalism based on organic solidarity, right-wing protesters asserted that their nation includes only "native" citizens and excludes all others. Antagonism toward the European Union arose, partly from the feeling that EU bureaucrats allied with multinational corporations, remained unaccountable to citizens within each nation, and supported the free movement of migrant workers across national borders. Given their stress on national solidarity, right-wing populists polarized political life between friend and enemy. They rejected expanding the civil liberties of those with "deviant" lifestyles, such as homosexuals. Enemies included communists, socialists, anarchists, union leaders, feminists, and left-wingers who backed immigrant rights. Support for the traditional patriarchal family hardly furthered gender equality.

Pledged to maintain order in a nation threatened by social unrest, right-wing protesters deferred to the hierarchical authority of the movement's heroic leader. Fearing threats to personal and national security, they wanted a powerful leader who embodied the collective national will, protected the people, and guided them toward national renewal. The leader needed not only loyal, disciplined followers but also a strong police and military to defend the nation against threats to its security. Hence, right-wingers preferred punitive policies—deportation, long prison sentences, harsh prison conditions—for criminal behavior, especially by immigrants.

In contrast to left socialists, right-wing populists placed lower priority on economic equality, particularly public policies that gave benefits to the "undeserving." They supported government provision of social services received by "deserving" native citizens who worked hard, produced, and supported their families. Rightist protesters claimed that foreign laborers reduced average wages, increased unemployment, and collected public benefits through fraudulent means. They deserved few if any government expenditures. Rightist movements showed greater agreement on the need for cultural assimilation than on opinions toward the market economy. Generally, they supported small-scale family businesses and domestic private enterprises that gave native citizens an opportunity to compete with other small firms, make money, and help industrious individuals gain upward mobility. According to them, economic inequalities served as an incentive to work harder. Right-wing populists rejected multinational corporations and international financial institutions that backed low-cost immigrant labor. Claiming that these bureaucratic institutions brought more perceived costs than benefits, rightist protesters opposed their dominance over the market economy.

Right-wing activists aimed to strengthen political efficacy among their followers. Small group networks in local families, neighborhoods, and voluntary associations shared information, grievances, and protest tactics. Mobilizing the fight against immigrants, leftists, and multiculturalists, right-wing leaders expressed the alienation toward government and established political parties felt by many Europeans who feared the modernization associated with globalization (Albertazzi 2009; Blitz 2010; Bornschier 2010, 37–49, 199–208; Caiani, della Porta, and Wagemann 2012, 103–213; Ceobanu and Escandell 2010; Fieschi, Morris, and Caballero 2012; Finseraas and Vernby 2011; Haegel 2009; Mudde 2013; Strømmen 2012; van Hiel 2012; Zaslove 2008).

However aggressive their rhetoric, most right-wing protesters have concentrated on consensual tactics. They used the Internet to communicate their message and to recruit followers, especially young men. Petitions, letters to government officials, marches, demonstrations, and coalitions with anti-immigrant populist parties formed the major tactics for attracting recruits. Increasing their electoral strength from 1980 through 2010, these parties included the Swiss People's Party, Italian Northern League, French National Front, Austrian Freedom Party, Belgian Vlaams Belang (Flemish Interest), Party for Freedom (Netherlands), Danish People's Party, Progress Party (Norway), and Finns Party.

Neo-Nazis tried to mobilize antagonism through aggressive tactics. Golden Dawn, a neo-Nazi Greek group, praised the 1967–1974 military dictatorship. Relying on armed militias, Golden Dawn activists committed violent acts against immigrants, leftists, gays, Jews, and Muslims. Elsewhere in Europe, neo-Nazis attacked Jews, Muslims, left-wing activists, homeless people, and immigrants, especially those from Asia, Africa, and the Middle East (Wheeler 2012).

Compared with left-wingers who protested austerity programs, rightist leaders gained stronger influence over policies that restricted immigrants' right to equality. Opportunities for effective resource mobilization outweighed obstacles. Divisions did arise over central government power, regional autonomy, and reliance on market solutions. In several societies like Belgium and Italy, regional loyalties clashed with national solidarity. Economic conflicts pitted individuals preferring an active central government against those who wanted private markets to supply social services.

Despite the factionalism, rightist protesters developed cohesion over the need to protect the nation's cultural identity against immigrants. Particularly when right-wing organizers came from highly educated business executives, managers, technicians, doctors, teachers, and lawyers, these leaders could more effectively influence public attitudes. Among the public, a majority of Europeans backed government restrictions on immigrants' rights to enter the country, become citizens, and freely practice their Muslim religion. Groups favoring this xenophobic stand included unemployed males, small business owners, and manual workers in domestic industries that lost jobs to foreign competition. Where the mass media gave favorable coverage to opposition against immigrants, rightist movements strengthened electoral support for allied right-wing populist parties. In parliamentary elections, they won from 10 to nearly 30 percent of the popular vote. Their most active supporters came from less formally educated men who felt lower trust in parliament, rejected globalization, and identified with the ideological right. Allies developed with center-right coalitional governing political parties, such as the Austrian People's Party, Conservative Party (Norway), Conservative and Liberal parties (Denmark), People of Liberty-Forza Italia (Italy), and the promarket Dutch VVD (People's Party for Freedom and Democracy). Under these alliances, policies for national exclusivism drew greater support from government leaders (Arter 2011, 1–28, 216–41; Caiani, della Porta, and Wagemann 2012, 36–102; Fieschi, Morris, and Caballero 2012; Gudbrandsen 2010; Koopmans, Michalowski, and Waibel 2012; Mavris 2012; van Spanje 2011; R. Wolin 2011).

United States

In the United States, the right-wing Tea Party movement secured policy influence because of its close ties with conservative Republican Party activists. Although Tea Partiers held diverse views, their economic policy beliefs reflected libertarian priorities that rejected equal outcomes. Values about economic justice partly derived from the writings of Friedrich Hayek. According to him, rather than enact redistributive programs that reduce economic inequalities, government leaders should strengthen the liberty of private entrepreneurs to make market decisions. From his perspective, government bureaucracies and labor unions, not private corporations, wield the dominant coercive power. Within the social-service state, the chief dangers to procedural liberty "come from inflation, paralyzing taxation, coercive labor unions, an ever increasing dominance of government in education, and a social service bureaucracy with far-reaching arbitrary powers" (Hayek 1960, 305). Contemporary Tea Party activists agreed with this assessment about the dangers of progressive taxes, high expenditures for social services, and arbitrary government decisions made by bureaucratic hierarchs. More than other Americans, they rejected government assistance to the needy, denied that business corporations make excessive profits, and refused to consider income inequality as a serious problem (Formisano 2012; Pew Research Center 2012).

Like the European anti-immigrant movements, the US Tea Party blended individual liberty with national exclusivism. It praised individuals who work hard, compete on the market, and achieve personal success. Yet along with this competitive individualism came a high emphasis on nationalism, with its focus on loyalty, allegiance, and uniform pro-American beliefs. Tea Partiers' exclusive interpretation of nationalism regarded African Americans, Latinos, immigrants, and Muslims as unequal members of the American community. Ideological polarization split the conservative in-group from out-groups: leftists, socialists, unionists, undocumented immigrants, cosmopolitan intellectuals, undisciplined youths, Muslims. Backed by evangelical Protestants, the Tea Party perceived Christians as the foundation of communal solidarity. Perceiving Christian values and the capitalist ethic as compatible, it wanted religious leaders to become politically active, participate in political debates, and win elective office. Their policymaking role would give them the opportunity to restore traditional American values: national pride, the importance of God in personal life, and the duty of parents to teach their children religious faith and obedience.

As illustrated by their active participation in the Republican Party, Tea Party members affirmed a high political efficacy. Many held lengthy experience in working for the Republican Party. Instead of being resigned to the established status quo, they sought to restore the party's conservative ideological purity and opposed Democratic leaders, especially President Barack Obama. Tea Party activists campaigned against expanded social-service benefits for poor people, immigrants, ethnic minorities, and youths. From the conservative perspective, low-income individuals should seek assistance from churches and private charities, not from government programs like food stamps and unemployment benefits. Even though disdaining government control over private business activities, Tea Party militants supported stricter government regulation over homosexual relations and especially over the legal right to an abortion (Campbell and Putnam 2011; M. Cohen 2012, 229; Parker and Barreto 2013, 102–258; Pew Research Center 2012; Skocpol and Williamson 2012, 189–205; Street and DiMaggio 2011, 27–93).

Tea Party tactics revolved around electoral participation, rallies, demonstrations, and confrontations with legislators at their public meetings. Although blasting Democrats for advocating Keynesian policies, Tea Party protesters also remained disenchanted with many incumbent Republicans who supposedly had compromised the conservative cause. During the 2010 primary congressional elections, their endorsements encouraged voters to select conservative Republicans who opposed compromises with Democratic officials. Particularly in districts that enjoyed relatively low unemployment rates and that incumbent centrist Democrats had won by narrow margins in the 2008 election, these tactics elected conservative Republicans to Congress. Financial resources came from wealthy corporate executives like Charles and David Koch as well as from leaders heading powerful interest groups, including FreedomWorks, Americans for Prosperity, State Policy Network, State Government Affairs Council, and the American Legislative Exchange Council. Groups like the Tea Party Patriots, Tea Party Nation, Tea Party Express, and Club for Growth spread the right-wing message throughout the United States. Fox TV News, radio talk programs, newspaper media like *The Wall Street Journal*, and numerous phone banks communicated Tea Party policy positions. Cohesion arose from shared ideological views and from support networks that included older, white, wealthy Republicans who identified themselves as ideological conservatives. Alliances with evangelical Protestant churches, private businesses, and especially the Republican Party furthered Tea Party protesters' influence over the policy agenda during 2011–2012. Not only the Republican majority in the House of Representatives but also right-wing Republicans who won control over state and local governments favored the Tea Party message (Abramowitz 2012; Arceneaux and Nicholson 2012; DiMaggio 2011, 125–49; Fang 2013, 83–123, 197–224; Gervais and Morris 2012; Parker and Barreto 2013, 66–101; Skocpol and Williamson 2012, 45–188; Street and DiMaggio 2011, 127–65).

Even if the Tea Party movement effectively organized resources that mobilized political enthusiasm among the Republican Party's conservative base, its tactics and policy stands alienated the general American public after 2010. Compared with Tea Party protesters, most Americans wanted religious leaders to confine their role to serving local parishioners, not engage in active partisan politics. Even within the Tea Party, a gap emerged between national leaders who adopted more libertarian stands and local activists who wanted to maintain social security and Medicare benefits. Given the growing income gap in the United States, the national Tea Party's support for reducing income taxes on the wealthy and decreasing government spending on social services like education, health care, and pensions aroused limited popular approval from the public, including many pragmatic Republicans who held a less conservative position toward political issues (Abramson, Aldrich, and Rohde 2012, 296–99, 304–12; Campbell and Putnam 2011; Karpowitz et al. 2011; Pew Research Center 2012).

Although the contemporary Tea Party took its name from the 1773 incident that dumped barrels of tea into the Boston Harbor, the modern Occupy movement has advocated policies more closely associated with the eighteenth-century revolutionaries. The British Parliament gave a monopoly to the East India Company over the sale of tea to the American colonists. Several parliamentarians held stock in that company, which allied with British government officials ruling the colonies. Rather than defending the private interests of company power, the original Boston Tea Party revolutionaries held town meetings and assemblies where they enacted policies that limited profits, controlled bread prices, and regulated manufactured products' quality. Wealthy professionals like Sam Adams led the Boston revolutionaries. Yet the main supporters of the Boston Tea Party comprised lower-status groups: artisans, shopkeepers, shoemakers, sailors, a few African Americans. Young men played the most active role in the struggle against the Loyalists and royalists for expanded political, economic, and cultural equality (Young 2011).

Unlike the modern Tea Party, the Occupy movement placed income inequality at the center of political discourse. Communications supported an interpretation of justice that stressed economic, political, and cultural equality. Believing that oligopolies, especially large financial institutions, wield excessive power over government policymakers, Occupiers sought higher taxes on the wealthy and corporations. Enhanced expenditures for social services took priority over programs to limit the federal deficit. According to Occupy protesters, labor unions should secure higher wages, more healthful working conditions, and enhanced control over company management. Politically, the general assemblies provided opportunities for all members to express their views, debate others, and reach a consensus through widespread participation. Culturally, the Occupy movement backed an inclusive position toward everyone: young, old, Hispanics, African Americans, whites, men, women, immigrants, citizens, students, professors, janitors, professionals. They should all hold equal status as valued human beings.

Opposition to hierarchy paralleled belief in extensive equality. Rejecting vertical authority, Occupiers preferred a horizontal form of governance that impeded deference to leaders' authority. Popular assemblies facilitated participatory democracy. Guided mainly by youths, several working groups shared authority to make decentralized decisions about food, health, sanitation, education, law, security, comfort, sustainability, facilitation, community relations, art, culture, and media communications.

Collectivism merged with individualism. Occupy protesters stressed the freedom for each individual to assert his or her views in general assemblies, affinity groups, and working groups. Yet the protesters also upheld a cooperative form of individualism whereby everyone recognized the need for mutual interdependence. A more universal ethos took precedence over the type of exclusive nationalism favored by the Tea Party. Through electronic media, Occupy protesters kept in contact with sympathizers in all parts of the world, including Western Europe, the Middle East, and Latin America. From their perspective, solidarity extended not only to the US nation but to human beings everywhere. In 2011 Occupy movements spread throughout the global community to more than eighty nations and two thousand cities, where protesters debated the most effective tactics to reduce inequality. Forming an electronic network that mobilized people across the globe, the People's Global Action members communicated information, ideas, and plans for political action (Hayduk 2012).

A division among Occupiers arose over tactics linked to political efficacy. Lacking confidence in government's power to enact egalitarian measures, some participants wanted the movement to remain independent from close ties to governments and political parties. Rather than identify with the Democratic Party, most activists viewed themselves as nonpartisan or backed the Green Party. For them, mass popular participation represented the best tactic for changing the political system. Other protesters affirmed stronger political efficacy about influencing the electoral process. Although skeptical of both major political parties, they favored policies more closely aligned with leftist Democrats than with conservative Republicans. Whatever their doubts about Democratic Party commitments, these Occupiers seemed willing to participate in electoral campaigns and press for candidates who supported egalitarian programs. Pragmatism took precedence over dedication to an idealistic cause.

Many Occupy protesters participated in disruptive tactics that usually involved nonviolent activities. Strikes, demonstrations, marches, encampments, and occupations of corporate headquarters, banks, and university buildings represented typical actions. These tactics revolved around the need to expand the space for political discourse, empowerment, and reconciliation of policy positions. For the activists, participatory democracy took precedence over representative government that emphasized electoral control but gave less attention to public policies that responded to a wide variety of popular demands, particularly those expressed by lower-income persons. The occupied space provided a stage for protesters to mobilize the audience behind their egalitarian agenda (Kohn 2013; Sennett 2012).

Given the divergence of groups within the movement that claimed to represent the "99 percent," the goals encompassed many different egalitarian objectives. Students sought reduced fees and lower interest charges on their debts. Antiwar veterans fought nonviolently for better public health services. Tenants demanded lower rents. The homeless occupied vacant houses. Homeowners wanted banks to reduce mortgage rates, cease foreclosures, and stop ordering evictions from residences. Through Strike Debt, the draft resistance movement mobilized diverse groups—home buyers, renters, students, firefighters—against the exorbitant interest rates, fees, and penalties imposed by creditors. The unemployed pursued increased job opportunities. Union activists struggled for higher wages, improved working conditions, and greater power to negotiate collective bargains with employers. Undocumented immigrants desired nondiscriminatory treatment, legal work permits, educational opportunities for their children, and speedier access to citizenship. Ecologists backed a more sustainable energy policy that reduced carbon emissions and provided new green jobs for workers.

Unlike the Tea Party protesters who convinced the Republican Party to support their policy agenda, the Occupy movement accomplished fewer policy achievements. Beginning its activities only in early 2011, it lacked the extensive resources, strong cohesion, and powerful allies of the Tea Party. Stronger opposition thwarted Occupiers' tactics. They had access to fewer financial resources, particularly those from wealthy contributors and private corporations. Whereas the Tea Party promoted ideological cohesion about explicit conservative beliefs, the Occupy movement included many diverse ideological groups that affirmed divergent priorities. For example, whereas Keynesians wanted to reform capitalist practices, socialists sought a more fundamental transformation of the American and global capitalist system. Other participants—anarchists, feminists, ecologists, herbalists, unionists, students, pacifists, left-wing church members, human-rights activists—lacked the strong agreement on goals and tactics needed to form an effective coalition.

Faced with powerful opposition, the Occupy movement suffered repression by police, urban officials, and their corporate allies. The tactics used by some Occupiers created greater opposition than did their goals. Nonviolent encampments, strikes, and building occupations caused disorder and inconvenience for many city residents, merchants, and corporate executives. Conservatives who pinned pejorative labels on Occupy protesters denounced them as "mobs, anarchists, terrorists, union thugs, and methadone felons." For many participants, disruptive tactics intimidated some potential joiners who supported Occupy goals. The Federal Bureau of Investigation and the Department of Homeland Security not only monitored actions by Occupy protesters but supplied information about them to financial institutions, corporations, and private security agencies. City police often destroyed Occupiers' property, such as tents, books, and health products. Pepper sprays, tear gas, beatings, encirclement, mobile blockades, preventive detention, expulsions, and orders that forbade entrance to specific areas restricted the space for Occupiers to pursue their protests. This repression, even against journalists observing the protests, attracted greater coverage in the world media and angered many participants. Coercion, however, impeded their opportunity to influence the policy process (Binelli 2012; DiMaggio and Street 2011; Hightower 2011; R. Kim 2011; M. Schwartz 2011; A. Taylor 2012).

CONCLUSION

Egalitarian protesters attained their greatest policy successes when opportunities exceeded constraints. Cultural values highlighted collective solidarity, low deference to hierarchical authority, high political efficacy, and a comprehensive perception that all people deserved equal human respect and treatment. Activists possessed several types of resources: political skills, finances, and informal networks of family members, friends, neighbors, and work colleagues. High cohesion cemented loyalty to the protest movement. It attracted several allies, including unions, leftist parties, some businesses, and especially the media. Coordinating organizations linked group allies with movement sympathizers. Neither government institutions nor private businesses wielded extensive coercive power over the egalitarian protesters. Along with corporate executives, many government officials backed programs for increasing social-service benefits (Lahusen 2013).

Immediately after World War II in most reconciliation systems, these opportunities held true. Until the mid-1970s, Keynesian policies secured full employment through raising aggregate demand, lowering interest rates, spending more on capital investment, and increasing wages. Fairly high equality emerged. Yet after 1980, with the growth of neoliberal priorities, the income gap widened. Particularly when the growth rate declined in 2008, nations that adopted austerity policies suffered greater income inequality. Neoliberal programs for reducing the deficit decreased capital investment, lowered growth rates, enlarged unemployment, and raised fiscal deficits as a share of GDP. Backed by neoliberal elites, austerity policies brought high unemployment, homelessness, personal debt, ill health, and low morale to many people.

Although deprivations motivated some frustrated individuals to mobilize behind public protests, structural constraints hindered the ability of egalitarian protesters to influence policy performance after 2008. Cultural values placed more emphasis on self-reliance, not collective solidarity, as the primary path to upward mobility. Many poor people felt resigned to capitalist institutions governed by hierarchical authority. Competitive efficiency on the global market took priority over cooperative equality. Organizations that rejected egalitarian policies held greater financial resources, communications facilities, and cohesion. Protesters secured fewer allies. Corporations wielded greater power over unions in the workplace and government offices. Unions and private businesses achieved less cooperation. When dominating the government, social democratic and labor parties backed many neoliberal programs preferred by the MNCs. Mass media often blasted egalitarian activists as undeserving malcontents who deserved little support. Fragmented by numerous conflicting values and interests, sympathizers became difficult to mobilize, particularly in societies split by rival ethnic-religious values. Unskilled laborers, skilled factory workers, clerks, retail salespersons, and employees in the informal sector could not easily organize class coalitions campaigning for egalitarian public programs. Even though the World Social Forum advocated greater global equality, the more influential World Economic Forum upheld neoliberal priorities backed by multinational corporations. Wealthy capitalists—managers, directors, senior administrators, chief executive officers—strengthened their solidarity through social networks. Similar club memberships, educational backgrounds, and lifestyles reinforced their cohesion (Amenta et al. 2010). Hence, neoliberal elites could mobilize their resources to influence government performance in reconciliation systems, where complex interactions between political democracy and capitalism shaped income distribution policies.

Chapter Six

Economic Inequality, Democracy, and Policy Dilemmas in Capitalist Societies

In *The Ragged Trousered Philanthropists*, Robert Tressell (1870–1911) portrayed the impact of capitalism and democracy on economic inequality. Taking place in southern England before World War I, the novel focused on arguments about the causes of poverty. Most workers for Rushton and Company Builders suffered from low wages, insecure jobs, limited employment opportunities, ill health, and dilapidated housing. Yet few painters, decorators, carpenters, plumbers, and bricklayers saw any alternative to the capitalist system. Several took a fatalistic orientation, which bred low efficacy and resignation to the status quo. Influenced by newspapers like the *Obscurer*, isolated individualists stressed the malignant influence of alcoholism, laziness, and excessive debt. For them, collective political activism offered no solution to their personal miseries. Other workers accepted the dominant elitist, hierarchical values of the wealthy elites. Feeling inferior to their "betters," they deferred to the hierarchical authority wielded by the capitalist class and regarded their subordinate status as natural, inevitable, and necessary for social order. Any prospect of greater income equality seemed impossible.

Frank Owen, the hero of the novel, attributed workers' inequality to structural conditions. A socialist decorator, he believed that the capitalist system caused poverty, economic inequalities, starvation, underemployment, ill health, short life expectancies, and political apathy among workers. Monopolies dominated both the economic and political systems. Private ownership of capital generated ruthless competition, high profits, low wages, and extensive surveillance of workers by managers. Employment opportunities remained volatile. Part-time, low-paid jobs offered few if any benefits such as health care. Owen wanted to raise workers' consciousness through political education so that they would understand the reason for their deprivation and take political action to transform current economic conditions (Tressell 1962).

Although around 60 percent of adult English men had the right to vote during the early 1900s, Owen did not believe that representative democracy would significantly reduce economic inequalities. Even if the two major political parties—Conservative and Liberal—promised work for the poor, few full-time jobs ever emerged. Wealthy capitalists from both parties gained election to city councils. Concerned to protect their property rights and their shares in major private corporations, neither Liberal nor Conservative candidates offered specific policy proposals for narrowing the income gap. Policy disputes revolved around competing arguments for free trade versus protectionism. Nationalistic patriots denounced foreigners for causing underemployment. Slogans accused the opposite party of acting like "scoundrels" and "fools." When a few socialists distributed leaflets, the two major parties hired bullies to attack the anticapitalist dissenters as "drunken loafers." Claiming that the protesters advocated unreasonable, impractical, violent policies that would bring atheism and "free love" to England, the bullies stoned Owen (Tressell 1962, 589). Like Étienne, he failed to realize his ambition to help establish a socialist commonwealth based on equality, collective solidarity, and political efficacy.

Written over a hundred years ago, Tressell's novel inspired readers who sought an alternative to capitalist injustices. A house painter and writer, Tressell died of tuberculosis at age forty in 1911. Buried in a pauper's grave, he never lived to see Owen's vision of socialism become an English reality. Despite Tressell's tragic life, the novel found readers throughout the world, including Britain, Western Europe, Eastern Europe, North America, Japan, and Africa. By the twenty-first century, it had sold over a million copies. Translations, stage dramas, BBC television productions, and radio programs spread the novel's themes. Tressell's critique of capitalism appealed to trade unionists who struggled for greater collective bargaining rights, higher wages, and improved access to health care and pensions. Feminists appreciated the emphasis on gender equality and respect for women. Leftist Christians approved Tressell's message that placed prophetic ideals over monetary profits. To socialists who perceived political education as a key requirement for enlightening the workers, his analysis highlighted the importance of overcoming political apathy, transcending differences, and creating collective solidarity (Anderson 2010; Cairnie and Walls 2008a, 2008b; J. Mitchell 1969, 121–42; Walls 2008).

Tressell probed a crucial dilemma faced by leaders working for systemic transformation. Income inequality still shapes people's health, educational opportunity, housing, and exposure to crime. Despite the unequal conditions, why do leftists face difficulties when they try to realize an alternative to the capitalist system? What cultural values and structural conditions affect the likelihood of egalitarian change? How do different policy strategies deal with the effects of political democracy and capitalism on income distribution?

Keynes and neoliberal theorists supported representative democracy and a capitalist market system. They upheld rule by educated experts, doubted the wisdom of extensive popular participation in public policymaking, and supported key elements of a market economy: decentralization, individualism, competition among autonomous private enterprises, and legal guarantees for private property rights. Both felt that such a pluralist economic system would ensure political liberty, free choice, and freedom for dissenters to express their views.

Despite their agreement on these issues, Keynes took a different position toward government's role in the economy than do most neoliberals today. A member of the Liberal Party, Keynes wanted to blend the liberal stress on individual freedom with some aspects of planning. For him, government authority should rest on consent, not coercion. Even if representative democracy needed experts that gave technical advice to government officials, he remained skeptical about elites' behavior to act decisively when faced by dire economic conditions, such as the massive unemployment that plagued Britain in the 1930s. According to Keynes, the Treasury dominated the civil service and cabinet, which produced policy stagnation. Populism hardly contributed to effective solutions. He rejected the "poison of popular politics" that caused government impotence and immobility (Keynes 1978, 155). Instead, he wanted Britain's democratic leaders to moderate their differences, pursue gradual reforms, and combine justice with efficiency. As a Liberal, he criticized the Conservative Party for its doctrinaire policies that opposed all new ideas. Although repudiating the Labour Party for stressing class struggle and nationalization, Keynes believed that a Liberal alliance with Labour would formulate more effective policies than a coalition with Conservative parliamentarians.

Opposed to both unregulated laissez-faire capitalism and centralized state socialism under Stalinist domination, Keynes preferred a decentralized planned economy in which government played an active role in stimulating capital investment, providing social services, and increasing aggregate demand. From his perspective, democratically elected agencies should not issue detailed regulations but instead prepare general guidelines and act only when decentralized administrators of government institutions failed to solve crucial economic problems. Independent banks should retain freedom from too many specific instructions by elected parliamentarians. Just as Keynes sought to reconcile justice with efficiency, so he preferred that government institutions and private enterprises form partnerships for expanding economic growth. In 1938 he urged President Franklin D. Roosevelt to treat business executives with kindness, strengthen their optimism, reassure them about government policies, and regard them as "domestic animals," not as "wolves and tigers" (Keynes 1982a, 438). According to Keynes, private enterprises should retain extensive independence and private profits but accept limited government regulations. Low-interest loans and high expenditures for capital investment would stimulate aggregate demand, enlarge employment opportunities, and promote economic growth. Public policies would expand knowledge, education, workers' training, geographic labor mobility, collective bargaining rights, and minimum wages. Keynes hoped that these policies, along with state-financed capital investment, would not only reduce high unemployment but narrow the income gap affecting capitalist economies during the 1930s (Keynes 1981a, 638–48; 1981b, 27; 1982a, 90–92, 131–32, 434–39, 492–500).

Unlike Keynes, neoliberal theorists reject a planned economy with extensive social services that reduce income inequalities. Instead, they want the partnership between government and private corporations to support policies advocated by capitalist business executives. For them, representative democracy must promote decentralized governance, entrepreneurship, skilled education, and opportunities for individual initiative. Competent judges should uphold laws that reduce corruption, enforce stable contracts, protect private property rights, and prevent social disorder. Allied with capitalist investors, government administrators can supply credit, provide grants, construct an infrastructure, supply research assistance for innovative technologies, and offer financial assistance to private banks faced with defaults on their loans. Policies for increasing equality, however, receive low priority. Neoliberals perceive comprehensive social-service spending as too generous and costly. Strong unions, collective bargaining rights, and workers' participation in management interfere with a flexible labor market that ensures innovation, high productivity, and rapid growth. To compete in a modern global market, private businesses need governments that practice fiscal discipline, incur minimal debts, facilitate world trade, and avoid tight controls over overseas financial investments (Hufbauer and Suominen 2010; Panitch and Gindin 2012, 1–21, 216–18, 275–340).

Throughout the world, the relationships among democracy, capitalism, and income distribution have shown divergent paths. Among the long-lasting political democracies in Western Europe, North America, and the Commonwealth, the most egalitarian outcomes arose since World War II in Scandinavian societies like Denmark, Sweden, Norway, and Finland. Their governments supported civil liberties, voluntary political participation, competitive elections, and social-group autonomy. Along with these democratic practices, a promarket capitalist economy gave private entrepreneurs extensive influence over domestic and global trade. Income distribution programs secured fewer benefits for immigrants who suffered high unemployment. Nevertheless, the generous, comprehensive, universal social services provided by public policymakers still produced fairly egalitarian results compared with other industrialized societies such as Britain and the United States. Public health and education systems encouraged the emergence of skilled labor sought by private enterprisers (Buchholz et al. 2009; Panić 2007). As a stronger democracy emerged during the early 1990s, South Korean government elites allied with private corporate executives to engineer rapid growth rates. The populace gained higher income equality and greater civil liberties than did Indians. By the late 1980s, military dictatorships in Latin American countries like Argentina, Brazil, Chile, and Uruguay had collapsed. Civilian political leaders enacted promarket economic policies. Even though ginis fell after 2000, a wide income gap exceeded levels in South Korea, Japan, and Western Europe.

To clarify the impact of capitalism and democracy on income distribution, the following sections explore three policy dilemmas faced by reconciliation leaders. How did procedural justice that ensures equal rights under the law affect distributive justice programs favoring more egalitarian outcomes? Why did policies for faster economic growth usually come at the expense of higher wages for workers? What perceptions shaped elected leaders' attitudes toward the interaction between representative democracy, which stresses electoral accountability, and participatory democracy that seeks greater popular involvement over the policy process? Power relations and public policies influenced the divergent ways that democratic leaders handle the cultural, economic, and political dilemmas.

CULTURAL DILEMMA: PROCEDURAL AND DISTRIBUTIVE JUSTICE

Cultural dilemmas involve the relative importance that reconciliation systems place on procedural and distributive justice. Whereas distributive justice upholds fair outcomes, procedural justice affirms the need for nondiscriminatory rules. Certain procedures contribute to representative democracy. Ideally, all individuals, whatever their social status, political power, income, gender, ethnicity, and religion, enjoy equal rights to fair treatment by authorities. Police officers, judges, and civil servants treat others with respect. They make decisions based on unbiased empirical evidence. Individuals gain access to accurate information about public policies. Free to express their opinions to political authorities, they can stage nonviolent challenges to government decisions without fearing arbitrary, coercive domination. All these procedures help ensure the free opportunity to participate in political life under a representative democracy.

Capitalism, however, rests on a different foundation of procedural justice. Compared with democratic procedures, capitalist rules place greater priority on hierarchy, elitism, and resignation to the impersonal laws of the market. Chief executive officers, managers, and supervisors stress the need for subordinate workers to show deference toward hierarchical authority. Social distance, secrecy, and monitoring of workers' behavior strengthen managerial elites, who claim to make decisions based on their superior meritocratic status. If workers challenge capitalist authority, they risk losing their jobs. Individual efficiency takes precedence over a communal feeling of solidarity with low-income people. Particularly when mergers and acquisitions strengthen conglomerates, isolated consumers lack the personal efficacy to influence market-based prices in a global capitalist market (G. Cohen 2009; Feygina and Tyler 2009; Hahnel 2009; Hayes 2012, 54–64, 181–91; Lovett 2009; Tyler 2011).

A dilemma between procedural and distributive justice especially arises when capitalist practices produce widespread income disparities. Most leaders and voters in reconciliation systems place a higher priority on procedural than distributive justice. Whatever their income or status, people prefer fair procedures ensuring that government officials treat them with equal respect. Yet in many capitalist societies, those who own the gold make the rules. Wealthy political elites use their resources to shape laws that affect their economic well-being. Hence, the distinction between process and outcomes becomes obscure. In societies where a wide gap separates rich from poor, the marginals suffer not only from economic inequalities but from procedural injustice. As graphically described in Tressell's novel, jobless persons, the underemployed, and the "undeserving poor" lack political power to transform their conditions. Stigmatized by their "betters," they often view procedural justice as an illusion, not an effective means for changing their economic outcomes. John Kenneth Galbraith (2000, 38) commented: "Nothing so denies a person liberty as the total absence of money." Both private economic exchanges and political interactions depend on cash as a crucial resource for achieving demands.

Marginal groups attain more equal procedural and distributive justice when they form cohesive sociopolitical networks that expand structural opportunities, raise expectations about political success, and form coalitions with other movements committed to egalitarian change. Under these conditions, political efficacy supersedes fatalism. Challenges to authority replace deference to hierarchical elites. Atomistic individualism with an emphasis on ruthless competition yields to egalitarian cooperation that affirms mutual benefits. However formidable the pragmatic difficulties of attaining procedural and distributive justice in a capitalist economy, Scandinavian political leaders have more effectively fulfilled these twin goals than policymakers in most other industrialized societies, particularly Britain and the United States (Andrain and Smith 2006, 105–118).

Compared with the British Labour Party, the Norwegian Labor Party achieved higher income equality and implemented more democratic freedoms. From 1945 through 2013, Labor prime ministers in Norway held power around 70 percent of that period. Labor's membership and ties with unions declined during recent years. Yet as the largest parliamentary party, it formed a red-red-green coalition with the Socialist Left and Center (agrarian) parties from 2007 to 2013. Labor governments in the early 2000s reconciled Keynesian programs with some aspects of neoliberalism, especially limited privatization, efficient operation of public enterprises, reliance on free trade, and overseas investment by Norwegian corporations. Government activism, however, remained strong. Financed partly by revenues from state-owned oil corporations, Norwegian social-service expenditures supplied comprehensive, universal benefits: pensions, health care, education, day care, child allowances, elder care. Paid parental leaves enabled over 90 percent of both mothers and fathers to care for their newborn children. Besides these generous expenditures, progressive tax revenues from corporate income as a share of GDP in 2010 totaled 10 percent—over three times higher than the rate for OECD countries (OECD 2012c, 109). Besides sizable budget surpluses, Norway's lack of membership in the European Union gave political leaders extensive independence to enact egalitarian fiscal and monetary programs. Compared with all OECD nations, Norway had the largest percentage of the labor force working for government agencies and public corporations. Even though private enterprises sought lower taxes and more privatized services, they established closer cooperative ties with unions than did Swedish corporations. Centralized, coordinated wage bargaining produced high wage equality even before taxes and transfers. Many union members, Lutheran clergy, ecologists, feminists, and academicians backed the Labor Party's egalitarian public policies. Like other Scandinavian governments, Norwegian administrations established equal opportunities for women, as indicated by the high proportion of women holding positions in parliament and cabinet ministries (Biermann and Kallset 2010; Gulbrandsen and Engelstad 2007; Hausmann, Tyson, and Zahidi 2012, 5, 10, 22, 55–56; Hill 2010, 83, 254, 347–51; Kenworthy 2011, 5–17, 33–101; Moschonas 2011; OECD 2011b, 195–99; OECD 2012b, 11, 26, 44–46, 68–69; Pontusson 2011; Strøm, Narud, and Valen 2007).

Distributive justice blended with procedural justice. Cultural values affirmed an egalitarian individualism that strengthened procedural consensus, tolerance of diverse lifestyles, and a high priority on popular participation in political decision making. Widespread participation in voluntary associations not only promoted high political efficacy but also a skeptical attitude toward hierarchical authority. Despite police discrimination against immigrants from non-European countries, political authorities usually encouraged peaceful challenges to government policies. The Labor, Center, and Socialist Left parties supported less restrictive immigration legislation than did the right-wing Progress Party or Conservative Party coalition governments. Compared with citizens from most other European nations, Norwegians maintained more extensive political participation, higher confidence in their political institutions, and greater support for democracy (Aalberg 2010; Andrain and Smith 2006, 10–11, 32–33, 49–50; Chemin 2011; Gudbrandsen 2010; P. Norris 2011, 88, 95–97; Rothstein 2011, 82–83, 135–36, 154–63; Welzel and Inglehart 2010).

After New Labour won control of the British House of Commons in 1997, it resisted combining procedural justice with egalitarian public policies. Many neoliberal programs from the previous Conservative administration remained. Prime Minister Tony Blair and Chancellor of the Exchequer Gordon Brown viewed raising growth rates, lowering inflation, and reducing poverty as more important than narrowing income disparities. According to them, equality meant opportunities to expand individual potential, not policies to increase equal shares. Individualism took precedence over collective solidarity stressed by unions. Rule by technical experts who possessed specialized computer knowledge supplanted popular participation in the policy process. Export competition in the global capitalist market required support for private corporations. Financial oligopolies gained extensive independence from ministerial or regulatory control. Promarket policies favored corporate executives, who received high salaries, large bonuses, and generous stock options. Whereas the income held by the richest 1 percent escalated under New Labour, less-wealthy individuals obtained far lower income raises. Regressive value-added taxes hurt poor people. Although poverty rates declined, greater income equality failed to result. Neither child and family tax credits nor higher government spending on health care and education as a proportion of GDP narrowed the income gap.

Even if capitalism thrived under New Labour, public officials showed less regard for civil liberties. Concerned about threats to national security, the Blair government made decisions that gave police the authority to detain individuals suspected of terrorism without any legal charge, trial, or conviction of a crime. Laws proscribed "antisocial" behavior. Those suffering the most arrests included low-income youths from South Asian and Middle Eastern backgrounds. British police used excessive force against protesters. Top Labour leaders stressed a more hierarchical interpretation of procedural justice than did the Norwegian Labor Party. Although the Labour government devolved authority to the Scottish, Welsh, and Northern Irish parliaments, within England the prime minister assumed centralized, hierarchical control over House of Commons members. The Blair government took an unsympathetic outlook toward the collective solidarity of unions when they challenged its policies. Neither Blair nor Brown, who became prime minister in 2007, saw any effective alternative system that could transform the capitalist market economy (Faucher-King and Le Galès 2010; Hutton 2010, 14–15, 139–71, 276–309; Mullard and Swaray 2010).

When a coalition of Conservatives and Liberal Democrats assumed control over the British government in May 2010, their policies neither strengthened procedural freedoms nor reduced income inequalities. As reflected in the harsh, arbitrary treatment imposed by police officers, judges, and court magistrates, punitive justice took priority over restorative justice. Coalition leaders showed a less egalitarian stance toward distributive justice than did the previous Labour administrations. The Conservative Party attacked the poor who needed social-service benefits as "scroungers and skivers." Determined to reduce fiscal deficits, the coalition government adopted a neoliberal perspective about the need for austerity budgets, means-tested programs, and "fiscal discipline." Policies raised the value-added tax and curbed people's tax credits but reduced the corporate income tax. Decreased expenditures went for the National Health Service (NHS), education, public legal assistance, and benefits for children, unemployed persons, renters, and the disabled. Greater privatization of NHS care by profit-oriented corporations triggered fewer treatments by general practitioners, longer waits for surgical operations, and wider regional inequalities. The central government slashed funds that financed social services implemented by nongovernmental associations and local councils, which closed public libraries, swimming pools, and lavatories. Tenants in public housing paid higher rents. Rail fares increased. Tuition fees for universities tripled. Antagonistic to unions, the Conservative chancellor of the exchequer placed a pay freeze on public-sector employees, reduced their pensions, and slashed their numbers. Restrictions on collective bargaining led to variable work schedules with more part-time, temporary, and insecure jobs.

British austerity policies caused declining real wages, higher joblessness, lower growth, and rising economic inequality under the coalition government. Its leaders expected that private corporations would spur capital investment. Instead, as aggregate demand fell, slower growth ensued. Unemployment rose. Resulting from higher consumer prices for food, electricity, and fuel, inflation rates exceeded wage increases. The poorest 40 percent of the population lost a larger proportion of their net income than did the richest tenth. Greater inequality particularly hurt single mothers, children, disabled persons, renters, and public employees (Amnesty International 2010, 339–42; Behr 2012; Blanchflower and Skidelsky 2011; Burns and Werdigier 2011; Finlayson 2013; Kisby 2010; Lyall and Cowell 2010; McKibbin 2013; Mulheirn 2013; Parker and Oakley 2010; Taylor-Gooby 2013; Taylor-Gooby and Stoker 2011).

Without a strong labor party, the United States lacked a powerful political organization to mobilize support behind egalitarian programs. Like British officials, many American leaders reduced expenditures for social services as a primary way to lower fiscal deficits. Cuts included programs for pensions, health care, public education, unemployment compensation, and financial assistance to the disabled. All these reductions widened the income gap. Elite power relationships produced this trend toward growing economic inequality. Especially in the private sector, union power declined. Corporations strengthened their influence over the media, government institutions, and both major political parties. Conglomerates controlled newspapers, radio stations, and television channels that communicated information favorable to private business activities. Corporate executives often held administrative posts in the executive branch and regulatory agencies. Administrators deferred to business expertise. Large corporate contributions financed electoral campaigns for legislators as well as for elected state and local judges. Lobbyists influenced and even helped write economic laws, rules, and regulations. Exemptions, long delays in implementing legal procedures, court cases against laws, and reduced funds for regulatory agencies weakened policies that limited income disparities (Taibbi 2012; Zandi 2008, 146–49).

Even if both Republican and Democratic leaders favored a capitalist market economy, leftist Democrats supported a more active government role for policies that adopted a comprehensive approach toward equality. Higher taxes on the wealthy, larger expenditures for social services, and increased government spending on public infrastructure and green energy (wind, solar) were among the Democratic preferences for distributive justice. Cultural tolerance upheld equal rights to gain a legal abortion, marry same-sex partners, and avoid orthodox religious prayers in public schools (Ellis and Stimson 2012, 90–148; Gerber et al. 2011; Haidt 2012; Pew Research Center 2012, 2013).

Hostile to an egalitarian agenda, right-wing Republican leaders allied with groups that opposed policies for narrowing the income gap. Dominant contributors included white evangelical Protestant churches, the National Rifle Association, and business corporations, including the Chamber of Commerce, National Federation of Independent Business, National Association of Manufacturers, and Club for Growth. Support also came from private equity corporations that controlled profitable gun manufacturing conglomerates, such as Freedom Group and Colt Defense (Sorkin 2012). Pressured by these organizations, Republican policymakers weakened unions, reduced public expenditures for low-income persons, and supported laws privatizing education, health care, pensions, police services, prisons, and defense. National Republican legislators passed laws that slashed funds for public education, health care, food stamps, children's assistance, and community development grants subsidizing poor residents' housing. Republican state officials not only weakened the power of public employees' unions but also the collective bargaining rights of unions in the private sector. As a result, wages declined. Unemployed workers secured lower compensation, faced stricter eligibility requirements, and received benefits that lasted a shorter time. Government regulators had less authority to curtail child labor, unhealthy working conditions, and discrimination against women and ethnic minorities. Corporations and the wealthy paid lower taxes (Lafer 2013; Weisman 2013). State government contracts supplied private corporations with low-cost prison labor, weapons, security guards, and correctional facilities. In overcrowded, understaffed, militarized detention centers, multinational corporations like GEO Group and G4S imposed punitive treatment on immigrants (Bernstein 2011; Weisman 2013; Western and Pettit 2010).

Procedural justice waned when Republican state legislators and governors took actions that strengthened their political power over the Democratic Party. Along with the Republican State Leadership Committee and the Republican Governors Association, the American Legislative Exchange Council (ALEC) prepared model bills for restricting electoral participation. Comprising corporate executives and mainly Republican state legislators, ALEC lobbied Republicans to pass laws that shortened early voting periods, hindered voter registration activities, required government-issued photo identification at the polls, and facilitated challenges to an individual's eligibility to vote. When Republican legislators denied county supervisors the financial resources for poll workers, machines, and translators, long waiting lines developed. Besides redistricting procedures that advantaged Republican candidates, all these restrictions impeded voting by young college students, low-income people, seniors, disabled persons, African Americans, Latinos, Latinas, former felons, and individuals who often moved from one place to another. Except for seniors, these groups preferred Democratic candidates and egalitarian public policies.

Unlike Democrats, Republicans participated more actively in politics. They voted at higher rates, made larger financial contributions to candidates, expressed greater interest in political matters, and more often discussed political issues with other people. Ideological consistency toward economic and cultural issues motivated participation by Republican activists. Hostile to Democratic control over government, they mobilized support for their conservative preferences that upheld private corporate power over workers, union activists, and poor people (Berman 2013; Bonica et al. 2013; DiNovella 2011; Ellis and Stimson 2012; Rogers and Dresser 2011).

Decisions by the Supreme Court affected both procedural and distributive justice. After World War II, court justices showed greater opposition to laws regulating private enterprise than during the earlier 1953–1974 era, when Keynesian values attracted broader elite appeal. Influenced by the National Chamber Litigation Center linked to the US Chamber of Commerce, justices decided cases about consumer protection, mergers, patents, collective action suits, securities law, and labor arbitration. Most decisions legitimated the economic rights of corporations vis-à-vis unionists, employees, consumers, and small-business owners. The 2010 *Citizens United v. Federal Election Commission* case rejected government bans that limited contributions made by private corporations to elections for government leaders, including state judges. Viewing corporations as "associations of citizens"—as persons with the right to free speech—the 5–4 court majority denied that Congress had the authority to "chill" political speech by corporations. Although the court extended the same right to unions, they lacked the financial resources, staff members, media outlets, and allies that corporations maintained. Other court decisions invalidated laws that facilitated class-based arbitration by consumers against large corporations like AT&T and by small-restaurant owners against American Express. According to the court's majority ruling, consumers lacked the right to sue a pharmaceutical manufacturer for selling a generic drug with noxious side effects. The Supreme Court held that a woman who suffered pay discrimination had no legal right to regain her lost wages. By a 5–4 vote, *Shelby County v. Holder* declared section 4 of the Voting Rights Act unconstitutional. Passed by Congress several times since 1965, the law required that states discriminating against ethnic minorities must gain the approval of federal government institutions—the Department of Justice or the three-judge US District Court in the District of Columbia—before states could change voting rules. As a result of this decision, several Republican state governments approved bills that imposed voting restrictions on poor people, African Americans, Hispanics, and students (Chemerinsky 2013; Cole 2013; Culpepper 2011, 1–24, 177–98; Greenwald 2011; Hartmann 2010, 14–44, 174–84; Liptak 2010; Stevens 2013).

The World Justice Project developed a Rule of Law index that compared several aspects of procedural justice in nearly one hundred nations. Measurements included three basic indicators: (1) fundamental rights to express opinions, join associations, practice one's religion, maintain personal privacy, achieve equal treatment under the law, resist forced labor, and bargain collectively with employers; (2) open government, especially freedom to participate in political life, petition the government, and gain official information; (3) civil justice—freedom from arbitrary, discriminatory, corrupt treatment that brings unreasonable delays. According to this index, the United States in 2012 gained a slightly lower score than did the United Kingdom. With its greater income equality, Norway ranked higher on all three indicators (Agrast et al. 2012, 12–18, 25–29, 123, 149–50, 158–61, 178). Besides achieving extensive procedural justice, Norwegian leaders enacted egalitarian public policies that mitigated people's economic losses when the real growth rate declined during the 2008–2009 financial crisis (IMF 2012b, 191; OECD 2013b, 37).

ECONOMIC DILEMMA: GROWTH AND EQUALITY

A key economic dilemma focuses on policymakers' attempts to find an effective relationship between high growth rates and income equality. If egalitarian political leaders want to finance generous, comprehensive social-service programs benefiting most citizens, high economic growth must emerge, mainly from high expenditures for capital investment that expands productivity. Particularly in developing nations, policy reliance on capital investment by domestic corporations, multinational corporations, and overseas financial institutions often raises the share of national income going to capitalists. Yet wage earners receive a lower proportion of the increased GDP. When more employees work part-time for subcontracted enterprises, underemployment results. Modern economies also depend on highly skilled technocrats processing complex information. Under these conditions, the income gap between skilled and less-skilled individuals widens. Even many college graduates find few jobs that require their advanced skills. Conflict divides lower-paid workers from wealthy capitalist managers who maintain close ties with government officials. Hence, leaders cannot easily enact egalitarian policies when low growth reduces tax revenues or rapid growth benefits mainly those with higher earnings. Skeptical about the need for wage equality and egalitarian redistribution programs, neoliberal leaders give priority to growth over more equal economic outcomes.

After World War II until 1973, most Western European policymakers followed Keynesian policies that achieved high growth rates, low unemployment, and extensive income equality under democratic institutions. The need to recuperate from wartime devastation stimulated aggregate demand. Capitalist managers and labor union heads cooperated to expand growth, secure generous wage settlements, and promote generous public social-service benefits. Corporations received lower profits as a proportion of the GDP than after 1980. Workers' share of national income rose. Compared with industrial corporations that manufactured goods, financial institutions exerted less policy influence. Social democratic, labor, and Christian democratic parties governed an activist state. Extensive social services and, to a lesser extent, progressive taxes limited income differences. Finances for the public programs came from rapid growth rates. Because of low unemployment, workers who earned high wages provided needed tax revenues.

From 1980 through the early twenty-first century, neoliberal policies gained approval in Western Europe. Government officials placed higher priority on curtailing inflation but less emphasis on narrowing the income gap. Capitalist managers instigated more adversarial interactions with weaker unions. As the manufacturing sector declined and services became more important, financial institutions won greater power over the policy process. Financial profits as a percentage of national income rose. Workers failed to gain such large increases in their wages. With the decline of leftist political parties, the government initiated policies that rewarded private corporations: lower business taxes, privatization, deregulation, a flexible labor market for more temporary, part-time jobs. Although these policies helped lower inflation, they scarcely achieved higher growth, lower unemployment, or greater income equality. Instead, higher growth rates occurred from 1950 through 1973 than from 1980 to 2010.

Unlike Western Europe, most Asian countries secured higher growth after 1973 than during the earlier 1950–1973 period. Until the 1990s, few Asian nations experienced democratic freedoms. Ruled by powerful military forces, a dominant political party, or a national patron, governments used authoritarian means to forge rapid growth. Technocrats dominated the policy process. Capitalist enterprises relied on the state to promote capital investment, an industrial infrastructure, and access to foreign investment. Policies rarely brought extensive benefits to the poor (Evans and Sewell 2013).

In the Republic of Korea (ROK), however, quasi-Keynesian programs used an activist government that redistributed land to small commercial farmers, expanded public educational opportunities, improved health-care services, and stimulated capital investment. These programs helped achieve higher growth and income equality. After 1992, elected civilian leaders became presidents and replaced rule by the military. Although they adopted some neoliberal features, government provision of social services increased and became more universal.

During the immediate postwar era, Indians lived under a more democratic regime than the South Koreans, but not until the early 1990s did policies begin to establish conditions for higher economic growth. The Ministry of Finance introduced neoliberal programs that deregulated government controls over private enterprises. Freer trade, expanded foreign investment, and enhanced opportunities for private entrepreneurs to gain upward mobility helped increase growth in the early 2000s. Unlike South Korea, however, rapid growth failed to reduce income inequalities (OECD 2013c, 37, 67, 79). Why did these two Asian societies experience different results after 1990?

Land, education, health, and capital investment policies produced high South Korean growth rates. After World War II, US military personnel supported land distribution programs that transferred land from Japanese colonial landlords and their few Korean allies to small-scale commercial farmers, who expanded agricultural productivity. Their savings helped finance urban industrial growth. Government subsidies and tax credits promoted the development of export industries. Influenced by their Confucian heritage, Japanese colonialism, and the American presence, Koreans placed a high priority on education. Educational enrollments in the primary, secondary, and university institutions rose, so by the early twenty-first century, most Koreans had attained literacy. As globalization became widespread, university education seemed the most effective way to gain upward economic mobility, high status, and job security. Korean parents contributed extensive private funds for educating their children. Hence, they gained the modern information-processing skills needed for increasing growth in the innovative, competitive global capitalist market. Policies that lowered infant mortality, raised life expectancy, and prevented diseases produced a healthy labor force, which also contributed to rapid growth rates. The high expenditures for capital formation by government, domestic corporations, and foreign investors raised growth.

Until the mid-2000s, Indians experienced lower growth because they gave lower priority to land redistribution, education, health, and capital investment than did Koreans. State governments redistributed land to only a few farmers. Landlessness became more common as the economy industrialized and local elites allowed corporations to acquire land for industrial development. Compared with South Korean officials, Indian policymakers allocated a lower percentage of the GDP for public education and health services. Indians relied on private funds to finance these benefits. Greater illiteracy, shorter life expectancy, and higher infant mortality rates resulted than in Korea. Conflicts among diverse families, castes, religions, and regions fragmented the Indian policy process. The geographic size, demographic diversity, multiple parties, federal system, and coalition governments impeded officials from taking decisive actions to expand the requirements for growth. Not until 2004 did capital investment reach over 30 percent of the GDP. Spurred by this investment, real GDP growth rates began to exceed 7 percent a year from 2004 to 2011 (IMF 2012a, 82; IMF 2012b, 191, 194; Maddison 2007b, 169, 345).

Higher growth failed to reduce India's income inequalities. Urban residents who secured a university education, learned modern information-processing skills, mastered the latest financial techniques, and became innovative entrepreneurs benefited from the movement toward global integration. Close ties with government officials strengthened their economic rewards. Less politically influential persons who worked as small farmers, agricultural wage workers, urban street vendors, laborers in the large informal sector, and employees for multinational corporations that subcontracted production to smaller subsidiaries received lower wages and fewer fringe benefits, whether public or private. Possessing weak influence, limited funds, and low memberships, unions could not improve the economic well-being of these informal and rural workers. Temporary contracts, low minimal wages, and lax enforcement of labor laws hindered workers' well-being. Income gaps divided individuals living in the poorer northeastern states from residents of the more prosperous southern regions. Women, scheduled castes (Dalits), tribal peoples, Muslims, and rural migrants to the cities suffered the lowest incomes and endured the most unequal treatment by government officials

(Bardhan 2009; Baru 2010; Kazmin 2012; Lamont 2011b; Mukherji 2009; Vakulabharanam 2010).

By contrast, high growth in South Korea led to income equality that resembled the Japanese level. Favorable land distribution, health, and especially education policies not only stimulated growth but also fairly egalitarian incomes relative to other Asian societies. An activist government led the drive for export-oriented industrialization and higher equality than under Japanese colonial rule. Like Indians, however, Koreans faced barriers to increased income equality when the movement toward neoliberal globalization began during the 1990s. A gap emerged between the formal and informal sector. Employees who held full-time, longer-lasting jobs in government institutions and private corporations secured higher salaries and more fringe benefits. Youths, even university graduates, had to take more part-time, temporary jobs in the growing informal sector. Middle-aged employees could no longer rely on lifetime positions. Faced with the constraints of global competition, domestic and multinational corporations reduced labor costs, increased layoffs, and limited collective bargaining rights (An and Bosworth 2013, 94–95, 121–22; Ash 2010; Chang 2010, 222–27; Haggard and Kaufman 2008, 135–39, 249–61; P. Kim 2010; S. Kim 2010; Lim 2010; Park and Mah 2011; Westra 2010).

Although South Korean and Indian leaders governed a representative democracy after 1990, their governments neither promoted inclusive political participation nor allowed extensive civil liberties. In both nations, competitive elections enabled different political parties to share power. The mass media criticized arbitrary government decisions. Nonviolent social groups could express their policy preferences. Despite this pluralist freedom, the armed forces, police, and security agencies still exercised significant influence. Facing threats from the northern communist government, ROK officials instituted national security laws that censored some media, restricted travel to the north, and gave police the authority to detain dissidents suspected of ties with the Democratic People's Republic of Korea. The police arrested journalists and union activists for "interfering with business." More migrant workers moved to South Korea from other Asian countries, including China, Mongolia, Vietnam, the Philippines, Indonesia, Bangladesh, and Pakistan. As a multicultural society began to emerge, immigrants suffered ethnic discrimination, low wages, forced overtime, frequent industrial accidents, arbitrary dismissals, verbal abuse, sexual harassment, and inadequate health treatment.

When Indian political authorities curtailed civil liberties, they justified their repressive policies by claiming the need to maintain security against groups that threatened the establishment. The Indian Official Secrets Act authorized censorship of "defamatory" behavior. Under the National Security Act, police and security forces harassed, detained, kidnapped, tortured, and killed dissidents. The Armed Forces Special Powers Act legalized coercive actions against journalists, human-rights activists, environmentalists, and dissenters. Counterinsurgency forces, antiterrorism squads, security agencies, paramilitary groups, and the army operated with limited civilian supervision. The landless poor, lower castes, tribal peoples, religious minorities (Christians, Muslims), Kashmiris, and women endured abusive treatment. They not only faced discrimination by landlords and private businesses but lacked access to public health care, educational opportunities, inexpensive loans, and legal services. Poverty, prejudice, and unequal legal treatment restricted the political participation of low-income marginals (Agrast et al. 2012, 55, 158–61; Amnesty International 2010, 166–70, 200–201; S. Banerjee 2012; Freedom House 2011, 300–306, 618–22; Mehta 2013; Narrain 2011; Navlakha 2011; Sang-Hun 2012).

POLITICAL DILEMMA: REPRESENTATIVE AND PARTICIPATORY DEMOCRACY

Reconciliation leaders confront the dilemma of choosing the degree of inclusive popular participation needed to operate an effective representative democracy. Policymakers preferring egalitarian programs seek a balance between effective, supportive government institutions and inclusive mass organizations: political parties, labor unions, consumer associations, social movements, and other voluntary associations. Besides rendering government officials accountable to voters, these popular organizations help policymakers formulate and implement egalitarian programs. Yet governing elites who fear mass involvement in the policy process and give priority to electoral competition among highly educated, wealthy activists may refrain from enacting redistributive programs that narrow the income gap. Although the next election enables voters to reelect incumbent leaders, reject them, or abstain from voting, the electoral process gives citizens little direct influence over the policy process.

An ideal democracy blends aspects of both representative and participatory democracy. Inclusive participation reinforces institutionalized competition. Procedural consensus regulates competition among government institutions, political parties, social groups, and protest movements, which claim to represent the public. Constitutions, laws, regulations, and informal customs restrain arbitrary, coercive power by political actors. They agree to reconcile their conflicts through peaceful means. These pluralist arrangements help ensure transparent decisions so that individuals can become enlightened about policy operations. Key resources, especially money and information, give them the opportunity for active participation in political life. Citizens have the freedom not merely to vote, campaign for candidates, and run for elective office. They can also express their views, join associations, deliberate key problems, identify tentative solutions, and influence the policy agenda about income distribution. Widespread, inclusive participation highlights important issues relevant to marginals, expands their group awareness of shared goals, and encourages public policymakers to become more responsive to demands for greater equality. Representative democracy grows stronger (Coppedge, Alvarez, and Maldonado 2008; Dahl 2006; Dahl and Levi 2009; Hildreth 2012; Schneider and Schmitter 2004; Weldon 2011, 1–29).

Three types of representation prescribe different roles for popular participation. Each type imposes constraints on egalitarian policymakers. First, *interpretive* representation places priority on dialogue, discourse, and communication between leaders and the populace. Representatives link the meaning of abstract ideological goals—freedom, equality, justice—to concrete policy proposals. Through rational public debates, they interpret the policy preferences held by their diverse constituents. Interpretive representation requires an informed, well-educated public that understands complex issues, perceives clear policy options, and can evaluate the merits of each alternative. Yet many citizens remain uninformed, disinterested, or overwhelmed by work, family life, and personal relationships. In many countries, the mass media transmit few messages about complex political issues. Political parties and government agencies give a positive "spin" to their performance. Ideological biases shape the perceptions of educated political activists. If weak leftist parties and protest movements lack the communications media to inform their followers, egalitarian themes hardly become important in public discourse.

Second, advocates of *proportional* representation want democratic institutions to enhance the equality of underrepresented groups so that government officeholders include leaders from the diverse population. For example, Scandinavian government agencies and political parties have mandated quotas to ensure that higher proportions of women run for elected office, head cabinet ministries, and become corporate executives. Indian laws expand opportunities for lower-caste individuals to gain a higher education and serve as elected legislators. In heterogeneous societies like Canada, Belgium, and Lebanon, accommodating leaders stress the need to provide representation for different ethnic, religious, and regional groups. Like interpretative representation, proportional representation poses obstacles to securing more egalitarian public policies. Not all members of the same gender, ethnicity, caste, religion, or region share the same policy preferences. Individuals have diverse identities: gender, ethnicity, religion, occupational class. The most important identities vary among specific individuals. Hence, their attitudes toward income equality also diverge within the same group. Ideology, kinship ties, and party affiliations influence their policy stands. The wealthiest, most highly educated members of a categorical group like gender usually become leaders of women's groups. Yet once in office, they may not support egalitarian programs. For them, gender conflict that increases women's representation takes precedence over class struggle that curtails income disparities. The greatest prospects for income redistribution programs occur when governing organizations merge gender with class equality.

Third, *policymaking* representation stresses the accountability of agents to their principals. Interactions among them prevail in different aspects of the policy process. Voters choose elected legislators and presidents, who ideally act as responsive agents. Parliamentarians (principals) depend on political party leaders (agents) to help guide their decisions. Civil servants remain accountable to cabinet ministers. Regulators often account for (justify) their decisions to both legislators and cabinet officials. In the judicial sphere, lawyers serve as agents for their clients. Among capitalist corporations, owners and directors have the obligation to represent shareholders' interests.

Dispersed power impedes clear accountability among reconciliation systems. Government officials decentralize power to regional and local agencies. Particularly in federal systems, courts retain extensive authority to check decisions made by elected leaders. Coalitional parties or factions within a single governing party need to reach a consensus about preferred policy options. Policy implementation takes place by several unelected institutions: civil services, regulatory agencies, quangos (quasi-nongovernmental organizations), auditing offices, ombudsmen, ombudswomen, corporations, unions. Neither elected leaders nor citizens can monitor the complex interactions of all these organizations. The public depends on the corporate media for information about government decisions. Yet in most reconciliation systems, coverage of complex political issues, especially policy implementation, remains scanty. As globalization expands, multinational corporations (MNCs) and international financial institutions make more decisions that affect everyone's lives, especially among developing nations. Dependent on trade and foreign investment, leaders face obstacles to holding the MNCs accountable. Threats of capital flight deter efforts to enact more-egalitarian policies that respond to popular demands.

Legislators remain more accountable to the wealthy and party activists than to poor people and the inactive public. Wealthy activists have greater resources: finances, information, expertise, complex organizations. Their more coherent, consistent policy preferences link local, national, and global issues. Ideological perspectives clearly define standards for evaluating candidates, especially the link between abstract promises and specific policy stands. Access to information gives the wealthy power to monitor legislators' behavior. When seeking policy goals through political parties, interest groups, and lobbies, active participants suffer little repression if they fail to gain their preferences. High benefits go to corporate elites who achieve success.

By contrast, poorer groups face higher costs but lower benefits when they struggle to render legislators accountable in a representative democracy. Although comprising greater numbers than the rich, poor people possess fewer resources, including money, cohesive organizations, strong party ties, and information. They often hold inaccurate information about the wealth of national residents, especially the wealthiest. A conceptual gap emerges between egalitarian ideals and specific proposals for attaining the goal of reducing income disparities. Inactive persons lack the ideological perspective, comprehensive information, and high education needed to monitor legislators' policy performance and vote against them if they reject the individual's preferences. Divergent values, interests, and policy preferences split poorer individuals. Not all of them support egalitarian programs. Activists who protest unequal conditions, strike, or disrupt social order risk repression, such as arrest, unemployment, or loss of income. Because costs outweigh benefits, poor, inactive persons cannot easily hold legislators accountable for their policy performance and make them responsive to popular preferences, especially for enhanced income equality (Cox 2009; Hayward 2009; Norton and Ariely 2011; Pettit 2009; Schmitter 2004; Taylor-Robinson 2010; Teorell 2006; Vieira and Runciman 2008).

Under the following structural conditions, policymakers will most likely enact egalitarian policies in a participatory democracy. Not just the wealthy but various economic groups control the government. Political parties mobilize low-income individuals, rural residents, and informal-sector workers for egalitarian ends. Besides organizing public employees and workers for large-scale private corporations, strong unions secure collective bargaining rights for those employed in smaller, informal enterprises. Corporate managers, union heads, and government officials coordinate negotiations about wages, fringe benefits, and working conditions. The mass media communicate egalitarian political views, not only ones upholding order, hierarchy, and elitism. Television, radio, newspapers, magazines, and the Internet transmit political information and egalitarian stands on crucial issues. Freedom for participation from below gives voluntary associations and protest movements opportunity to stimulate popular activism for egalitarian policies (Lipset and Lakin 2004, 143–68; Mazzuca 2010; Pitkin 2004; Pontusson and Rueda 2010). As best exemplified by Norway, these conditions promoting income equality lead to a more participatory type of representative democracy.

Opposed to equal economic outcomes, neoliberals claim that capitalism and representative democracy strengthen each other. From their perspective, competition, organizational pluralism, voluntary exchanges, and laws protecting private property and stable contracts not only expand capitalism but also facilitate representative democracy. Whereas consumers in a competitive market can freely purchase goods or services, voters in a representative democracy have the freedom to choose their elected leaders, who promise to enact desired policies in exchange for political support. Just as laws of contract restrain economic entrepreneurs, so constitutionalism curtails arbitrary behavior by government officials. Pluralist organizations in both the market and political life decentralize decision making, promote innovation, and expand freedom. Voluntary exchanges on the market resemble voluntary political participation. Seeking to realize their policy preferences through collective political action, citizens join voluntary associations that aim to influence policymakers.

According to egalitarian activists, the logical premises of neoliberalism clash with actual empirical conditions. Drawing parallels between the economic and political market, neoliberals downplay the importance of citizenship. They assume that candidates function as sellers who treat voters as consumers. In practice, however, the electoral market enables voters the opportunity to accept or reject candidates, not the right to purchase a specific policy. When buying a television set, consumers obtain information about its price, quality, and expected performance from friends, dealers, magazines, and the Internet. By contrast, electoral choices supply voters with less information about past policy performance or expected results of policy promises made during a campaign.

In most capitalist economies, government officials, political party leaders, and private corporate executives exert the greatest influence over policy performance. Executive officials, judges, and government bureaucrats, not legislators, make crucial decisions about income inequality. When Tressell wrote his novel, small family businesses employed more workers than today. With the growth of mergers, acquisitions, conglomerates, and concentrated industries, corporations possess the money, organizational expertise, and control over advertising to affect political party actions, candidates' policy promises, and government officials' decisions. Personal leaders in small groups and informal networks dominate both government and private corporate hierarchies. Making secret decisions, political patrons bring high benefits to powerful corporate clients.

By privatizing, deregulating, and limiting public provision of social services, government authorities who favor neoliberalism deter widespread voluntary participation. Associations representing low-income workers, unemployed persons, uneducated youths, women, immigrants, and indigenous peoples retain limited opportunity to shape the implementation of laws that affect income distribution. Few worker-owned cooperatives teach the interpersonal skills needed for political engagement. When individualist values reinforce isolation and ethnic, religious, and gender cleavages fragment cross-class coalitions, policymakers can enact neoliberal programs without countervailing pressures from inclusive participation that supports egalitarian policies (Andrain and Smith 2006, 57–61; Brown 2011; Chong and Gradstein 2007; Crouch 2011; Dahl 2006, 63–67; Harvey 2010, 119–39, 215–60; Malleson 2013; Manzetti 2009, 247–65; Mirowski 2013, 50–88; Przeworski 2010, 66–98; Savoie 2010, 192–241; Streeck 2011; Wolff 2012, 1–16, 139–79; S. Wolin 2008, 1–68, 259–92).

Comparisons of Chile with Uruguay clarify the barriers to transforming economic conditions under representative democracy. An urbanized, well-educated population lives in both South American nations. Contemporary government leaders relied on a private market economy with many state-owned enterprises (SOEs). Public-private partnerships shared decision-making authority. Adopting key neoliberal features, left-wing and rightist governments supported free trade, greater foreign investment, and privatization of some social services and SOEs. Prudent fiscal policies recently secured fairly balanced budgets. Throughout the twentieth century, Chileans and Uruguayans usually lived under a representative democracy. Political freedom promoted civil liberties, independent courts, and competitive elections. Different political parties alternated in government office. Committed to a peaceful reconciliation strategy of resolving conflicts, leaders formed governing coalitions with other parties, particularly in Chile. Negotiators' pragmatic attitudes triumphed over dogmatic ideologies.

Despite this democratic history, during the early 1970s military coups overthrew the reconciliation systems. From late 1973 to early 1990, the armed forces ruled Chile. The dictatorship suppressed political parties, labor unions, and leftist organizations. Among voluntary associations, the Roman Catholic Church retained the greatest freedom to protest against human-rights violations. Arrests, imprisonment, torture, and "disappearances" paralyzed opponents. Besides suppressing political freedom, the Pinochet regime pursued neoliberal economic policies that worsened Chile's income inequality. The Uruguayan military dictators pursued similar tactics except that arrested citizens endured fewer deaths but higher imprisonment rates per one thousand persons than did Chileans. Lasting from 1973 through 1984, the armed forces imposed brutal torture. Security agencies monitored "thought crimes." In the secular society, Roman Catholic bishops had limited independence to campaign against state repression that victimized leftist parties, unions, student groups, and newspapers.

In both countries, divisions within the military elite, domestic economic crises, and international pressures eventually convinced the armed forces to replace their bureaucratic-authoritarian regime with a reconciliation system governed by elected civilian leaders. During late 1984, Uruguayans chose competitive political parties for elective government offices. A coalition of political parties led by Christian Democrats and Socialists won the 1989 elections in Chile. Even though the Chilean military retained some perquisites, the civilian leaders gradually reduced the armed forces' power, limited their economic privileges, and prosecuted some top military officers, police, and security agents for violating human rights. Expanding growth and curtailing inflation took main priority. Economic policies also concentrated on reducing unemployment, poverty, and social risks, particularly by the elderly, children, women, and very poor individuals (Andrain 1994, 148–53; 2011, 151–203; Drake 2009, 1–51, 201–43; Freedom House 2011, 142–45, 721–24; M. Loveman 1998; Solimano 2012, 50–88). Whereas Chilean Socialists emphasized the primacy of representative over participatory democracy, Uruguayan policymakers secured a blend of the two types. Opportunities for public participation helped establish greater income equality than in Chile.

When two Socialist Party presidents—Ricardo Lagos and Michelle Bachelet—led the Chilean Concertación government (2001–2010), institutional constraints hindered their attempts to implement egalitarian policies. Technocrats preferred neoliberal programs for development. Particularly for those in the Finance Ministry and Central Bank of Chile, increasing growth, price stability, and the export trade took precedence over reducing unemployment and expanding equal outcomes. Multinational corporations dominated the capital-intensive copper industry, which gained high profits but paid low wages to the miners. Workers in other export industries such as forest products, wine, and salmon also earned low wages. Allied with influential right-wing political parties, especially the Independent Democratic Union, private business conglomerates controlled mining, pharmaceutical industries, health corporations, banks, insurance firms, private pension funds, and the media. Prominent families—Luksic, Paulmann, Matte, Piñera—dominated these conglomerates, which endured few government regulations. They wielded extensive power over public policymakers, who granted the oligopolies favorable subsidies, licenses, and tax credits.

The Socialist Party lacked the resources and cohesion possessed by Chile's capitalist elites. It relied on corporate donations to finance electoral campaigns. No strong alliance merged Socialist leaders with organized groups, especially trade unions. Legal restrictions impeded their freedom to organize public-sector workers; one-half had temporary contracts. Private unions could collectively bargain with employers only in each firm, not at the industry level. Socialist officials disagreed over the extent to which an activist government should provide comprehensive, generous public services. Within the Concertación administration, Socialists needed to gain cooperation from Christian Democratic and Party for Democracy leaders, who showed less enthusiasm for income redistribution measures than did Lagos or Bachelet. They had to compromise not only with other parties in the Concertación but with the rightist parties that held extensive influence in the two-house legislature, particularly the Senate.

The Socialist presidency continued many promarket, neoliberal policies introduced under the Pinochet regime and accepted by Christian Democratic presidents who headed the coalition governments from 1990 to 2000. The government subsidized private grammar and secondary schools. Public municipal schools lacked funds and skilled teachers needed to raise student performance. Charging high fees, private pension organizations depended on the volatile stock market for sufficient funds to finance workers' retirement. Regressive tax policies imposed high value-added taxes but low corporate and personal income taxes. Many rich people avoided tax payments. Generous tax credits went to foreign investors.

Some policies enacted by the Lagos and Bachelet administrations did reduce the wide income gap. Increased expenditures for public health services and pensions as well as a higher minimum wage brought gains to the poor. Programs for health care and pensions became more public and inclusive. Expanded preschool education helped women who worked for pay. As a partial result of these policies, the gini declined from .55 to .52 between 2003 and 2009. Women, informal-sector workers, and the self-employed achieved slightly greater income. Yet men, formal-sector employees, those working for large corporations, and investors, financiers, managers, and technocrats still secured the highest economic rewards (Borzutsky 2010; ECLAC 2011a, 75; Ewing and Kay 2011; Fairfield 2010; Ffrench-Davis 2010, 174–208, 268–77; Huber, Pribble, and Stephens 2010; Huber and Stephens 2012, 170–83, 194–206, 253–57; Mainwaring and Scully 2010; Paredes and Pinto 2009; Pérez Caldentey 2012; Pribble 2011; Pribble and Huber 2011; Roberts 2011; Sehnbruch 2010; Solimano 2012, 74–155; Teichman 2012, 151–58, 185; Weeks and Borzutsky 2012).

Facing opposition from the Chilean corporate elite, military officers, and right-wing political party leaders, the Socialist Party presidents gave greater importance to representative than to participatory democracy. The populist mobilization during the brief Allende Socialist presidency deterred the Lagos and Bachelet governments from encouraging widespread popular participation that demanded fundamental transformations in Chile's economy. Instead, the primary objective focused on preserving democracy, enacting constitutional reforms, winning elections, and avoiding conflicts with the conservative opposition. Procedural consensus involved making compromises that mollified business elites. Negotiations among powerful social networks occurred in hierarchical settings.

Opposed to hierarchical rule, groups lacking close ties with dominant elites staged popular protests. Unions struck for increased wages. University students protested higher tuition fees. The Mapuches organized sit-ins, hunger strikes, and land seizures. Demanding collective rights, they rejected privatization by both multinational and domestic corporations. Their protests denounced timber industries and hydroelectric power corporations that acquired indigenous ancestral lands for exploitation. Although the Bachelet administration granted some land to the Mapuches, it used internal security laws inherited from the Pinochet regime to repress protests. Chilean policymakers did not encourage inclusive mass popular participation by unions, ecologists, and indigenous poor peoples (Carruthers and Rodriguez 2009; Funk 2012; Vergara 2009).

The elitist trend continued after Sebastián Piñera won the January 2010 presidential election by 52 percent of the popular vote. The billionaire gained a doctorate at Harvard University, taught economics to Chileans, established a prosperous credit-card business, and managed the Bank of Taka. Sharing control over mining, energy, and retail corporations, Piñera became wealthy under the neoliberal policies enacted by the Pinochet administration. When his brother José Piñera served as labor minister during bureaucratic-authoritarian rule, he formulated policies that privatized pensions, curtailed union rights, and repressed popular resistance to these policies. Even if President Piñera hardly sought to restore past authoritarian practices, his right-wing Coalition for Change, unlike the socialist government, showed a stronger commitment to hierarchical neoliberal principles. Wealthy business executives dominated the cabinet. Privatizing social services, granting tax credits for foreign private investment, and instituting a more flexible labor market took precedence over expanding political participation. Student protests against high university fees, low public financing, and increased debts for students expressed their discontent with neoliberal policies that had privatized and decentralized education. Calling on the national Ministry of Education to restructure the system, protesters demanded more-equal access to educational facilities. Not only students but teachers, union members, left-wing party activists, and government employees demonstrated for greater workers' rights, higher pensions, and more spending on public health care and education. Even though President Piñera admitted that Chile faced "excessive" and "immoral" inequalities, his government tried to restrict protesters' political participation. Police officers attacked protesters with tear gas and water cannons laced with chemicals. Police on horseback trampled demonstrators (Barrionuevo 2011; Bonnefoy 2012; Pilger 2010; Piñera 2011).

By contrast, representative democracy in Uruguay promoted greater popular participation than in Chile. Structural conditions strengthened opportunities for egalitarians to implement their policy preferences. During the early twentieth century, Uruguay enacted such generous social-service programs that the nation became known as the "Switzerland of Latin America." Political parties, especially the Colorados, supported policies that produced a higher degree of income equality and greater civil liberties than in most other Latin American societies except Costa Rica. After the twelve-year period (1973–1984) of military domination, political repression, and economic deprivation, three major parties competed for power: the Colorado, Nacional (Blanco), and Frente Amplio (Popular Front—the most leftist of the three).

In the 2004 and 2009 elections, the Frente Amplio (FA) gained control of the presidency and the legislature. The FA comprised a coalition of several different factions, including socialists, communists, left-wing Catholics, ecologists, and former urban guerrillas (Tupamaros) who had abandoned violence for a peaceful way to power. The first FA president, Tabaré Vásquez, a physician who formerly served as Montevideo mayor, instituted several egalitarian policies. His successor, José Mujica, an ex-Tupamaros activist, won the 2009 election for president and continued the programs for participatory democracy and income redistribution for the poor. He also retained such neoliberal programs as foreign direct investment, competitive foreign trade, and trade surpluses. Despite the numerous ideological factions within the Frente Amplio, most leaders took a pragmatic position toward public policies. They reconciled conflicts, negotiated compromises, and secured interpersonal trust. Unlike Chilean Socialists, FA leaders benefited from less powerful business groups, a stronger alliance with labor unions, weaker opposition parties, and a more activist policy commitment by the presidency and legislature. Hence, the Frente Amplio could mobilize support for its egalitarian programs.

The FA government provided more public, universal, generous benefits for education, health care, family assistance, and pensions than did Chilean Socialists. During 2006–2007, public expenditures for social services as a share of the GDP totaled 21 percent in Uruguay but 12 percent in Chile (ECLAC 2011a, 221). Unemployment insurance, maternity benefits, and disability/sickness allowances as well as spending on education and health care all produced greater equality. Family allowances particularly helped Uruguayan women and children. Progressive tax policies lowered the value-added tax (VAT) but raised taxes on income and profits as a share of total taxation. Unions actively supported the Frente Amplio. As in Norway, wage councils composed of union heads, business leaders, and government officials negotiated wage settlements, labor conditions, and safety issues. Egalitarian results ensued. From 2005 to 2010, the minimum wage rose. Unemployment rates fell. The gini declined to .42—the lowest income inequality in all Latin America except Venezuela.

Despite more equality, real GDP growth rates between 2005 and 2011 increased by 5.9 percent a year in Uruguay, compared with 4.5 percent in Chile. High growth rates resulted from exports of beef, lamb, dairy products, soya, timber, cellulose, and software. Public revenues funded inexpensive laptops for all schoolchildren. Government agencies also financed the development of computer firms. Video games became an important technically advanced export (Bucheli et al. 2013; ECLAC 2011a, 42, 76, 221–26; Huber and Stephens 2012, 183–86, 199–205; IMF 2012b, 195; Lanzaro 2011;

OECD/ECLAC/CIAT 2012, 69, 72; Olesker 2009b; Pribble 2013, 70–132, 172–83).

By merging support for representative democracy with inclusive popular participation, Uruguay's leftist leaders helped narrow income disparities. Rather than fearing participatory democracy, FA activists relied on group mobilization to enhance their egalitarian programs. Compared with the Chilean power structure, Uruguayan organizations provided greater scope for the FA and party members to influence government decisions. Given the urbanized, highly educated population, individuals had access to political information, social networks, and political organizations that encouraged participation. Unions played a more influential role than in Chile. Whereas during 2008 only 16 percent of Chilean wage earners belonged to a union and collective bargaining covered 11 percent, in Uruguay union density reached 22 percent. Collective bargaining included nearly 90 percent of salaried employees (Reinecke and Valenzuela 2011, 195). Peaceful negotiations observed democratic rules. Citizens influenced public policies through diverse social movements that included students, feminists, environmentalists, and human-rights activists.

FA leaders responded to popular demands for social improvements and maintained open access to the policy process. Decentralization policies gave power to municipal government agencies and neighborhood councils in Montevideo. Acting as political entrepreneurs, neighborhood activists bargained with city officials for concrete benefits. Local citizens established centers for youths, seniors, women, children, and the disabled. Community-managed centers provided health care. Cultural centers offered artistic productions. Job-creation programs lowered unemployment. Reliant on personal networks, participants in several districts improved public lighting, paved streets, trash collection, sewage facilities, and public transportation.

Not only poor residents but upper- and middle-income groups benefited from enhanced political involvement. Frequent referenda and popular initiatives gave the public an opportunity to decide key policies except those about taxes. The Frentistas strongly supported referenda that rejected privatization of state-owned enterprises and reduction of public-pension increases. Reacting against some neoliberal privatization measures of previous administrations, FA voters preferred that public institutions own such enterprises as water works, electricity, railroads, telecommunications, and oil refinement.

Favorable economic performance led to high satisfaction with democratic institutions. According to national sample surveys conducted throughout Latin America during 2007–2008, only one-fifth of Uruguayans, compared with nearly half the Chileans, perceived their country's income distribution as very unjust. Perceptions of justice coincided with democratic satisfaction. Over 70 percent of Uruguay's residents expressed satisfaction with the operation of democratic institutions and regarded democracy as more preferable than any other type of government. A lower proportion of Chileans voiced such positive attitudes toward satisfaction with democracy and preference for democracy as a superior governmental form (Altman 2011, 140–202; Alvarez Rivadulla 2012; Canel 2010; Daude and Melguizo 2012, 544; ECLAC 2009, 79; Goldfrank 2011, 121–64; Madrid, Hunter, and Weyland 2010; McDonald and Weinstein 2011; Mondak et al. 2011; P. Norris 2011, 90–97; OECD 2010a, 150; Olesker 2009a; Reygadas and Filgueira 2010; Romero 2013d; Webber 2013).

CONCLUSION

Income distribution has close connections to political democracy and capitalism as well as to human development. Measured by life expectancy at birth, years of education, and gross national income per person, the highest human development during 2010 occurred in nations with the most democratic governments that regulated capitalist operations. Among the twenty countries topping the human development index (HDI), most showed fairly egalitarian incomes, especially in northwestern Europe. Living in wealthy societies, their citizens possessed the high formal education and good health that encouraged active political involvement. Scandinavians gained the highest rankings on statistical indicators measuring children's well-being, women's rights, personal freedom, social tolerance, interpersonal trust, confidence in national institutions, and opportunities for upward economic mobility. Besides these social conditions, public policies secured low homicide rates in Scandinavia (Adamson 2012, 2–13; Corak 2013; Legatum Institute 2010; OECD 2008, 205; OECD 2011b; OECD 2011g, 90–93; Save the Children 2011; Stiglitz 2012, 18; UNDP 2010; UNODC 2011, 111; Wilkinson and Pickett 2009, 129–209).

According to the 2012 World Justice Project Rule of Law index, nations with the greatest income equality also ranked highest on commitment to civil liberties, open government, and civil justice. The most egalitarian societies—Norway, Sweden, Denmark, Finland—secured the highest scores on procedural justice. China, Russia, India, and Turkey, which showed the weakest commitment to democratic legal freedoms, faced the widest income gap. Among Latin American countries, Uruguayan policymakers most effectively combined income equality with procedural justice (Agrast et al. 2012, 159–61, 180–81).

In Western Europe, Norwegian officials selected the policy options that best reconciled the cultural, economic, and political dilemmas of democracy. Cultural values blended procedural with distributive justice. Voters elected leaders who implemented public policies supplying generous, comprehensive, and universal social services, thereby producing egalitarian outcomes.

Economic decisions attained both growth and equality. Widespread political participation strengthened representative democracy. Resources derived from widespread prosperity, health, and education provided individuals with opportunities to participate in collective political action. Popular attitudinal support for civil liberties and for inclusive participation in political life, local communities, and the workplace motivated people to strengthen democratic institutions. Interpersonal trust among citizens encouraged them to organize behind efforts to make government actions more accountable and responsive. Opposed to hierarchical authority, Norwegians upheld legal restraints on arbitrary power. A relatively efficient, honest bureaucracy treated residents in an impartial way, which strengthened greater confidence in government institutions, encouraged more-peaceful protests, and promoted greater social equality than experienced by most other countries (Clausen, Kraay, and Nyiri 2011; Rothstein 2011, 82–83, 121–63, 207–25; Sejersted 2011).

Unlike Northern Europe, developing nations achieved a weaker balance among democracy, capitalism, and economic equality. Chinese and Russian capitalism developed without a firm democratic foundation. After the collapse of state socialism, the income gap widened. During the 1970s and 1980s, Latin American bureaucratic-authoritarian regimes used extensive coercion to enforce capitalist policies that raised income differences. Yet those societies like Uruguay, Chile, and Argentina that gained fairly high rankings on human development democratized after the military relinquished its political power. Competitive elections and civil liberties emerged. Infant mortality declined. Attendance rose at primary schools. Particularly in Uruguay, expanded popular participation encouraged the effective operation of representative government. Uruguayans upheld attitudes that supported gender equality, personal tolerance, political freedom, and inclusive participation. Frente Amplio legislators enacted laws that legalized the sale of marijuana. Women seeking a first-trimester abortion and couples desiring to marry a same-sex partner gained the legal freedom to fulfill these rights. Although India operated a capitalist economy, powerful regional, religious, caste, kinship, and gender cleavages curtailed participatory democracy, peaceful reconciliation of conflicts, and egalitarian policies. India's low HDI hindered government attempts to narrow the income gap (Inglehart and Welzel 2009; Kääriäinen and Lehtonen 2006; Romero 2013c; Schneider and Soskice 2009; Smith and Ziegler 2007; UNDP 2010, 58–99, 142–55; Welzel and Inglehart 2005, 2010).

Whatever a nation's score on human development, the same groups throughout the world endured the greatest suffering from income inequalities. These groups included children, women, uneducated individuals, indigenous peoples, migrant laborers, and workers in the informal economy. Public policies only marginally improved their wages, health status, housing conditions, life satisfaction, and support from social networks. Even in wealthy industrialized nations, low-income persons faced difficulties gaining access to quality health care, attending a university, earning an adequate income, and securing a stable job (OECD 2011b, 34–35). In less-developed societies, access to both private and public benefits remained scanty. Marginals secured few benefits from global economic integration. Poor people had limited influence over the public-policy agenda. Wealthy, highly educated, middle-aged elites dominated government policymaking. Artisans, merchants, and small-scale family businesses could not effectively compete with large domestic enterprises or multinational corporations. For many low-income groups, the ideals of democracy and capitalism conflicted with the realities of income inequality. Viewing the current situation as unjust, they held opinions that favored more egalitarian public policies.

Chapter Seven

Public Opinion, Social Science, and Income Distribution Policies

What causes poverty? First presented in 1905, *Major Barbara* by George Bernard Shaw gives three different answers: rational self-interest, religious values, and capitalist structures that mobilize opposition to egalitarian policies. The play's major characters illustrate these explanations. Andrew Undershaft, an arms manufacturer, defends the capitalist virtues of efficiency, energy, innovation, self-control, personal responsibility, pragmatism, and the competitive pursuit of profits. Opposed to trade unions and socialism, he views money as the rational means to food, clothing, children's care, and the happy life (Shaw 2008, 103). Rather than viewing poverty as a blessing, Undershaft sees it as a vice that causes malnutrition, ill health, bad housing, and crime (Shaw 2008, 103, 161–62).

Undershaft's daughter Barbara takes an opposite position from her father, especially in the first two acts. A member of the Salvation Army, she perceives Christian values, not economic self-interest, as the only way to attain eventual relief from poverty. Poor individuals must abandon alcohol, work hard, and live by spiritual values: compassion, kindness, forgiveness, empathy, generosity, peace, hope, faith. Through spiritual consciousness and behavior, Major Barbara seeks to uplift the person to God.

Adolphus Cusins, the fiancé of Major Barbara, aims to transform social structures so that income inequalities will no longer produce misery. He wants democratic institutions that will enable the "common people" to overcome the political, economic, and cultural oligarchies that wield power for their special interests, not for the general good. Committed to ending labor exploitation, capital punishment, unjust wars, and British imperialism, he recognizes that power—the necessary ingredient for structural transformation—can produce not only good outcomes but evil results. As a low-income teacher of Greek literature, he needs money to support his future wife, Barbara. Despite his ambivalence toward power, Cusins agrees to work for Undershaft's enterprise that manufactures weapons (Shaw 2008, 154–75).

The play *Major Barbara* recognized the link between the need for money and power as a means to reduce the income gap. For Shaw, neither religious rhetoric nor personal righteousness would achieve greater income equality. Instead, activists should mobilize public support for egalitarian policies such as a minimum wage and a universal lifetime pension. He believed that programs like these would provide everyone a reasonable income (Shaw 2008, 10–25). Pledged to organize support for socialist policies, Shaw helped establish in 1886 the Fabian Society, which conducted social science research. His friends Beatrice and Sidney Webb, influential Fabian Society founders, assumed that social structures, not an individual's defective character, caused poverty. In 1900 Shaw, the Webbs, and other left-wingers organized the Labour Representation Committee, which later became the Labour Party.

Another of Shaw's plays, *Pygmalion*, highlights the causal attributions that lead the public to prefer programs that help the "deserving poor." A poor flower girl, Eliza Doolittle, becomes a fair lady under the tutelage of Professor Henry Higgins. She has a father calling himself one of the "undeserving poor." Rejecting "middle class morality," he claims to need as much money as deserving folk have. Ironically, by the end of the play, this garbage collector becomes wealthy by exchanging witticisms with upper-class elites. Although denounced as déclassé by the middle class and scarcely admired by public opinion, the father overcomes deprivation by using his interpersonal skills (Shaw 2008, 227–28, 299–300). Today perceptions of deservedness still affect cross-national opinions about policies toward social-service expenditures. Especially when individuals regard stigmatized groups as "lazy freeloaders," approval for government assistance declines (Petersen 2012).

PUBLIC OPINION TOWARD INCOME DISTRIBUTION POLICIES

The resource mobilization perspective offers the most plausible explanation for the impact of public opinion on social-service policies. Egalitarian activists achieved the greatest success when they devised flexible, pragmatic tactics. Social forums that generated cooperation among diverse groups helped communicate inspirational messages over the media. Demands for increased job opportunities, lower personal debt, and stricter regulation of financial institutions represented popular issues. Allies, especially groups with extensive resources, mobilized backing for the cause.

Key resources for organizing popular support behind egalitarian policies included communication of cultural values and personal interests. Cultural values shaped causal attributions about fairness. If individuals perceived income inequality as extensive, unjust, and harmful to the "deserving poor," stronger approval emerged for generous, comprehensive, universal social services. Sample surveys asked respondents to compare actual and fair incomes of different occupations, like an unskilled factory worker and chief executive officer of a large corporation. In nearly all countries, most people wanted to reduce income gained by the rich. Greater disagreement emerged about incomes that the poor should have. Compared with Norwegians, who agreed about ideal minimum incomes, Americans voiced more polarized attitudes. Whereas left-wing Democratic activists supported egalitarian government policies, wealthy right-wing ideologues viewed income differences as empirically limited and ethically fair. Hence, they opposed government actions that lessened economic inequalities (Abramowitz 2010; Bartels 2008, 252–303; Blendon and Benson 2011; Gilens 2012, 162–92; Mann and Ornstein 2012, 43–58, 102–3; Mettler 2011; Newport 2011; Osberg and Smeeding 2006; Page and Jacobs 2009a, 95–109; Pew Research Center 2012; Whyte 2010a; 2010b, 43–67, 163–79).

In the United States and other nations, ideological identifications shaped attitudes toward economic equality. Right-wing ideologues who accepted market-based risks and assumed that poverty stemmed from individual defects rejected egalitarian programs as unfair. For them, such policies deterred honesty, hard work, personal initiative, responsibility, and opportunity to earn more money. Left-wing identifiers blamed poverty on social and political conditions beyond personal control: corporate injustice, labor exploitation, discrimination, unequal opportunities, inadequate educational facilities, failure of government institutions to provide economic security. From this perspective, public policies could change structural conditions and thereby achieve a fairer society (Fridberg 2012, 146–49; Hjerm and Schnabel 2012, 185–86; Jost and Kay 2010).

Changes, however, did not occur unless leaders mobilized resources behind an egalitarian message that envisioned an ideal society based on social solidarity. As a pilot fighting with the Allies against Nazi Germany during World War II, the French author Antoine de Saint-Exupéry (1986, 205) viewed all persons as "inhabitants of the same planet, passengers on the same ship." Rather than isolated from one another on different planets, individuals share a common fate. According to Saint-Exupéry, before political action begins, a vision should guide the work. Just as love of the sea motivates shipbuilders, so an idealistic cause must mobilize supporters. Comradeship unites the heterogeneous passengers behind the same general ideals, such as pursuit of the common good (Saint-Exupéry 1940, 45–46, 287–95; 1948, 205–7; 1986, 116–17). After 1980 with the growth of neoliberal priorities that stressed competitive individualism, the income gap widened. Capitalist economies alternated between boom and bust. As James K. Galbraith (2012, 148) commented: "A rising tide may lift all boats, but recent business cycles have been more like waves, whereby certain sectors and areas ride the peaks before crashing to the shore."

Mobilizing support for egalitarian attitudes required not only an idealistic vision but effective organizations, such as strong leftist parties, social movements, unions, and supportive media. These organizations highlighted the link between personal interests and public policies. People's discontent with their current living standards raised support for programs that reduced income differences. Persons who presently experienced or expected future risks—unemployment, economic insecurity, sickness, income loss—preferred policies benefiting those who needed jobs, pensions, child care, and health care. When an individual perceived that vulnerable groups faced inadequate income and deserved government assistance, that person viewed such programs as desirable (Adams, Green, and Milazzo 2012, 515; Blekesaune 2013; Blofield and Luna 2011; Blomberg et al. 2012; Kulin and Svallfors 2013; Rehm, Hacker, and Schlesinger 2012; Svallfors, Kulin, and Schnabel 2012).

The quest for greater income equality arose when mobilizing organizations rejected hierarchy, affirmed political efficacy, and blended individual independence with collective solidarity. They opposed deference to private corporations, ecclesiastical hierarchies, and government bureaucracies benefiting wealthy elites. Egalitarians transmitted media messages that affirmed political efficacy, not fatalistic resignation to poverty. To overcome poverty, they encouraged a feeling that all people, whatever their income, gender, religion, ethnicity, and occupational status, shared common values. Instead of blaming migrant laborers for low wages, activists affirmed an inclusive nationalism that upheld compassion, empathy, tolerance, diversity, and universal standards. For them and Keynes, investments that promote the public good became more important than speculation securing high private profits for the rich (Bowles and Polanía-Reyes 2012; Keynes 1972, 224–29, 292–94; Kulin and Svallfors 2013; Lepianka, Gelissen, and van Oorschot 2010; Sachweh 2012; S. Schwartz 2012; Staerklé, Likki, and Scheidegger 2012; Whyte and Han 2008; Zaidi 2009).

Recent cross-national sample surveys indicate that public attitudes more closely resembled the preferences of Keynes than proposals favored by neoliberals. Few respondents viewed capitalism as a highly efficient system that needed no regulation. Instead, most individuals favored increasing government activism that would narrow income differences and regulate private corporations. These policy preferences took priority over austerity programs, such as regressive taxes and lower social service spending on pensions, education, health care, and subsidized food prices (Arnold and Samuels 2011; BBC 2009, 2010; Blofield and Luna 2011; Chaffin 2013; ECLAC 2009, 19–22; Jaeger 2009; Loveless and Whitefield 2011; Morgan and Kelly 2010; Svallfors 2012b, 14; Whyte 2010b, 68–91).

Egalitarian leaders relied on the media to communicate their policy positions. Keynes viewed the media as a "mysterious, oracular force" that often decided the general policy agenda, if not specific technical details. Recommending that the media educate the public, he nevertheless acknowledged its deficiencies. For him, rather than highlight a leader's "sensational statement or rash words," the media should supply the context, communicate accurate information, and present reasonable arguments about desirable, feasible policy options (Keynes 1980a, 204, 447–48; 1981a, 474–75; 1982a, 360). Today television, radio, newspapers, the Internet, tablets, and mobile phones transmit information that affirms desirable values and describes conditions, no matter how accurate the report. Through political discourse, activists try to mobilize support for an egalitarian agenda. If they expect to influence public opinion, they must communicate information about preferred policies that supporters find accessible, understandable, and important to their personal and national experiences. Seeking to strengthen agreement with desired policies, mobilizers focus on information that reinforces a person's preferred issue stance. Demonstrations, marches, rallies, factory occupations, sit-ins, strikes, and boycotts exemplify mobilizing activities that attract the most attention. Intended to rouse potential followers from their political apathy, these activities may stimulate countermobilization efforts that weaken commitment to the egalitarian cause.

Social networks play a key role in mobilizing support for attitudes on income distribution. At the local level, activists depend on family members, friends, neighbors, and coworkers who share similar policy preferences about enhanced or curtailed economic equality. At the national and global level, financiers, multinational corporate executives, neoliberal economists, and government ministers participate in such organizations as the World Economic Forum (WEF). At its annual meetings, WEF social networks pressure policymakers to implement programs for expanding growth, lowering inflation, and curbing government deficits. To these neoliberal elites, reducing unequal incomes hardly represents a top priority. Faced with limited resources, international unions lack the powerful worldwide networks that effectively campaign for less inequality.

Even though political leaders seek public support for their policy preferences, neither the general public nor poor people have exerted decisive power over income distribution policies. During the early twenty-first century, leaders in both society and government made the crucial decisions about economic equality. Programs to expand equal opportunities and increase social-service benefits for education, health care, and retirement pensions attracted greater leadership support than did policies for distributing equal income shares. Political activists, party leaders, and especially high-ranking government officials—civil servants, presidents, prime ministers—assumed major responsibility for making public policy. Compared with the public, these elites had clearer policy stands, more intense ideological commitments, and greater information about complex issues such as ways that monetary programs affected income distribution. When voters chose their elected leadership, they could not determine actual policies. Leaders usually remained influenced by powerful groups in society, especially private corporations and media conglomerates. Combining power with intensity, these groups largely controlled the policy agenda. If they intensified their opposition to egalitarian programs, policymakers hesitated to implement such policies unless rival groups like left-wing political parties, unions, voluntary associations, and social movements mobilized support for them (Ellis 2013).

Legislators underestimated the appeal of egalitarian policies even in the United States, where universal social-service programs drew less support than in most other countries. Sample surveyors found widespread popularity for progressive taxes and generous government spending on social benefits. Particularly if these policies increased equal opportunities for education and jobs, secured a fairer society, and went to individuals regarded as most deserving, Americans' support rose. Over 60 percent favored measures that assisted the poor and placed higher taxes on the rich, including corporate income. More than two-thirds preferred a higher minimum wage, retraining for unemployed workers, early childhood education, good public schools for children, financial aid for college education, child-care assistance, expansion of health-care coverage for uninsured children, and measures giving everyone access to health care. Only around one-quarter of respondents wanted to reduce expenditures for these programs or reduce taxes on the rich. Whereas nearly 50 percent of Americans in 2008 believed that government had the responsibility to reduce income disparities between rich and poor, merely 13 percent of wealthy respondents shared this policy preference (Ellis and Stimson 2012, 27, 147–56; Jones et al. 2012, 39–43; McCall 2013, 109–36, 186–232; Page, Bartels, and Seawright 2013; Page and Jacobs 2009a, 49–93; Pew Research Center 2013). Dominated by wealthy contributors who played an active political role, government officials implemented fiscal decisions that increased austerity. In 2010 over thirty state governments, mainly those led by wealthy right-wing Republicans, decreased expenditures for public health, children's health benefits, public education, and services for the elderly and disabled (Austin 2010). According to Katherine S. Newman and Elisabeth S. Jacobs (2010, 116): "Over the last three decades, the American political economy has become both vastly richer and vastly more unequal. . . . Rising tides lifted the yachts, but did very little for the rowboats."

Although popular attitudes all over the world resisted neoliberal austerity programs, the division of power among many dispersed organizations hindered strategies for making government policies more responsive to public opinion. Federal systems with influential courts shared power among central, regional, and local institutions. When several different parties governed a parliamentary system, voters could not hold a single party responsible for policy performance. Opposing parties often controlled the executive and legislature in countries where voters elected a president. With the neoliberal stress on decentralization, deregulation, and privatization, central government power declined. Private corporations received generous government contracts. Regulatory agencies secretly made decisions without approval by elected political leaders. Quasi-nongovernmental organizations escaped accountability. Under these fragmented conditions, corporate directors, lawyers, and financiers with cohesive policy positions wielded greater influence over income distribution programs than did the general public (Soroka and Wlezien 2010a, 2010b).

THE IMPACT OF POLICIES ON INCOME EQUALITY

Fiscal and monetary policies influenced national income equality. Even though particular historical conditions diverged among different societies, higher government expenditures for inclusive public education, health care, child care, parental leave, elder care, and housing usually secured greater equality. Even progressive taxes yielded a less important effect than did generous, comprehensive, inclusive expenditures. Yet taxes on personal income, corporate profits, capital gains, dividends, and financial transactions raised revenues that helped finance social-service benefits. Rather than support a countercyclical approach when growth rates declined and unemployment rose, government officials who enacted austerity policies faced the unequal consequences analyzed by Keynes during the 1930s depression. Not only fiscal programs but monetary decisions affected income distribution. Greater equality emerged when consumers and small businesses gained access to low interest rates. Strict government regulation of financial institutions as well as government provision of social services proved more effective in reducing economic inequalities than did deregulation and privatization welcomed by neoliberals. When banks won more independence from elected government leaders after 1980, deregulation policies exacerbated the financial crisis that erupted during 2008.

Labor-market policies shaped both wages and income after expenditures and taxes. The power that private corporations exercised over labor unions affected wage settlements, pensions, health-care services, and rights to participate in collective bargaining. More equal results occurred when government officials supported strong, centralized unions with nationwide collective bargaining rights. Wage increases matched gains in overall productivity. When a high minimum wage and generous unemployment compensation exceeded inflation rates, poorer workers benefited. Training in advanced technical skills, especially information processing, created job opportunities in a global capitalist economy marked by intensified competition. Trade policies that increased exports based on labor-intensive manufacturing lowered unemployment and heightened equality. The same outcome ensued when foreign direct investment that produced goods and services took precedence over speculative financial flows throughout the world. If foreign investors paid high wages to employees who worked forty hours per week in long-lasting jobs, equality rose when both government and private corporations supplied inexpensive social-service benefits like health care and pensions (ILO 2013, 27–116; UNCTAD 2012, 1–168).

Since World War II, three different types of political systems—elitist mobilization, bureaucratic-authoritarian, reconciliation—shaped income distribution policies in Central and Eastern Europe, Asia, and Latin America. In Maoist China and the Soviet Union under Stalin, communist party leaders and government bureaucrats implemented state socialist programs that engineered more income equality than did the previous or successive noncommunist regimes. Aiming to achieve rapid industrialization, bureaucratic-authoritarian systems followed a program of developmental capitalism. State bureaucrats allied with private corporate capitalists to suppress workers' rights. Chinese elites fused private markets with party-state direction of economic growth. Policies of the Chinese Communist Party widened the income gap, especially between rural areas and more industrialized urban regions. The military officials who dominated South Korea from 1961 through 1993 enacted policies for land redistribution, inclusive education, high capital investment, and labor-intensive manufacturing. Hence, they attained greater income equality than did the Chilean armed forces who ruled during the 1973–1989 period. Across developing countries, reconciliation systems merged pluralist arrangements with elitist features. Income distribution policies mainly arose from political leaders' value priorities as well as from power relationships among government institutions, competitive political parties, private corporations, and unions.

Global patterns of interdependence affected the complex ways that domestic political systems produced decisions toward income distribution. Culturally, the global media of communication transmitted diverse information, values, and perceptions about equality. Economically, foreign trade, overseas investment, and worldwide labor migration shaped income differences. Politically, the nation-state retained power over policies about trade, foreign investment, and especially recruitment of immigrant workers. Its decisions primarily influenced income within specific countries. Yet even the most powerful nation-states could not impose their will on domestic priorities, whether in their own countries or overseas. Since 1990, increased trade, investment, and information flows have heightened global interdependence. Such international institutions as the International Monetary Fund, World Bank, and World Trade Organization as well as regional development banks and multinational corporations enlarged the national income gap. They represented the interests of wealthy creditors more than debtors, particularly low-income consumers and small businesses. Austerity programs favored by financial institutions widened national income inequalities. Neither global union organizations nor worldwide leftist movements like the World Social Forum could mobilize resources behind protests that secured more egalitarian policies.

The resource mobilization perspective helps comprehend protests against economic inequality in China, India, Latin America, Western Europe, and the United States. The goals and tactics of protest movements affected their success in narrowing income differences. As demonstrated all over the world, a protest movement most effectively attained egalitarian goals when its political leaders communicated an appealing ideological vision to a mobilized audience and when structural opportunities outweighed constraints. If the movement skillfully used its resources, expanded internal cohesion, secured key allies, and escaped repression, prospects for success increased.

Three policy dilemmas confronted reconciliation leaders when they coped with the interactions among capitalism, democracy, and economic inequality. First, how did procedural justice that ensures equal justice under the law affect distributive justice programs favoring more egalitarian outcomes? Among three industrialized capitalist economies, Norwegian government policymakers more successfully reconciled this tension than did British or American officials, who secured lower income equality and fewer civil liberties. Second, what policies for rapid economic growth led to higher wages for workers? By enacting programs that promoted inclusive education, public access to computer services, and capital investment for the export of labor-intensive manufactured goods, South Korean reconciliation leaders secured more equal wages than did officials in the poorer Indian society, where caste, regional, religious, gender, and class cleavages fragmented the policy process. Third, what conditions shaped leaders' perceptions about the connection between representative democracy, which stresses competitive elections, and participatory democracy, which seeks greater popular involvement in government decision making? Among two social democratic governments in the southern cone of Latin America—Uruguay and Chile—Uruguayan leftist officials formulated fiscal policies that more effectively combined participatory with representative democracy but still obtained greater income equality. They fused Keynesian ideas with some principles advocated by neoliberal economists.

THE ROLE OF THE SOCIAL SCIENTIST IN THE POLICY PROCESS

Keynesian and neoliberal economists adopted different views about the role of the social scientist in the policy process. Both used theories as cognitive maps that depicted destination points, optional routes (rules, institutions, policies), and the probability of easily reaching a specific location. For Keynesians, the goals involved lowering unemployment and reducing economic inequalities. Private corporations, labor unions, and activist governments should cooperate behind policies that ensure reciprocal tradeoffs. Because the volatile capitalist world constantly changes, future outcomes remain uncertain. Hence, economists cannot make accurate predictions. By contrast, neoliberals attach greater priority to achieving low inflation, high corporate profits, and rapid growth. Through relying on market mechanisms, not on government regulation or provision of social services, the economy will realize efficiency, productivity, and innovation. Under efficient market hypotheses, past conditions serve as a fairly accurate guide to future situations. Hence, quantitative models can accurately calculate future effects (Andrain and Apter 1995, 9–10; Blyth 2013, 38–45).

Since the early 1980s, neoliberals exerted greater influence over the policy process than did Keynesians. Economists supporting financial deregulation, privatization, low business taxes, labor-market flexibility, weak union power, lower wages, and reduced expenditures for social services helped legitimate austerity programs. Despite public protests against the inegalitarian outcomes of austerity, neoliberal economists in universities, research institutes, private corporations, and financial institutions won support from government authorities. Social scientists with stronger egalitarian commitments attained less policy influence. Criticizing the austerity programs preferred by many leaders in the United States and Europe, Keynesian economist Paul Krugman observed: "To the extent that policymakers and elite opinion in general have made use of economic analysis at all, they have, as the saying goes, done so the way a drunkard uses a lamppost: for support, not illumination" (Krugman 2013, 73).

With his long tenure as a civil servant in the British Treasury, Keynes played a more active government role than do most contemporary Keynesians. This political experience led him to envision a multifaceted role for economists. From his perspective, they should synthesize the diverse features of mathematics, history, politics, and philosophy. Ideally, the social scientist blends opposite tendencies—general perspectives with specific conditions, temporal realities with eternal aspirations, the present situation with past events and future expectations. By so doing, the "master-economist" becomes "as aloof and incorruptible as an artist, yet sometimes as near the earth as a politician" (Keynes 1924, 322).

Unlike Keynes, who supported a regulated capitalist economy that would narrow the income gap, Karl Marx (1818–1883) believed that political economists should transform the capitalist system into a communist society. Relying on interpretations of the young Hegelians, Marx's doctoral dissertation analyzed Greek philosophers. During the mid-1840s, he asserted: "The philosophers have only *interpreted* the world, in various ways; the point is to *change* it" (Marx 1975, 423). A letter written during the same decade sketched his notion of the philosopher's role: "If we have no business with the construction of the future or with organizing it for all time there can still be no doubt about the task confronting us at present: the *ruthless criticism of the existing order*, ruthless in that it will shrink neither from its own discoveries nor from conflict with the powers that be" (Marx 1975, 207). Intellectuals must therefore act to reform the workers' consciousness, demystify popular illusions about capitalist realities, forge class struggle, and secure a political revolution that terminates class privileges in a capitalist society. This mobilization process involved collective action by a workers' political party and several other organizations: labor unions, cooperatives, newspapers, and small group networks (Sperber 2013, 48–70, 354–61; S. Wolin 2004, 409–35).

Through his books, newspaper articles, letters, and social networks, Marx tried to convert his theories into political practice. He wrote policy proposals first for the Communist League and later for the International Working Men's Association (IWMA). It backed egalitarian reforms to increase the suffrage, institute a progressive income tax, strengthen unions, shorten the workday, improve workplace conditions, and end capitalist exploitation of child, female, and prisoners' labor. After the advanced stage of communism had achieved high productivity and economic abundance, Marx expected that the class privileges of capitalism would disappear, especially the gap between high profits secured by private corporations and low wages paid to workers (Marx 1974, 81–92, 270, 346–48, 373–75; 1975, 257; Sperber 2013, 354–61, 537–38).

Antonio Gramsci (1891–1937), who adapted Marx's theories to Italian conditions, also focused on linking radical intellectuals with political action. A founder of the Italian Communist Party (PCI), Gramsci sought to educate workers so that they attained a higher consciousness about the meaning of political, economic, and cultural realities in Italy after World War I. He struggled to reconcile optimism of the will with pessimism of the intellect (Gramsci 1994, 1:299). Opposed to fatalism, passivity, inertia, and historical determinism, he recognized the objective constraints—political repression, party divisions, backward economic conditions, cultural misconceptions—that prevented an immediate fulfillment of socialist objectives. These included higher wages for workers, collective bargaining rights for them, improved working conditions, land for southern peasants, and receipt of inexpensive credit. Gramsci wanted the PCI to communicate a powerful political discourse affirming the will, energy, resilience, initiative, and activism needed to surmount obstacles. In this task, intellectuals who criticized existing structural conditions under capitalism played a crucial role. They should take a nondogmatic approach that affirmed critical thinking, experimentation, unconventional ideas, and practical means to attain socialist goals.

Gramsci's eclectic perspective on theory partly derived from close friends like Piero Sraffa, an Italian economist. First meeting him at the University of Turin, Gramsci took courses in linguistics, Italian literature, Greek literature, economics, and philosophy. His broad intellectual background prepared him to see the complexities that linked politics, economics, and culture. From 1919 until Gramsci's death, Sraffa had the wealth to supply him with newspapers, journals, and books. Between 1927 and 1963, Sraffa lectured and conducted research at Cambridge University, where he gave suggestions to Keynes about passages in his manuscript that needed clarification (Keynes 1973a, 207–9; 1979, 157–58). Visiting Gramsci in prison, Sraffa brought him the works of Keynes as well as classical economists such as Ricardo and Malthus.

As fascist control over Italy intensified, Gramsci envisioned the PCI heading a broad alliance that opposed fascism, mobilized for socialist reconstruction, and revitalized Italian society. Rather than operate in the dictatorial way that Lenin advocated, the PCI should conduct its activities in a reciprocal form of political education. Just as party intellectuals teach the students, so the PCI must learn from them about the most effective ways to fulfill egalitarian socialist objectives. That task included not just material benefits but also treatment of workers and poor peasants with greater respect and dignity (Gramsci 1994, 1:67, 317, 356; 2000, 147–64; Rosengarten 1994, xxi, 10–27; Santucci 2010).

Max Weber (1864–1920) assumed that social scientists have the main responsibility to understand and interpret the policy process, not to use theory for transforming society or abolishing capitalism. According to him, policymaking involves the complex, changing interactions among goals, means, and outcomes. Like other individuals, political leaders form their values based on cultural meanings of life. Their goals, including material interests, stem from diverse, heterogeneous worldviews. The social scientist should clarify these values, indicate their consistency, and specify the complex relationships among them. Weber also held that social scientists must analyze the appropriate, effective ways to attain policy goals. They can examine the possible outcomes, both intended and unintended, that may result from policies, regulations, strategies, and communications aiming to narrow the income gap. When making decisions, leaders rely on practical, not scientific, judgments about possible qualitative results in an ever-changing capitalist world. Hence, social scientists should focus on clarifying theoretical perspectives about the historical changes that emerge from specific policies in diverse contexts. The search for an interpretive understanding of some effect like income inequality can help explicate the human behavior of political actors and the social interactions that influence their policies (Bruun and Whimster 2012, xi–xxviii; Weber 2012, 100–138, 315–17, 349–50).

Even if Weber attacked the Prussian bureaucratic dictatorship for repressing trade unions and denying workers the right to participate in economic management, he scarcely advocated a socialist revolution, especially one led by Marxists. Instead, Weber supported a liberal capitalist economy that ensured peaceful bourgeois competition on the world market. Although preferring neither laissez-faire nor socialist policies, he sought rational measures that would lessen the inequalities arising from a person's individual and structural conditions (Roth 2005, 39–40; Titunik 2005; Wright 2005).

CONCLUSION

To expand their policy influence, social scientists who seek more income equality must mobilize resources that support redistributive programs. Effective organizations rally support from the general public as well as mass media (radio, television, Internet), research institutes, labor unions, ecological associations, consumer groups, and private businesses. They not only communicate cultural values but shape individual preferences. Through these organizations, egalitarian researchers can enlarge their political power over policymakers, however formidable the obstacles.

The difficulties of measuring power impede efforts to test resource mobilization assumptions. Rather than a thing, political power indicates a relationship among several leaders, groups, organizations, movements, and institutions, both domestic ones and those in the global arena. Personal networks formulate major government and corporate decisions in hierarchical organizations that remain closed to the public. How can the social scientist uncover the precise indicators measuring the influence exercised by such powerful structures? Resource mobilization theorists also neglect the complex ways that these structures transform specific types of resources—time, energy, money, knowledge, organizational skills—into collective political action and public policies. Political power means the effective use of resources to coordinate action, organize support, and overcome resistance. Analysts face problems devising accurate, reliable, valid indicators of these complex variables (Opp 2009, 91–160; White 2009).

Whereas this book has explained basic trends about political power, public policies, and the income gap, future research should clarify important issues—a task recommended by Weber. Particularly among developing nations, indicators of people's income remains missing, incomplete, or limited to urban residents. To assess the policies of other countries, statisticians need more standardized indicators of income for comparative analysis. Organizational power often diverges at different stages of the policy process, such as placing issues for consideration on the policy agenda, formulating alternatives, choosing the option viewed as most feasible, implementing the policy, and evaluating its outcome. Social scientists can more easily observe policy formulation than implementation of complex programs, particularly monetary and regulatory decisions made in secret sessions. What techniques will best enable researchers to measure the impact of business corporations on such administrative regulations? Throughout the world, different types of capitalism give priority to state guidance, competitive markets, and coordination among government officials, corporate managers, and union leaders. How does each type influence democratic institutions? As the capitalist market becomes more globalized, social scientists should explore the reciprocal ways that international institutions affect people's lives, including the way that international electronic media expand popular participation. What global conditions motivate individuals to protest their discontent? When egalitarian movements mobilize for political action, which tactics will likely yield an egalitarian outcome? Clarification of such issues will help explain the connections between political power and economic inequality in capitalist societies.

References

Aalberg, Toril. 2010. "Norway." *European Journal of Political Research* 49 (December): 1113–21.

Abraham, Vinoj. 2007. "Growth and Inequality of Wages in India: Recent Trends and Patterns." *Indian Journal of Labour Economics* 50 (October–December): 927–41.

Abramowitz, Alan I. 2010. *The Disappearing Center: Engaged Citizens, Polarization, and American Democracy*. New Haven, CT: Yale University Press.

———. 2012. "Grand Old Tea Party: Partisan Polarization and the Rise of the Tea Party Movement." In *Steep: The Precipitous Rise of the Tea Party*, edited by Lawrence Rosenthal and Christine Trost, 195–211. Berkeley: University of California Press.

Abramson, Paul R., John H. Aldrich, and David W. Rohde. 2012. *Change and Continuity in the 2008 and 2010 Elections*. Washington, DC: Congressional Quarterly.

Acharya, Arnab, Aaron Schneider, and Cecilia Ugaz. 2006. "The Political Economy of Inequality: The Privatisation of Utilities in Latin America." In *Overcoming Inequality in Latin America*, edited by Ricardo Gottschalk and Patricia Justino, 140–72. New York: Routledge.

Adams, James, and Lawrence Ezrow. 2009. "Who Do European Parties Represent? How Western European Parties Represent the Policy Preferences of Opinion Leaders." *Journal of Politics* 71 (January): 206–23.

Adams, James, Jane Green, and Caitlin Milazzo. 2012. "Has the British Public Depolarized Along with Political Elites? An American Perspective on British Public Opinion." *Comparative Political Studies* 45 (April): 507–30.

Adamson, Peter. 2012. *Measuring Child Poverty: New League Tables of Child Poverty in the World's Richest Countries*. Report Card 10. Florence, Italy: UNICEF Innocenti Research Centre.

Addabbo, Tindara, Fahima Aziz, and Jack Reardon. 2011. "The Effect of the Financial Crisis on the Italian and US Labour Markets." In *The Legacy of the Crash: How the Financial Crisis Changed America and Britain*, edited by Terrence Casey, 198–217. London: Palgrave Macmillan.

Admati, Anat, and Martin Hellwig. 2013. *The Bankers' New Clothes: What's Wrong with Banking and What to Do about It*. Princeton, NJ: Princeton University Press.

Agarwala, Rina. 2008. "Reshaping the Social Contract: Emerging Relations between the State and Informal Labor in India." *Theory and Society* 37 (August): 375–408.

Aglietta, Michel. 2012. "The European Vortex." *New Left Review*, no. 75 (May–June): 15–36.

Agnew, John. 2009. *Globalization and Sovereignty*. Lanham, MD: Rowman & Littlefield.

Agrast, Mark David, Juan Carlos Botero, Joel Martinez, Alejandro Ponce, Christine S. Pratt, and Kelly Roberts. 2012. *World Justice Project Rule of Law Index*. Washington, DC: World

Justice Project. http://worldjusticeproject.org/sites/default/files/WJP_Index_Report_2012.pdf.

Akerlof, George A., and Robert J. Shiller. 2009. *Animal Spirits: How Human Psychology Drives the Economy, and Why It Matters for Global Capitalism*. Princeton, NJ: Princeton University Press.

Albertazzi, Daniele. 2009. "Reconciling 'Voice' and 'Exit': Swiss and Italian Populists in Power." *Politics* 29 (February): 1–10.

Albo, Gregory. 2007. "Neoliberalism and the Discontented." In *Socialist Register 2008: Global Flashpoints*, edited by Leo Panitch and Colin Leys, 354–72. New York: Monthly Review.

Albo, Greg, and Bryan Evans. 2010. "From Rescue Strategies to Exit Strategies: The Struggle over Public Sector Austerity." In *Socialist Register 2011: The Crisis This Time*, edited by Leo Panitch, Greg Albo, and Vivek Chibber, 283–308. New York: Monthly Review.

Alemán, José. 2008. "Labor Market Deregulation and Industrial Conflict in New Democracies: A Cross-national Analysis." *Political Studies* 56 (December): 830–56.

Alpert, Daniel, Robert Hockett, and Nouriel Roubini. 2011. *The Way Forward: Moving from the Post-bubble, Post-bust Economy to Renewed Growth and Competitiveness*. Washington, DC: New America Foundation. http://newamerica.net/sites/newamerica.net/files/policydocs/NAF--The_Way_Forward--Alpert_Hockett_Roubini.pdf.

Altman, David. 2011. *Direct Democracy Worldwide*. New York: Cambridge University Press.

Alvaredo, Facundo, Anthony B. Atkinson, Thomas Piketty, and Emmanuel Saez. 2013. "The Top 1 Percent in International and Historical Perspective." *Journal of Economic Perspectives* 27 (Summer 2013): 3–20.

Álvarez, Alejandra Machín. 2012. "'Think Global, Act Local': Neighborhood and Town Assemblies." In *From Cairo to Wall Street: Voices from the Global Spring*, edited by Anya Schiffrin and Eamon Kircher-Allen, 126–32. New York: New Press.

Alvarez Rivadulla, María José. 2012. "Clientelism or Something Else? Squatter Politics in Montevideo." *Latin American Politics and Society* 54 (Spring): 37–63.

Amenta, Edwin, Neal Caren, Elizabeth Chiarello, and Yang Su. 2010. "The Political Consequences of Social Movements." *Annual Review of Sociology* 36: 287–307.

Amnesty International. 2009. *Disposable Labour: Rights of Migrant Workers in South Korea*. London: Amnesty International Publications.

———. 2010. *Amnesty International Report 2010: The State of the World's Human Rights*. London: Amnesty International Publications.

An, Chong-Bum, and Barry Bosworth. 2013. *Income Inequality in Korea: An Analysis of Trends, Causes, and Answers*. Cambridge, MA: Harvard University Asia Center.

An, Mi-young. 2009. "The Gender Impact of National Pension Reforms in the Republic of Korea." *International Social Security Review* 62 (April/June): 77–99.

Anderlini, Jamil. 2011. "Subsidies at Heart of New Deal." *Financial Times*, June 1, 2.

Andersen, Torben M., Bengt Holmström, Seppo Honkapohja, Sixten Korkman, Hans Tson Söderström, and Juhana Vartiainen. 2007. *The Nordic Model: Embracing Globalization and Sharing Risks*. Helsinki, Finland: Taloustieto Oy.

Anderson, Vicki. 2010. "The Story of a Book." In Robert Tressell, *The Ragged Trousered Philanthropists*, adapted play by Howard Brenton, iv–v. London: Nick Hern.

Andeweg, Rudy B. 2003. "Beyond Representativeness? Trends in Political Representation." *European Review* 11 (May): 147–61.

Andrain, Charles F. 1980. *Politics and Economic Policy in Western Democracies*. North Scituate, MA: Duxbury.

———. 1994. *Comparative Political Systems: Policy Performance and Social Change*. Armonk, NY: M. E. Sharpe.

———. 2008. *Political Justice and Religious Values*. New York: Routledge.

———. 2011. *Political Change in the Third World*. London: Routledge.

Andrain, Charles F., and David E. Apter. 1995. *Political Protest and Social Change: Analyzing Politics*. New York: New York University Press.

Andrain, Charles F., and James T. Smith. 2006. *Political Democracy, Trust, and Social Justice: A Comparative Overview*. Lebanon, NH: University Press of New England.

Andreas, Joel. 2010. "A Shanghai Model? On Capitalism with Chinese Characteristics." *New Left Review*, no. 65 (September–October): 63–85.
Anner, Mark. 2008. "Meeting the Challenges of Industrial Restructuring: Labor Reform and Enforcement in Latin America." *Latin American Politics and Society* 50 (Summer): 33–65.
———. 2011. *Solidarity Transformed: Labor Responses to Globalization and Crisis in Latin America*. Ithaca, NY: Cornell University Press.
Anxo, Dominique, and Harald Niklasson. 2008. "The Swedish Model: Revival after the Turbulent 1990s?" Discussion paper no. 189. Geneva: International Institute for Labour Studies, International Labour Organization.
Appel, Hilary. 2006. "International Imperatives and Tax Reform: Lessons from Postcommunist Europe." *Comparative Politics* 39 (October): 43–62.
Apter, David E. 1971. *Choice and the Politics of Allocation*. New Haven, CT: Yale University Press.
———. 2006. "Duchamp's Urinal: Who Says What's Rational When Things Get Tough?" In *Oxford Handbook of Contextual Political Analysis*, edited by Robert E. Goodin and Charles Tilly, 767–96. New York: Oxford University Press.
Arceneaux, Kevin, and Stephen P. Nicholson. 2012. "Who Wants to Have a Tea Party? The Who, What, and Why of the Tea Party Movement." *PS: Political Science & Politics* 46 (October): 700–710.
Arnold, Jason Ross, and David J. Samuels. 2011. "Evidence from Public Opinion." In *The Resurgence of the Latin American Left*, edited by Steven Levitsky and Kenneth M. Roberts, 31–51. Baltimore, MD: Johns Hopkins University Press.
Arsenault, Amelia, and Manuel Castells. 2008. "Switching Power: Rupert Murdoch and the Global Business of Media Politics." *International Sociology* 23 (July): 488–513.
Arter, David. 2011. *Inside the Radical Right: The Development of Anti-Immigrant Parties in Western Europe*. New York: Cambridge University Press.
Ash, Robert F. 2010. "Economy" [of South Korea]. In *The Far East and Australasia 2011*, 42nd ed., edited by Lynn Daniel, 652–72. London: Routledge.
Asian Development Bank. 1989. *Asian Development Outlook 1989*. Manila, Philippines: Asian Development Bank.
Atasoy, Yildiz. 2007. "The Islamic Ethic and the Spirit of Turkish Capitalism Today." In *Socialist Register 2008: Global Flashpoints*, edited by Leo Panitch and Colin Leys, 121–40. New York: Monthly Review.
Atkinson, Anthony B., Thomas Piketty, and Emmanuel Saez. 2011. "Top Incomes in the Long Run of History." *Journal of Economic Literature* 49 (March): 3–71.
Austin, Algernon. 2010. "Budget Cuts and Our Children's Future." *American Prospect* 21 (November): A18–19.
Babb, Sarah. 2007. "Embeddedness, Inflation, and International Regimes: The IMF in the Early Postwar Period." *American Journal of Sociology* 113 (July): 128–64.
Bacarro, Lucio. 2008. "Labour Institutions and Inequality." In *World of Work Report 2008*, 71–113. Geneva: Institute for Labour Studies, International Labour Organization.
Backhouse, Roger F., and Bradley W. Bateman. 2011. *Capitalist Revolutionary: John Maynard Keynes*. Cambridge, MA: Harvard University Press.
Bafumi, Joseph, and Michael C. Herron. 2010. "Leapfrog Representation and Extremism: A Study of American Voters and Their Members in Congress." *American Political Science Review* 104 (August): 519–42.
Baker, Wayne. 2005. *America's Crisis of Values: Reality and Perception*. Princeton, NJ: Princeton University Press.
Banerjee, Debdas. 2007. "Trends in Wage and Income Differentials." *Indian Journal of Labour Economics* 50 (October–December 2007): 891–902.
Banerjee, Sumanta. 2011. "West Bengal's Next Quinquennium, and the Future of the Indian Left." *Economic & Political Weekly* 46 (June 4): 14–19.
———. 2012. "From Parliamentary to Paramilitary Democracy." *Economic & Political Weekly* 47 (January 7): 16–19.
Barbara, Vanessa. 2013. "Brazil's Vinegar Uprising." *New York Times*, June 22, A17.

Barbieri, Paolo. 2009. "Flexible Employment and Inequality in Europe." *European Sociological Review* 25 (December): 621–28.

Barboza, David. 2011a. "Truck Drivers in Shanghai Plan to Resume Protests." *New York Times*, April 25, A6.

———. 2011b. "Weak Link in an Export Chain." *New York Times*, April 29, B1, B6.

———. 2013. "Loan Practices of China's Banks Raising Concern." *New York Times*, July 2, A1, A3.

Barboza, David, and Hiroko Tabuchi. 2010. "Labor Strife Signals Shift in China." *New York Times*, June 9, B1, B8.

Bardhan, Pranab. 2009. "Notes on the Political Economy of India's Tortuous Transition." *Economic & Political Weekly* 44 (December 5): 31–36.

Barr, Robert R. 2009. "Populists, Outsiders and Anti-Establishment Politics." *Party Politics* 15 (January): 29–48.

Barratt, Craig. 2009. *Trade Union Membership 2008*. London: Department for Business Enterprise and Regulatory Reform, URN.

Barrionuevo, Alexei. 2011. "With Kiss-Ins and Dances, Young Chileans Push for Reform." *New York Times*, August 5, A4.

Barry, Frank. 2009. "Foreign Direct Investment and Labor Markets." In *Princeton Encyclopedia of the World Economy*, edited by Kenneth A. Reinert and Ramkishen S. Rajan, 464–70. Princeton, NJ: Princeton University Press.

Bartels, Larry M. 2008. *Unequal Democracy: The Political Economy of the New Gilded Age*. New York: Russell Sage Foundation.

Bartlett, Bruce. 2012. *The Benefit and the Burden: Tax Reform—Why We Need It and What It Will Take*. New York: Simon & Schuster.

Baru, Sanjaya. 2010. "Economy [of India]." In *South Asia 2011*, 8th ed., edited by Jillian O'Brien, 275–87. London: Routledge.

Bastagli, Francesca. 2011. "Conditional Cash Transfers as a Tool of Social Policy." *Economic & Political Weekly* 46 (May 21): 61–66.

Bauder, Harald. 2011. "The Regulation of Labor Markets through Migration." In *Migration in the Global Political Economy*, edited by Nicola Phillips, 41–60. Boulder, CO: Rienner.

Baumgartner, Frank R., Jeffrey M. Berry, Marie Hojnacki, David C. Kimball, and Beth L. Leach. 2009. *Lobbying and Policy Change: Who Wins, Who Loses, and Why*. Chicago: University of Chicago Press.

BBC (British Broadcasting Corporation). 2009. *BBC World Service Poll: Wide Dissatisfaction with Capitalism—Twenty Years after Fall of Berlin Wall*, November 9. http://www.worldpublicopinion.org/pipa/pdf/nov09/BBC_BerlinWall_Nov09_rpt.pdf.

———. 2010. *BBC World Service Poll: Governments Misspend More than Half of Our Taxes—Global Poll*, September 27. http://www.worldpublicopinion.org/pipa/pdf/sep10/BBCEcon_Sep10_rpt.pdf.

Beck, Ulrich. 2013. *German Europe*. Translated by Rodney Livingstone. Cambridge: Polity.

Becker, Gary S., and Richard A. Posner. 2009. *Uncommon Sense*. Chicago: University of Chicago Press.

Beeson, Mark, and André Broome. 2008. "Watching from the Sidelines? The Decline of the IMF's Crisis Management Role." *Contemporary Politics* 14 (December): 393–409.

Behr, Rafael. 2012. "The Dying of the Middle-Class Dream." *New Statesman* 141 (November 2–8): 24–28.

Béland, Daniel, and Robert Henry Cox. 2011. "Introduction: Ideas and Politics." In *Ideas and Politics in Social Science Research*, edited by Daniel Béland and Robert Henry Cox, 3–20. New York: Oxford University Press.

Belton, Catherine, and Charles Clover. 2012. "Putin's People." *Financial Times*, May 31, 7.

Beramendi, Pablo, and Thomas R. Cusak. 2009. "Diverse Disparities: The Politics and Economics of Wage, Market, and Disposable Income Inequalities." *Political Research Quarterly* 62 (June): 257–75.

Berman, Ari. 2013. "Conservatives Take Aim at Voting Rights." *Nation* 296 (February 25): 11–17.

Bermeo, Nancy, and Jonas Pontusson. 2012. "Coping with Crisis: An Introduction." In *Coping with Crisis: Government Reactions to the Great Recession*, edited by Nancy Bermeo and Jonas Pontusson, 1–31. New York: Russell Sage Foundation.

Bernardi, Fabrizio, and Luis Garrido. 2008. "Is There a New Service Proletariat? Post-industrial Employment Growth and Social Inequality in Spain." *European Sociological Review* 24 (July): 299–313.

Bernstein, Nina. 2011. "Immigrant Crackdowns Turn into Big Business." *New York Times*, September 29, A1, A11.

Bernstein, Shai, Josh Lerner, and Antoinette Schoar. 2013. "The Investment Strategies of Sovereign Wealth Funds." *Journal of Economic Perspectives* 27 (Spring): 219–38.

Bhushan, Prashant. 2012. "Legitimising Tax Avoidance." *Economic & Political Weekly* 47 (March 3): 37–40.

Biermann, Wolfgang, and Kristine Kallset. 2010. "'Everyone on Board!' The Nordic Model and the Red-Red-Green-Coalition—A Transferable Model of Success?" *Internationale Politik und Gesellschaft*, no. 4: 167–91.

Binelli, Mark. 2012. "The Battle for the Soul of Occupy." *Rolling Stone*, no. 1158 (June 7): 62–69.

Birdsall, Nancy, Nora Lustig, and Darryl McLeod. 2012. "Declining Inequality in Latin America: Some Economics, Some Politics." In *Routledge Handbook of Latin American Politics*, edited by Peter Kingstone and Deborah J. Yashar, 158–80. New York: Routledge.

Bivens, Josh, and Lawrence Mishel. 2013. "The Pay of Corporate Executives and Financial Professionals as Evidence of Rents in Top 1 Percent Incomes." *Journal of Economic Perspectives* 27 (Summer): 57–77.

Blackburn, Robin. 2011. "Crisis 2.0." *New Left Review*, no. 72 (November–December): 33–62.

Blackhurst, Richard. 2009. "World Trade Organization." In *Princeton Encyclopedia of the World Economy*, edited by Kenneth A. Reinhart and Ramkishen S. Rajan, 1185–91. Princeton, NJ: Princeton University Press.

Blanchflower, David. 2011. "Portugal Is Cutting Its Way Deeper into Crisis. Could Britain Follow?" *New Statesman* 140 (April 4): 15.

Blanchflower, David, and Robert Skidelsky. 2011. "Vince Cable Is Working. The Coalition Isn't." *New Statesman* 140 (January 24): 37–38.

Blekesaune, Morten. 2013. "Economic Strain and Public Support for Redistribution: A Comparative Analysis of 28 European Countries." *Journal of Social Policy* 42 (January): 57–72.

Blendon, Robert, and John Benson. 2011. "Partisan Conflicts among the Public on the Economy and Budget Deficit in 2011." *Challenge* 54 (September–October): 5–17.

Blind, Peride Kaleağasi. 2007. "A New Actor in Turkish Democratization: Labor Unions." *Turkish Studies* 8 (June): 289–311.

Blitz, James. 2010. "Poll Reveals High Level of Hostility to Immigrants in Europe." *Financial Times*, September 7, 4.

Block, Fred. 2012a. "There Was No Baby in This Bathwater: A Reply to Critics." In *Political Power and Social Theory*, vol. 23, edited by Julian Go, 323–34. Bingley, UK: Emerald Group.

———. 2012b. "Varieties of What? Should We Still Be Using the Concept of Capitalism?" In *Political Power and Social Theory*, vol. 23, edited by Julian Go, 269–91. Bingley, UK: Emerald Group.

Blofield, Merike, and Juan Pablo Luna. 2011. "Public Opinion on Income Inequalities in Latin America." In *The Great Gap: Inequality and the Politics of Redistribution in Latin America*, edited by Merike Blofield, 147–81. University Park: Pennsylvania State University Press.

Blomberg, Helena, Johanna Kallio, Olli Kangas, Christian Kroll, and Mikko Niemelä. 2012. "Attitudes among High-Risk Groups." In *Contested Welfare States: Welfare Attitudes in Europe and Beyond*, edited by Stefan Svallors, 58–80. Stanford, CA: Stanford University Press.

Blyth, Mark. 2013. *Austerity: The History of a Dangerous Idea*. New York: Oxford University Press.

Bochel, Hugh, and Andrew Defty. 2007. "MPs' Attitudes to Welfare: A New Consensus?" *Journal of Social Policy* 36 (January): 1–17.

Boeri, Tito, and Jan van Ours. 2008. *The Economics of Imperfect Labor Markets*. Princeton, NJ: Princeton University Press.

Boito, Armando Júnior. 2007. "Le gouvernement lula et l'ascension politique de la grande bourgeoisie intérieure brésilienne." *Lusotopie* 14 (November): 43–60.

Bolzendahl, Catherine. 2011. "Beyond the Big Picture: Gender Influences on Disaggregated and Domain-Specific Measures of Social Spending, 1980–1999." *Politics & Gender* 7 (March): 35–70.

Bonanno, Alessandro, and Douglas H. Constance. 2008. *Stories of Globalization: Transnational Corporations, Resistance, and the State*. University Park: Pennsylvania State University Press.

Bondgraham, Darwin. 2012. "We Have Your City. Pay Up, or Else!" *Dollars & Sense*, no. 300 (May/June): 11–18.

Bonica, Adam, Nolan McCarty, Keith T. Poole, and Howard Rosenthal. 2013. "Why Hasn't Democracy Slowed Rising Inequality?" *Journal of Economic Perspectives* 27 (Summer): 103–24.

Bonnefoy, Pascale. 2012. "Volunteers Keep Watch on Protests in Chile." *New York Times*, August 27, A6.

Bornschier, Simon. 2010. *Cleavage Politics and the Populist Right: The New Cultural Conflict in Western Europe*. Philadelphia, PA: Temple University Press.

Borzutzky, Silvia. 2010. "Socioeconomic Policies: Taming the Market in a Globalized Economy." In *The Bachelet Government: Conflict and Consensus in Post-Pinochet Chile*, edited by Silvia Borzutzky and Gregory B. Weeks, 87–116. Gainesville: University Press of Florida.

Boughton, James M. 1998. "Harry Dexter White and the International Monetary Fund." *Finance & Development* 35 (September): 39–41.

Bourdieu, Pierre. 1986. "The Forms of Capital." In *Handbook of Theory and Research for the Sociology of Education*, edited by John G. Richardson, 241–58. Westport, CN: Greenwood.

———. 1998a. *Acts of Resistance: Against the Tyranny of the Market*. Translated by Richard Nice. New York: New Press.

———. 1998b. *Practical Reason: On the Theory of Action*. Stanford, CA: Stanford University Press.

Bowles, Samuel, and Herbert Gintis. 1986. *Democracy and Capitalism: Property, Community, and the Contradictions of Modern Social Thought*. New York: Basic.

Bowles, Samuel, and Sandra Polanía-Reyes. 2012. "Economic Incentives and Social Preferences: Substitutes or Complements?" *Journal of Economic Literature* 50 (June): 368–425.

Boyer, Robert. 2012. "The Four Fallacies of Contemporary Austerity Policies: The Lost Keynesian Legacy." *Cambridge Journal of Economics* 36 (January): 283–412.

Bradsher, Keith. 2010. "An Independent Labor Movement Stirs in China." *New York Times*, March 11, A1, A4.

Brady, David. 2009. *Rich Democracies, Poor People: How Politics Explain Poverty*. New York: Oxford University Press.

Braithwaite, Tom, Brooke Masters, and Jeremy Grant. 2011. "A Shield Asunder: Financial Regulation." *Financial Times*, May 20, 7.

Brekke, Idunn, and Arne Mastekaasa. 2008. "Highly-Educated Immigrants in the Norwegian Labor Market: Permanent Disadvantage?" *Work, Employment and Society* 22 (September): 507–26.

Bresser-Pereira, Luiz Carlos. 2012. "For a Heterodox Mainstream Economics: An Academic Manifesto." *Journal of Post Keynesian Economics* 35 (Fall): 2–20.

Brinton, Mary C. 2011. *Lost in Transition: Youth, Work, and Instability in Postindustrial Japan*. New York: Cambridge University Press.

Brody, David. 2010. "A Tale of Two Labor Laws." *Dissent* 57 (Spring): 63–68.

Brooks, Clem, and Jeff Manza. 2006. "Social Policy Responsiveness in Developed Democracies." *American Sociological Review* 71 (June): 474–94.

———. 2007. *Why Welfare States Persist: The Importance of Public Opinion in Democracies*. Chicago: University of Chicago Press.

Brown, Wendy. 2011. "We Are All Democrats Now . . ." In *Democracy in What State?* by Giorgio Agamben, Alain Badiou, Daniel Bensaïd, Wendy Brown, Jean-Luc Nancy, Jacques Rancière, Kristin Ross, and Slavoj Žižek, 44–57. New York: Columbia University Press.

Bruun, Hans Henrik, and Sam Whimster. 2012. "Introduction." In *Max Weber: Collected Methodological Writings*, edited by Hans Henrik Bruun and Sam Whimster, translated by Hans Henrik Bruun, xi–xxviii. New York: Routledge.

Buchanan, Paul G. 2008. "Preauthoritarian Institutions and Postauthoritarian Outcomes: Labor Politics in Chile and Uruguay." *Latin American Politics and Society* 50 (Spring): 59–89.

Bucheli, Marisa, Nora Lustig, Máximo Rossi, and Florencia Amábile. 2013. "Social Spending, Taxes and Income Redistribution in Uruguay." CEQ working paper no. 10. New Orleans, LA: Center for Inter-American Policy and Research, Tulane University. http://stonecenter.tulane.edu/uploads/Bucheli_et_al_URU_SocialSpending_Taxes_Redist_Aug_31_2012_FINAL-1347378266.pdf.

Buchholz, Sandra, Dirk Hofäcker, Melinda Mills, Hans-Peter Blossfeld, Karin Kurz, and Heather Hofmeister. 2009. "Life Courses in the Globalization Process: The Development of Social Inequalities in Modern Societies." *European Sociological Review* 25 (February): 53–71.

Buck, Tobias. 2012. "Spain's Deepening Lack of Hope Takes Its Toll." *Financial Times*, November 6, 4.

Buğra, Ayşe, and Osman Savaşkan. 2012. "Politics and Class: The Turkish Business Environment in the Neoliberal Age." *New Perspectives on Turkey*, no. 46 (Spring): 27–63.

Bulard, Martine. 2013. "South Korea's Corporate Dynasty." *Le Monde diplomatique*, English edition, no. 1307 (July): 1–3.

Bull, Benedicte. 2008. "Policy Networks and Business Participation in Free Trade Negotiations in Chile." *Journal of Latin American Studies* 40 (May): 195–224.

Burchardt, Hans-Jürgen. 2010. "The Latin American Paradox: Convergence of Political Participation and Social Exclusion." *Internationale Politik und Gesellschaft*, no. 3: 40–51.

Burns, John F., and Julia Werdigier. 2011. "Britain's Economy Stalls, Prompting Attacks on Cameron's Strict Austerity Cure." *New York Times*, January 26, A10.

Busch, Andreas. 2009. *Banking Regulation and Globalization*. New York: Oxford University Press.

Büthe, Tim, and Walter Mattli. 2011. *The New Global Rulers: The Privatization of Regulation in the World Economy*. Princeton, NJ: Princeton University Press.

Byrd, Scott C., and Lorien Jasny. 2010. "Transnational Movement Innovation and Collaboration: Analysis of World Social Forum Networks." *Social Movement Studies* 9 (November): 355–72.

Cahill, Damien. 2008. "Hegemony and the Neoliberal Historical Bloc: The Australian Experience." In *Hegemony: Studies in Consensus and Coercion*, edited by Richard Howson and Kylie Smith, 201–17. New York: Routledge.

Cai, Yongshun. 2010. *Collective Resistance in China: Why Popular Protests Succeed or Fail*. Stanford CA: Stanford University Press.

Caiani, Manuela, Donatella della Porta, and Claudius Wagemann. 2012. *Mobilizing on the Extreme Right: Germany, Italy, and the United States*. New York: Oxford University Press.

Cain, J. Salcedo, Rana Hasan, Rhoda Magsombol, and Ajay Tandon. 2010. "Accounting for Inequality in India: Evidence from Household Expenditures." *World Development* 38 (March): 282–97.

Cairnie, Julie, and Marion Walls. 2008a. "Introduction." In *Revisiting Robert Tressell's Mugsborough: New Perspectives on "The Ragged Trousered Philanthropists,"* edited by Julie Cairnie and Marion Walls, 1–11. Amherst, NY: Cambria.

———. 2008b. "Towards Universal Interdependence: The Internationalism of Tressell's Text." In *Revisiting Robert Tresell's Mugsborough: New Perspectives on "The Ragged Trousered Philanthropists,"* edited by Julie Cairnie and Marion Walls, 173–97. Amherst, NY: Cambria.

Campbell, David E., and Robert D. Putnam. 2011. "Crashing the Tea Party." *New York Times*, August 17, A21.

Campbell, John L. 2011. "The US Financial Crisis: Lessons for Theories of Institutional Complementarity." *Socio-Economic Review* 9 (April): 211–34.

Canel, Eduardo. 2010. *Barrio Democracy in Latin America: Participatory Decentralization and Community Activism in Montevideo*. University Park: Pennsylvania State University Press.

Carabelli, Anna M., and Mario A. Cedrini. 2010. "Keynes and the Complexity of International Relations in the Aftermath of World War I." *Journal of Economic Issues* 44 (December): 1009–27.

Carbaugh, Bob, and Koushik Ghosh. 2011. "Reforming the U.S. Tax System." *Challenge* 54 (March/April): 61–79.

Card, David. 2009. "Immigration and Inequality." *American Economic Review: Papers & Proceedings* 99 (May): 1–21.

Cárdenas, Mauricio, and Guillermo Perry. 2011. "Fiscal Policy in Latin America." In *Oxford Handbook of Latin American Economics*, edited by José Antonio Ocampo and Jaime Ros, 266–92. New York: Oxford University Press.

Cardim de Carvalho, Fernando J. 2008–2009. "Keynes and the Reform of the Capitalist Social Order." *Journal of Post Keynesian Economics* 31 (Winter): 191–211.

Carrión, Maria. 2013. "Brazil's Poor Pay World Cup Penalty." *Progressive* 77 (July): 26–29.

Carroll, William K. 2009. "Tracking the Transnational Capitalist Class: The View from on High." In *Hegemonic Transitions, the State and Crisis in Neoliberal Capitalism*, edited by Yildiz Atasoy, 43–69. London: Routledge.

———. 2010. *The Making of a Transnational Capitalist Class: Corporate Power in the Twenty-First Century*. London: Zed.

Carruthers, David, and Patricia Rodriguez. 2009. "Mapuche Protest, Environmental Conflict and Social Movement Linkage in Chile." *Third World Quarterly* 30 (4): 743–60.

Carvalho Filho, José Juliano de, and Maria Luisa Mendonça. 2007. "Agrarian Policies and Rural Violence in Brazil." *Peace Review: A Journal of Social Justice* 19 (January–March): 77–85.

Cassidy, John. 2009. *How Markets Fail: The Logic of Economic Calamities*. New York: Farrar, Straus & Giroux.

Castells, Manuel. 2011. "The Crisis of Global Capitalism: Toward a New Economic Culture?" In *Business as Usual: The Roots of the Global Financial Meltdown*, edited by Craig Calhoun and Georgi Derluguian, 185–209. New York: New York University Press.

———. 2012. *Networks of Outrage and Hope: Social Movements in the Internet Age*. Malden, MA: Polity.

Castillo, Juan C. 2009. "¿Cuál es la brecha salarial justa? Opinión pública y legitimación de la desigualdad económica en Chile." *Estudios Públicos*, no. 113 (Summer): 237–66.

Castorina, Emilia. 2007. "The Contradictions of 'Democratic' Neoliberalism in Argentina: A New Politics from 'Below'?" In *Socialist Register 2008: Global Flashpoints*, edited by Leo Panitch and Colin Leys, 265–83. New York: Monthly Review.

Centeno, Miguel A., and Joseph N. Cohen. 2010. *Global Capitalism: A Sociological Perspective*. Cambridge: Polity.

Ceobanu, Alin M., and Xavier Escandell. 2010. "Comparative Analyses of Public Attitudes toward Immigrants and Immigration Using Multinational Survey Data: A Review of Theories and Research." *Annual Review of Sociology* 36: 309–28.

Chaffin, Joshua. 2013. "Berlin's Dominant Role Raises Hackles, Poll Says." *Financial Times*, June 24, 3.

Chambers, David, and Elroy Dimson. 2013. "John Maynard Keynes, Investment Innovator." *Journal of Economic Perspectives* 27 (Summer): 213–28.

Chandrasekhar, S., and Abhiroop Mukhopadhyay. 2010. "Poverty and Well-Being in Indian Cities during the Reforms Era." *Poverty & Public Policy* 2 (2):189–209.

Chang, Ha-Joon. 2008. *Bad Samaritans: The Myth of Free Trade and the Secret History of Capitalism*. New York: Bloomsbury.

———. 2010. *23 Things They Don't Tell You about Capitalism*. London: Allen Lane.

Charlton, Andrew. 2008. "Capital Market Liberalization and Poverty." In *Capital Market Liberalization and Development*, edited by José Antonio Ocampo and Joseph E. Stiglitz, 121–38. New York: Oxford University Press.

Chase, Kerry A. 2008. "Moving Hollywood Abroad: Divided Labor Markets and the New Politics of Trade in Services." *International Organization* 62 (Fall): 653–87.

Chatterjee, Partha. 2008. "Democracy and Economic Transformation in India." *Economic & Political Weekly* 43 (April 19): 53–62.

Checchi, Daniele, and Cecilia García-Peñalosa. 2008. "Labour Market Institutions and Income Inequality." *Economic Policy* 23 (October): 601–49.

Chemerinsky, Erwin. 2013. "Justice for Big Business." *New York Times*, July 2, A21.

Chemin, Anne. 2011. "Norway Lets Fathers Do Their Share." *Guardian Weekly*, July 22, 28.

Chen, Jie, and Bruce J. Dickson. 2010. *Allies of the State: China's Private Entrepreneurs and Democratic Change*. Cambridge, MA: Harvard University Press.

Chen, Wenhong, and Barry Wellman. 2005. "Minding the Cyber-Gap: The Internet and Social Inequality." In *The Blackwell Companion to Social Inequalities*, edited by Mary Romero and Eric Margolis, 523–45. Oxford, UK: Blackwell.

Choi, Young Jun. 2008. "Pension Policy and Politics in East Asia." *Policy & Politics* 36 (January): 127–44.

Chong, Alberto, and Mark Gradstein. 2007. "Inequality and Institutions." *Review of Economics and Statistics* 89 (August): 454–65.

Christensen, Paul T. 2013. "Russia as Semiperiphery: Political Economy, the State, and Society in the Contemporary World System." In *The Political Economy of Russia*, edited by Neil Robinson, 169–89. Lanham, MD: Rowman & Littlefield.

Chwieroth, Jeffrey M. 2010. *Capital Ideas: The IMF and the Rise of Financial Liberalization*. Princeton, NJ: Princeton University Press.

Cinoli, Marlo, Annalisa Primi, and Maurizio Pugno. 2006. "A Low-Growth Model: Informality as a Structural Constraint." *CEPAL Review*, no. 88 (April): 85–102.

Clark, Rob. 2011. "World Economic Inequality in the Global Era: New Estimates, 1990–2008." *Social Problems* 58 (November): 565–92.

Clarke, Peter. 2009. *Keynes: The Rise, Fall, and Return of the 20th Century's Most Influential Economist*. New York: Bloomsbury.

Clarke, Simon. 2007. "The State of the Russian Unions." *Journal of Labor Research* 28 (Spring): 275–99.

Clausen, Bianca, Aart Kraay, and Zsolt Nyiri. 2011. "Corruption and Confidence in Public Institutions: Evidence from a Global Survey." *World Bank Economic Review* 25 (June): 212–49.

Cleary, Edward. 2007. *Mobilizing for Human Rights in Latin America*. Bloomfield, CT: Kumarian.

Cohen, Daniel. 2012. *The Prosperity of Vice: A Worried View of Economics*. Translated by Susan Emanuel. Cambridge, MA: MIT Press.

Cohen, G. A. 2009. *Why Not Socialism?* Princeton, NJ: Princeton University Press.

Cohen, Martin. 2012. "The Future of the Tea Party: Scoring an Invitation to the Republican Party." In *Steep: The Precipitous Rise of the Tea Party*, edited by Lawrence Rosenthal and Christine Trost, 212–41. Berkeley: University of California Press.

Cole, David. 2013. "Equality and the Roberts Court: Four Decisions." *New York Review of Books* 60 (August 15): 28–30.

Collins, Stephen D. 2010. "Indigenous Rights and Internal Wars: The Chiapas Conflict at 15 Years." *Social Science Journal* 47 (December): 773–88.

Coloma, Tristan. 2013. "Erdogan Goes Too Far." *Le Monde diplomatique*, no. 1307 (July): 7.

Conyon, Martin J., John E. Core, and Wayne R. Guay. 2011. "Are U.S. CEOs Paid More Than U.K. CEOs? Inferences from Risk-Adjusted Pay." *Review of Financial Studies* 24 (February): 402–38.

Cook, Linda J. 2007. *Postcommunist Welfare States: Reform Politics in Russia and Eastern Europe*. Ithaca, NY: Cornell University Press.

Coppedge, Michael, Angel Alvarez, and Claudia Maldonado. 2008. "Two Persistent Dimensions of Democracy: Contestation and Inclusiveness." *Journal of Politics* 70 (July): 632–47.

Corak, Miles. 2013. "Income Inequality, Equality of Opportunity, and Intergenerational Mobility." *Journal of Economic Perspectives* 27 (Summer): 79–102.
Cornia, Giovanni Andrea. 2011. "Economic Integration, Inequality and Growth: Latin America vs. the European Economies in Transition." United Nations Department of Economic and Social Affairs Working Paper No. 101. New York: UNDESA.
Cortez Ruiz, Carlos. 2010. "The Struggle towards Rights and Communitarian Citizenship: The Zapatista Movement in Mexico." In *Citizenship and Social Movements: Perspectives from the Global South*, edited by Lisa Thompson and Chris Tapscott, 160–83. London: Zed.
Coşar, Simten, and Aylin Özman. 2008. "Representation Problems of Social Democracy in Turkey." *Journal of Third World Studies* 25 (Spring): 233–52.
Cox, Gary W. 2009. "Swing Voters, Core Voters, and Distributive Politics." In *Political Representation*, edited by Ian Shapiro, Susan C. Stokes, Elisabeth Jean Wood, and Alexander S. Kirshner, 342–57. New York: Cambridge University Press.
Crabtree, James. 2012. "Bollygarchs at Bay." *Financial Times*, June 6, 7.
Crouch, Colin. 2008. "What Will Follow the Demise of Privatised Keynesianism?" *Political Quarterly* 79 (October–December): 476–87.
———. 2009. "Privatised Keynesianism: An Unacknowledged Policy Regime." *British Journal of Politics and International Relations* 11 (August): 382–99.
———. 2011. *The Strange Non-death of Neoliberalism*. Cambridge: Polity.
Cullen, Francis T., James D. Unnever, Kristie R. Blevins, Jennifer A. Pealer, Shannon A. Santana, Bonnie S. Fisher, and Brandon K. Applegate. 2009. "The Myth of Public Support for Capital Punishment." In *Public Opinion and Criminal Justice*, edited by Jane L. Wood and Theresa A. Gannon, 73–95. Portland, OR: Willan.
Culpepper, Pepper D. 2011. *Quiet Politics and Business Power: Corporate Control in Europe and Japan*. New York: Cambridge University Press.
Cunningham, Maura Elizabeth, and Jeffrey N. Wasserstrom. 2011. "Interpreting Protest in Modern China." *Dissent* 58 (Winter): 13–18.
Dahl, Robert A. 2006. *On Political Equality*. New Haven, CT: Yale University Press.
Dahl, Robert A., and Margaret Levi. 2009. "A Conversation with Robert A. Dahl." *Annual Review of Political Science* 12: 1–9.
Dahlström, Carl. 2009. "The Bureaucratic Politics of Welfare State Crisis: Sweden in the 1990s." *Governance* 22 (April): 217–38.
Daley, Suzanne. 2012. "Spain Recoils as Its Hungry Forage Trash Bins for a Next Meal." *New York Times*, September 25, Al, A6.
Dalrymple, William. 2012. "After the Blackout." *New Statesman* 141 (October 12–18): 23–29.
Dalton, Russell, Alix van Sickle, and Steven Weldon. 2010. "The Individual-Institutional Nexus of Protest Behaviour." *British Journal of Political Science* 40 (January): 51–73.
Danopoulos, Constantine P., and Boris Znidaric. 2007. "Informal Economy, Tax Evasion, and Poverty in a Democratic Setting: Greece." *Mediterranean Quarterly* 18 (Spring): 67–84.
Das, Raju J. 2007. "Looking, but Not Seeing: The State and/as Class in Rural India." *Journal of Peasant Studies* 34 (July/October): 408–40.
Daude, Christian, and Ángel Melguizo. 2012. "Taxation and Democracy in Latin America." In *Oxford Handbook of Latin American Political Economy*, edited by Javier Santiso and Jeff Dayton-Johnson, 532–56. New York: Oxford University Press.
Davis, Deborah, and Feng Wang. 2009. "Poverty and Wealth in Postsocialist China: An Overview." In *Creating Wealth and Poverty in Postsocialist China*, edited by Deborah S. Davis and Feng Wang, 3–19. Stanford, CA: Stanford University Press.
Davis, Gerald F., and J. Adam Cobb. 2010. "Corporations and Economic Inequality around the World: The Paradox of Hierarchy." *Research in Organizational Behavior* 30: 35–53.
Deaton, Angus, and Jean Drèze. 2005. "Poverty and Inequality in India: A Re-examination." In *The Great Indian Poverty Debate*, edited by Angus Deaton and Valerie Kozel, 428–65. New Delhi: Macmillan.
Dedeoglu, Saniye. 2012. "Equality, Protection or Discrimination: Gender Equality Policies in Turkey." *Social Politics* 19 (Summer): 269–90.
De la Merced, Michael J. 2012. "Understanding Libor." *New York Times*, July 11, B4.

De la Torre, Rodolfo. 2008. "Economic Polarisation and Governability in Mexico." *Well-Being and Social Policy* 4 (1): 1–27.

Della Porta, Donatella. 2009a. "Democracy in Movement: Some Conclusions." In *Democracy in Social Movements*, edited by Donatella della Porta, 262–74. Houndmills, Basingstoke, UK: Palgrave Macmillan.

———. 2009b. "Global Justice Movement Organizations: The Organizational Population." In *Democracy in Social Movements*, edited by Donatella della Porta, 16–43. Houndmills, Basingstoke, UK: Palgrave Macmillan.

Dellepiane-Avellaneda, Sebastian. 2010. "Good Governance, Institutions and Economic Development: Beyond the Conventional Wisdom." *British Journal of Political Science* 40 (January): 195–224.

Demiralp, Seda. 2009. "The Rise of Islamic Capital and the Decline of Islamic Radicalism in Turkey." *Comparative Politics* 41 (April): 315–35.

Dent, David W. 1999. *The Legacy of the Monroe Doctrine: A Reference Guide to U.S. Involvement in Latin America and the Caribbean*. Westport, CT: Greenwood.

———. 2008. *Hot Spot Latin America*. Westport, CT: Greenwood.

Deshpande, Lalit, Anoop Kumar Satpathy, and Sudha Deshpande. 2007. "Personal Income Distribution and Heterogeneity of Labour Markets in India." *Indian Journal of Labour Economics* 50 (October–December): 903–26.

Dev, S. Mahendra, and C. Ravi. 2007. "Poverty and Inequality: All-India and States, 1983–2005." *Economic & Political Weekly* 42 (February 10): 509–21.

Dewan, Torun, and Kenneth A. Shepsle. 2008a. "Review Article: Recent Economic Perspectives on Political Economy, Part I." *British Journal of Political Science* 38 (April): 363–82.

———. 2008b. "Review Article: Recent Economic Perspectives on Political Economy, Part II." *British Journal of Political Science* 38 (July): 543–64.

Dickens, Charles. 2003. *Little Dorrit*. Rev. ed. Edited by Stephen Wall and Helen Small. London: Penguin.

Dickson, Bruce J. 2008. *Wealth into Power: The Communist Party's Embrace of China's Private Sector*. New York: Cambridge University Press.

DiMaggio, Anthony. 2011. *The Rise of the Tea Party: Political Discontent and Corporate Media in the Age of Obama*. New York: Monthly Review.

DiMaggio, Anthony, and Paul Street. 2011. "Occupy Wall Street, Mass Media and Progressive Change in the Tea Party Era." *Economic & Political Weekly* 46 (November 19): 10–14.

Di Martino, Kirsten. 2011. "China: Ensuring Equal Access to Education and Health Care for Children of Internal Migrants." In *Children without a State: A Global Human Rights Challenge*, edited by Jacqueline Bhabha, 279–305. Cambridge, MA: MIT Press.

Dinerstein, Ana Cecilia. 2007. "Workers' Factory Takeovers and New State Policies in Argentina: Towards an 'Institutionalisation' of Non-Governmental Public Action?" *Policy and Politics* 35 (July): 529–50.

DiNovella, Elizabeth. 2011. "The Group behind the Republican Takeover." *Progressive* 75 (November): 26–29.

Dion, Michelle L. 2010. *Workers and Welfare: Comparative Institutional Change in Twentieth-Century Mexico*. Pittsburgh, PA: University of Pittsburgh Press.

Dion, Michelle L., and Vicki Birchfield. 2010. "Economic Development, Income Inequality and Preferences for Redistribution." *International Studies Quarterly* 54 (June): 315–34.

Dixit, Avinash. 2009. "Governance Institutions and Economic Activity." *American Economic Review* 99 (March): 5–24.

Donaghy, Maureen M. 2011. "Do Participatory Governance Institutions Matter? Municipal Councils and Social Housing Programs in Brazil." *Comparative Politics* 44 (October): 83–102.

Dostoevsky, Fyodor. 2005. *"The Double" and "The Gambler."* Translated by Richard Pevear and Larissa Volokhonsky. New York: Vintage.

Douglas, Mary, and Steven Ney. 1998. *Missing Persons: A Critique of the Social Sciences*. Berkeley: University of California Press.

Douglas-Fairhurst, Robert. 2011. *Becoming Dickens: The Invention of a Novelist*. Cambridge, MA: Belknap.

Drake, Paul W. 2009. *Between Tyranny and Anarchy: A History of Democracy in Latin America, 1800–2006*. Stanford, CA: Stanford University Press.

Drèze, Jean, and Amartya Sen. 2013. *An Uncertain Glory: India and Its Contradictions*. Princeton, NJ: Princeton University Press.

Dumas, Charles. 2010. *Globalisation Fractures: How Major Nations' Interests Are Now in Conflict*. London: Profile.

Duménil, Gérard, and Dominique Lévy. 2011. *The Crisis of Neoliberalism*. Cambridge, MA: Harvard University Press.

Dunn, Bill. 2009a. *Global Political Economy: A Marxist Critique*. London: Pluto.

———. 2009b. "Myths of Globalisation and the New Economy." *International Socialism*, no. 121 (Winter): 75–97.

Dyer, Geoff, David Pilling, and Henny Sender. 2011. "A Strategy to Straddle the Planet." *Financial Times*, January 18, 6.

Easson, Angus. 1999. Introduction to *Little Dorrit* by Charles Dickens, xxiii–xxxv. London: J. M. Dent.

Easter, Gerald M. 2008. "Capacity, Consent and Tax Collection in Post-Communist States." In *Taxation and State-Building in Developing Countries: Capacity and Consent*, edited by Deborah A. Bräutigam, Odd-Helge Fjeldstad, and Mick Moore, 64–88. New York: Cambridge University Press.

ECLAC (Economic Commission for Latin America and the Caribbean). 2009. *Panorama Social de América Latina*. Santiago, Chile: United Nations.

———. 2011a. *Social Panorama of Latin America*. Santiago, Chile: United Nations.

———. 2011b. *Statistical Yearbook for Latin America and the Caribbean*. Santiago, Chile: United Nations.

Ehrenreich, Barbara. 2008. *Nickel and Dimed: On (Not) Getting By in America*. New York: Henry Holt.

———. 2009. "A Homespun Safety Net." *New York Times* Week in Review, July 12, 9.

Ekkehard, Ernst, and Verónica Escudero. 2008. "The Role of Financial Globalization." In *World of Work Report 2008: Income Inequalities in the Age of Financial Globalization*, 30–68. Geneva: International Institute for Labour Studies, International Labour Organization.

Ellis, Christopher. 2013. "Social Context and Economic Biases in Representation." *Journal of Politics* 75 (July): 773–86.

Ellis, Christopher, and James A. Stimson. 2012. *Ideology in America*. New York: Cambridge University Press.

Elster, Jon. 2007. *Explaining Social Behavior: More Nuts and Bolts for the Social Sciences*. New York: Cambridge University Press.

Elveren, Adem Y. 2008. "Social Security Reform in Turkey: A Critical Perspective." *Review of Radical Political Economics* 40 (Spring): 212–32.

Emrence, Cem. 2008. "After Neo-liberal Globalization: The Great Transformation of Turkey." *Comparative Sociology* 7 (1): 51–67.

Epifani, Paolo, and Gino Gancia. 2008. "The Skill Bias of World Trade." *Economic Journal* 118 (July): 927–60.

Ertuğrul, Kürşad. 2012. "AKP's Neo-Conservatism and Politics of Otherness in Europe-Turkish Relations." *New Perspectives on Turkey*, no. 46 (Spring): 157–86.

Esping-Andersen, Gøsta. 2007a. "More Inequality and Fewer Opportunities? Structural Determinants and Human Agency in the Dynamics of Income Distribution." In *Global Inequality: Patterns and Explanations*, edited by David Held and Ayse Kaya, 216–51. Cambridge: Polity.

———. 2007b. "Sociological Explanations of Changing Income Distributions." *American Behavioral Scientist* 50 (January): 639–58.

EU (European Union). 2012. *Employment and Social Developments in Europe 2011*. Brussels, Belgium: European Commission.

Evans, Peter B., and William H. Sewell Jr. 2013. "Neoliberalism: Policy Regimes, International Regimes, and Social Effects." In *Social Resilience in the Neoliberal Era*, edited by Peter A. Hall and Michèle Lamont, 35–68. New York: Cambridge University Press.

Ewing, Christina, and Stephen J. Kay. 2011. "Postretrenchment Politics: Policy Feedback in Chile's Health and Pension Reforms." *Latin American Politics and Society* 53 (Winter): 67–99.

Faiola, Anthony. 2010. "China Buys Up 'Bargain-Basement' Greece and Extends Its Global Reach." *Guardian Weekly*, June 18, 9.

Fairfield, Tasha. 2010. "Business Power and Tax Reform: Taxing Income and Profits in Chile and Argentina." *Latin American Politics and Society* 52 (Summer): 37–71.

———. 2011. "Business Power and Protest: Argentina's Agricultural Producers Protest in Comparative Context." *Studies in Comparative International Development* 46 (December): 424–53.

Fang, Lee. 2013. *The Machine: A Field Guide to the Resurgent Right*. New York: New Press.

Farrant, Andrew, Edward McPhail, and Sebastian Berger. 2012. "Preventing the 'Abuses' of Democracy: Hayek, the 'Military Usurper' and Transitional Dictatorship in Chile?" *American Journal of Economics and Sociology* 71 (July): 513–38.

Faucher-King, Florence, and Patrick Le Galès. 2010. *The New Labour Experiment: Change and Reform under Blair and Brown*. Translated by Gregory Elliott. Stanford, CA: Stanford University Press.

Fernandes, Bernardo Manaçano. 2009. "The MST and Agrarian Reform in Brazil." *Socialism and Democracy* 23 (November): 90–99.

Feygina, Irina, and Tom R. Tyler. 2009. "Procedural Justice and System-Justifying Motivations." In *Social and Psychological Bases of Ideology and System Justification*, edited by John T. Jost, Aaron C. Kay, and Hulda Thorisdottir, 351–70. New York: Oxford University Press.

Ffrench-Davis, Ricardo. 2010. *Economic Reforms in Chile: From Dictatorship to Democracy*. 2nd ed. Houndmills, Basingstoke, UK: Palgrave Macmillan.

Fieschi, Catherine, Marley Morris, and Lila Caballero. 2012. *Recapturing the Reluctant Radical: How to Win Back Europe's Populist Vote*. London: Counterpoint. http://counterpoint.uk.com/wp-content/uploads/2013/02/E-version-Recapturing-the-Reluctant-Radical-September-2012.pdf.

Finlayson, Alan. 2013. "From Blue to Green and Everything in Between: Ideational Change and Left Political Economy after New Labour." *British Journal of Politics and International Relations* 15 (February): 70–88.

Finseraas, Henning, and Kåre Vernby. 2011. "What Parties Are and What Parties Do: Partisanship and Welfare State Reform in an Era of Austerity." *Socio-Economic Review* 9 (October): 613–38.

Fitzgerald, F. Scott. 1926. "The Rich Boy." *Red Book Magazine* 46 (January): 27–32, 144, 146; 46 (February): 75–79, 122, 124–26.

———. 1945. *The Crack-Up*. Edited by Edmund Wilson. New York: New Directions.

Flores-Macías, Gustavo A. 2012. *After Neoliberalism? The Left and Economic Reforms in Latin America*. New York: Oxford University Press.

Fontana, Giuseppe, and Malcolm Sawyer. 2011. "Fiscal Austerity: Lessons from Recent Events in the British Isles." *Challenge* 54 (March/April): 42–60.

Formisano, Ronald P. 2012. *The Tea Party*. Baltimore, MD: Johns Hopkins University Press.

Förster, Michael, David Jesuit, and Timothy Smeeding. 2005. "Regional Poverty and Income Inequality in Central and Eastern Europe: Evidence from the Luxembourg Income Study." In *Spatial Inequality and Development*, edited by Ravi Kanbur and Anthony J. Venables, 211–47. New York: Oxford University Press.

Foster, John Bellamy, and Robert W. McChesney. 2012. "The Global Stagnation and China." *Monthly Review* 63 (February): 1–28.

France, Anatole. 1964. *Le lys rouge*. Paris: Calmann-Lévy.

Frank, Dana. 2012. "Honduras: Which Side Are We On?" *Nation* 294 (June 11): 11–17.

Frank, Joseph. 1995. *Dostoevsky: The Miraculous Years 1865–1871*. Princeton, NJ: Princeton University Press.

———. 2010. *Dostoevsky: A Writer in His Time*. Edited by Mary Petrusewicz. Princeton, NJ: Princeton University Press.

Franz, Barbara. 2007. "Guest Workers and Immigration Reform: The Rise of a New Federalism in America?" *New Political Science* 29 (September): 349–68.

Frazier, Mark W. 2010. *Socialist Insecurity: Pensions and the Politics of Uneven Development in China*. Ithaca, NY: Cornell University Press.

Freedom House. 2011. *Freedom in the World 2011: The Annual Survey of Political Rights & Civil Liberties*. Lanham, MD: Rowman & Littlefield.

Freeland, Chrystia. 2012. *Plutocrats: The Rise of the New Global Super-Rich and the Fall of Everyone Else*. New York: Penguin.

Freire, André. 2008. "Party Polarization and Citizens' Left-Right Orientations." *Party Politics* 14 (March): 189–209.

Frey, Ada Freytes, and Karina Crivelli. 2011. "Challenging Traditional Female Roles through Social Participation: Tensions in Women's Experiences in Argentina's Picketing Movements." In *Gender & Globalization: Patterns of Women's Resistance*, edited by Erica G. Polakoff and Ligaya Lindio-McGovern, 233–58. Whitby, ON: De Sitter Publications.

Fridberg, Torben. 2012. "Legitimacy of the System and Support for the Welfare State." In *The Future of the Welfare State: Social Policy Attitudes and Social Capital in Europe*, edited by Heikki Ervasti, Jørgen Goul Andersen, Torben Fridberg, and Kristen Ringdal, 134–52. Cheltenham, UK: Edward Elgar.

Friedman, Eli, and Ching Kwan Lee. 2010. "Remaking the World of Chinese Labour: A 30-Year Retrospective." *British Journal of Industrial Relations* 48 (September): 507–33.

Friedman, Jeffrey, and Wladimir Kraus. 2011. *Engineering the Financial Crisis: Systemic Risk and the Failure of Regulation*. Philadelphia: University of Pennsylvania Press.

Froissart, Chloé. 2009. "The Rise of Migrant Workers' Collective Actions: Toward a New Social Contract in China." In *Social Movements in China and Hong Kong: The Expansion of Protest Space*, edited by Khun Eng Kuah-Pearce and Gilles Guiheux, 155–78. Amsterdam, Netherlands: Amsterdam University Press.

Funk, Kevin. 2012. "Review Article: 'Today There Are No Indigenous People' in Chile? Connecting the Mapuche Struggle to Anti-neoliberal Mobilizations in South America." *Journal of Politics in Latin America* 4 (2): 125–40.

Galbraith, James K. 2007. "Global Inequality and Global Macro Economics." In *Global Inequality: Patterns and Explanations*, edited by David Held and Ayse Kaya, 148–75. Cambridge: Polity.

———. 2012. *Inequality and Instability: A Study of the World Economy Just before the Great Crisis*. New York: Oxford University Press.

Galbraith, James K., Sara Hsu, and Wenjie Zhang. 2009. "Beijing Bubble, Beijing Bust: Inequality, Trade, and Capital Inflow into China." *Journal of Current Chinese Affairs* 38 (2): 3–26.

Galbraith, John Kenneth. 2000. "*The Progressive* Interview." By Amitabh Pal. *The Progressive* 64 (October): 35–38.

Ganghof, Steffen. 2008. "The Politics of Tax Structure." In *Divide and Deal: The Politics of Distribution in Democracies*, edited by Ian Shapiro, Peter A. Swenson, and Daniela Donno, 72–98. New York: New York University Press.

Ganguly-Scrase, Ruchira, and Timothy J. Scrase. 2008. "Hegemony, Globalisation, and Neoliberalism: The Case of West Bengal, India." In *Hegemony: Studies in Consensus and Coercion*, edited by Richard Howson and Kylie Smith, 184–200. New York: Routledge.

Garay, Candelaria. 2007. "Social Policy and Collective Action: Unemployed Workers, Community Associations, and Protest in Argentina." *Politics & Society* 35 (June): 301–28.

Garfinkel, Irwin, Lee Rainwater, and Timothy Smeeding. 2010. *Wealth & Welfare States: Is America a Laggard or Leader?* New York: Oxford University Press.

Gaspari, Elio. 2013. "Let Them Eat Soccer." *New York Times*, June 26, A23.

Gasparini, Leonardo, Guillermo Cruces, and Leopoldo Tornarolli. 2009. "Recent Trends in Income Inequality in Latin America." Working paper, Society for the Study of Economic Inequality (ECINEQ), no. 132. Palma de Mallorca, Spain: Society for the Study of Economic Inequality. http://www.ecineq.org/milano/WP/ECINEQ2009-132.pdf.

Gasparini, Leonardo, and Nora Lustig. 2011. "The Rise and Fall of Income Inequality in Latin America." In *Oxford Handbook of Latin American Economics*, edited by José Antonio Ocampo and Jaime Ros, 691–714. New York: Oxford University Press.

Gautney, Heather. 2009. "Is Another State Possible?" In *Democracy, States, and the Struggle for Global Justice*, edited by Heather Gautney, Omar Dahbour, Ashley Dawson, and Neil Smith, 205–34. New York: Routledge.

Genschel, Philipp, and Peter Schwarz. 2011. "Tax Competition: A Literature Review." *Socio-Economic Review* 9 (April): 339–70.

Gerber, Alan S., Gregory A. Huber, David Doherty, and Conor M. Dowling. 2011. "The Big Five Personality Traits in the Political Arena." *Annual Review of Political Science* 14: 265–87.

Gerlach, Knut, and Wolfgang Meyer. 2010. "Wage Effects of Works Councils and Collective Agreements in Germany." In *Labor in the Era of Globalization*, edited by Claus Brown, Barry Eichengreen, and Michael Reich, 295–316. New York: Cambridge University Press.

Gervais, Bryan T., and Irwin L. Morris. 2012. "Reading the Tea Leaves: Understanding Tea Party Caucus Membership in the US House of Representatives." *PS: Political Science & Politics* 45 (April): 245–50.

Ghosh, Jayati. 2011. "Cash Transfers as the Silver Bullet for Poverty Reduction: A Sceptical Note." *Economic & Political Weekly* 46 (May 21): 67–71.

Gilbert, Christopher L., and David Vines. 2009. "World Bank." In *Princeton Encyclopedia of the World Economy*, edited by Kenneth A. Reinert and Ramkishen S. Rajan, 1174–80. Princeton, NJ: Princeton University Press.

Gilens, Martin. 2012. *Affluence and Influence: Economic Inequality and Political Power in America*. Princeton, NJ: Princeton University Press; New York: Russell Sage Foundation.

Giles, Chris. 2011. "Spectre of Stagnating Incomes Stalks Globe." *Financial Times*, June 28, 4.

Gillan, Michael. 2007. "Strange Company? Organised Labour and the Politics of Liberalisation in India." In *Labour, the State, Social Movements and the Challenge of Neo-liberal Globalisation*, edited by Andrew Gamble, Steve Ludlam, Andrew Taylor, and Stephen Wood, 110–28. Manchester, UK: Manchester University Press.

Glenn, John. 2008. "Global Governance and the Democratic Deficit: Stifling the Voice of the South." *Third World Quarterly* 29 (March): 217–38.

———. 2009. "Welfare Spending in an Era of Globalization: The North-South Divide." *International Relations* 23 (March): 27–50.

Glyn, Andrew. 2009. "Functional Distribution and Inequality." In *Oxford Handbook of Economic Inequality*, edited by Wiemer Salverda, Brian Nolan, and Timothy M. Smeeding, 101–26. New York: Oxford University Press.

Goldfrank, Benjamin. 2011. *Deepening Local Democracy in Latin America: Participation, Decentralization, and the Left*. University Park: Pennsylvania State University Press.

Goldfrank, Benjamin, and Andrew Schrank. 2009. "Municipal Neoliberalism and Municipal Socialism: Urban Political Economy in Latin America." *International Journal of Urban and Regional Research* 33 (June): 443–62.

Gomory, Ralph, and Richard Sylla. 2013. "The American Corporation." *Daedalus* 142 (Spring): 102–18.

Goñi, Edwin, J. Humberto López, and Luis Servén. 2011. "Fiscal Redistribution and Income Inequality in Latin America." *World Development* 39 (September): 1558–69.

Gorshkov, M. K. 2010. "The Low-Income Strata in the Social Structure of Russian Society." *Sociological Research* 49 (January–February): 41–63.

Gorton, Gary B. 2013. *Misunderstanding Financial Crises: Why We Don't See Them Coming*. New York: Oxford University Press.

Gough, Orla, and Roberta Adami. 2012. "Welfare Systems and Adequacy of Pension Benefits in Europe." *Social Policy & Society* 11 (January): 41–53.

Gourevitch, Peter. 2013. "Afterword: Yet More Hard Times? Reflections on the Great Recession in the Frame of Earlier Times." In *Politics in the New Hard Times: The Great Recession in Comparative Perspective*, edited by Miles Kahler and David A. Lake, 253–74. Ithaca, NY: Cornell University Press.

Gower, Richard, Caroline Pearce, and Kate Raworth. 2012. "Left Behind by the G20? How Inequality and Environmental Degradation Threaten to Exclude Poor People from the Benefits of Economic Growth." Oxfam Briefing Paper no. 157. Oxford, UK: Oxfam International. http://www.oxfam.org/sites/www.oxfam.org/files/bp157-left-behind-by-the-g20-190112-en.pdf.

Gramsci, Antonio. 1994. *Letters from Prison*, 2 vols. Edited by Frank Rosengarten. Translated by Raymond Rosenthal. New York: Columbia University Press.

———. 2000. *The Gramsci Reader: Selected Writings 1916–1935*. Edited by David Forgacs. New York: New York University Press.

Greenhouse, Steven. 2013. "Fighting Back against Wretched Wages." *New York Times* Sunday Review, July 28, 7.

Greenwald, Glenn. 2011. *With Liberty and Justice for Some*. New York: Metropolitan.

Griffith-Jones, Stephany. 2009. "Capital Flows to Developing Countries." In *Princeton Encyclopedia of the World Economy*, edited by Kenneth A. Reinert and Ramkishen S. Rajan, 158–63. Princeton, NJ: Princeton University Press.

Gudbrandsen, Frøy. 2010. "Partisan Influence on Immigration: The Case of Norway." *Scandinavian Political Studies* 33 (September): 248–70.

Guillén, Mauro F., and Sandra L. Suárez. 2010. "The Global Crisis of 2007–2009: Markets, Politics, and Organizations." In *Markets on Trial: The Economic Sociology of the U.S. Financial Crisis*, Research in the Sociology of Organizations, vol. 30A, edited by Michael Lounsbury and Paul M. Hirsch, 257–79 (Bingley, UK: Emerald Group).

Gulbrandsen, Trygve, and Fredrik Engelstad. 2007. "Elite Consensus on the Norwegian Welfare State Model." In *Norway in Transition: Transforming a Stable Democracy*, edited by Øyvind Østerud, 194–214. London: Routledge.

Gustafsson, Björn. 2008. "The Swedish Model in the Era of Integration and Globalisation." In *Institutions for Social Well-Being: Alternatives for Europe*, edited by Lilia Costabile, 176–97. New York: Palgrave Macmillan.

Gwartney, James, Joshua Hall, and Robert Lawson. 2010. *Economic Freedom of the World: 2010 Annual Report*. Vancouver, BC: Fraser Institute.

Ha, Eunyoung. 2012. "Globalization, Government Ideology, and Income Inequality in Developing Countries." *Journal of Politics* 74 (April): 541–57.

Hacker, Jacob S., and Paul Pierson. 2010. *Winner-Take-All Politics: How Washington Made the Rich Richer—and Turned Its Back on the Middle Class*. New York: Simon & Schuster.

Haegel, Florence. 2009. "Right-Wing Parties in France and in Europe." In *Politics in France and Europe*, edited by Pascal Perrineau and Luc Rouban, 217–33. New York: Palgrave Macmillan.

Haggard, Stephan, and Robert R. Kaufman. 2008. *Development, Democracy, and Welfare States: Latin America, East Asia, and Eastern Europe*. Princeton, NJ: Princeton University Press.

Hahnel, Robin. 2009. "Why the Market Subverts Democracy." *American Behavioral Scientist* 52 (March): 1006–22.

Haidt, Jonathan. 2012. *The Righteous Mind: Why Good People Are Divided by Politics and Religion*. New York: Pantheon.

Hakhverdian, Armèn. 2009. "Capturing Government Policy on the Left-Right Scale: Evidence from the United Kingdom, 1956–2006." *Political Studies* 57 (December): 720–45.

Hardin, Russell. 2009. "Utilitarian Aggregation." *Social Philosophy and Policy* 26 (Winter): 30–47.

Harris, Edward, and Frank Sammartino. 2011. *Trends in the Distribution of Household Income between 1979 and 2007*. Washington, DC: Congressional Budget Office.

Hart, Austin. 2010. "Death of the Partisan? Globalization and Taxation in South America, 1990–2006." *Comparative Political Studies* 43 (March): 304–28.

Hartmann, Thom. 2010. *Unequal Protection*. 2nd rev. ed. San Francisco: Berrett-Koehler.

Harvey, David. 2005. *A Brief History of Neoliberalism*. New York: Oxford University Press.

———. 2007. "Neoliberalism as Creative Destruction." *Annals of the American Academy of Political and Social Science* 610 (March): 22–44.

———. 2010. *The Enigma of Capital and the Crises of Capitalism*. London: Profile.

Haufler, Virginia. 2010. "Corporations in Zones of Conflict: Issues, Actors, and Institutions." In *Who Governs the Globe?* edited by Deborah D. Avant, Martha Finnemore, and Susan K. Sell, 102–30. New York: Cambridge University Press.

Häusermann, Silja. 2010. "Solidarity with Whom? Why Organised Labour Is Losing Ground to Continental Pension Politics." *European Journal of Political Research* 49 (March): 223–56.

Häusermann, Silja, Georg Picot, and Dominik Geering. 2013. "Review Article: Rethinking Party Politics and the Welfare State—Recent Advances in the Literature." *British Journal of Political Science* 43 (January): 221–40.

Hausmann, Ricardo, Laura D. Tyson, and Saadia Zahidi. 2012. *The Global Gender Gap Report 2012*. Geneva: World Economic Forum.

Hay, Colin. 2008. "Globalization's Impact on States." In *Global Political Economy*, 2nd ed., edited by John Ravenhill, 314–45. New York: Oxford University Press.

Hayduk, Ron. 2012. "Global Justice and the OWS: Movement Connections." *Socialism and Democracy* 26 (July): 43–50.

Hayek, Friedrich A. 1960. *The Constitution of Liberty*. Chicago: University of Chicago Press.

Hayes, Christopher. 2012. *Twilight of the Elites: America after Meritocracy*. New York: Crown.

Hayter, Susan, and Bradley Weinberg. 2011. "Mind the Gap: Collective Bargaining and Wage Inequality." In *The Role of Collective Bargaining in the Global Economy: Negotiating for Social Justice*, edited by Susan Hayter, 136–86. Cheltenham, UK: Edward Elgar.

Hayward, Clarissa Rile. 2009. "Making Interest: On Representation and Democratic Legitimacy." In *Political Representation*, edited by Ian Shapiro, Susan C. Stokes, Elisabeth Jean Wood, and Alexander S. Kirshner, 111–35. New York: Cambridge University Press.

Hein, Eckhard. 2011. "Redistribution, Global Imbalances, and the Financial and Economic Crisis: The Case for a Keynesian New Deal." *International Journal of Labour Research* 3 (1): 51–73.

Hemingway, Ernest. 1936. "The Snows of Kilimanjaro: A Long Story." *Esquire* 6 (August): 27, 194–201.

Hemmings, F. W. J. 1991. Introduction to *Germinal* by Émile Zola, v–xxii. London: Penguin.

Henry, James S. 2012. *The Price of Offshore Revisited: New Estimates for "Missing" Global Private Wealth, Income, Inequality, and Lost Taxes*. London: Tax Justice Network. http://taxjustice.net.

Hensman, Rohini. 2011. *Workers, Unions, and Global Capitalism: Lessons from India*. New York: Columbia University Press.

Hessel, Stéphane. 2011. *Time for Outrage: Indignez vous!* Translated by Marion Duvert. New York: Twelve.

Hieda, Takeshi. 2013. "Politics of Childcare Policy Beyond the Left-Right Scale: Post-industrialisation, Transformation of Party Systems and Welfare State Restructuring." *European Journal of Political Research* 52 (June): 483–511.

Hightower, Jim. 2011. "From Occupy Wall Street to Occupy Nation in Just Two Months." *Hightower Lowdown* 13 (November): 1–4.

Hildreth, R. W. 2012. "Word and Deed: A Deweyan Integration of Deliberative and Participatory Democracy." *New Political Science* 34 (September): 295–320.

Hill, Steven. 2010. *Europe's Promise: Why the European Way Is the Best Hope in an Insecure Age*. Berkeley: University of California Press.

Hille, Kathrin. 2013. "China: Citizens United." *Financial Times*, July 30, 5.

Hilton, Isabel. 2013. "Football, Riches and Protest." *New Statesman* 142 (June 28–July 4): 22–27.

Hjerm, Mikael, and Annette Schnabel. 2012. "Social Cohesion and the Welfare State: How Heterogeneity Influences Welfare State Attitudes." In *The Future of the Welfare State: Social Policy Attitudes and Social Capital in Europe*, edited by Heikki Ervasti, Jørgen Gould Andersen, Torben Fridberg, and Kristen Ringdal, 172–93. Cheltenham, UK: Edward Elgar.

Ho, Karen. 2009. *Liquidated: An Ethnography of Wall Street*. Durham, NC: Duke University Press.

Holt-Giménez, Eric, and Ray Patel. 2009. *Food Rebellions! Crisis and the Hunger for Justice*. Oxford, UK: Pambazuka.

Hook, Leslie. 2011. "Rising Fuel Prices Leave China's Drivers Stuck in First Gear." *Financial Times*, April 25, 2.

Hope, Kerin. 2012. "Grim Effects of Austerity Show on the Streets of Greece." *Financial Times*, February 18/19, 2.

Hopkin, Jonathan, and Mark Blyth. 2012. "What Can Okun Teach Polanyi? Efficiency, Regulation and Equality in the OECD." *Review of International Political Economy* 19 (February): 1–33.

Houlder, Vanessa. 2013. "Momentum Builds for Tax Transparency." *Financial Times*, June 17, 2.

Howard, Christopher. 2009. "Making Taxes the Life of the Party." In *The New Fiscal Sociology: Taxation in Comparative and Historical Perspective*, edited by Isaac William Martin, Ajak K. Mehrotra, and Monica Prasad, 86–100. New York: Cambridge University Press.

Huang, Yasheng. 2008. *Capitalism with Chinese Characteristics: Entrepreneurship and the State*. New York: Cambridge University Press.

———. 2011. "China: Getting the Rural Issues Right." In *New Ideas on Development after the Financial Crisis*, edited by Nancy Birdsall and Francis Fukuyama, 85–110. Baltimore, MD: Johns Hopkins University Press.

Huber, Evelyne, Thomas Mustillo, and John D. Stephens. 2008. "Politics and Social Spending in Latin America." *Journal of Politics* 70 (April): 420–36.

Huber, Evelyne, François Nielsen, Jenny Pribble, and John D. Stephens. 2006. "Politics and Inequality in Latin America and the Caribbean." *American Sociological Review* 71 (December): 943–63.

Huber, Evelyne, Jennifer Pribble, and John D. Stephens. 2010. "The Chilean Left in Power: Achievements, Failures, and Omissions." In *Leftist Governments in Latin America: Successes and Shortcomings*, edited by Kurt Weyland, Raúl L. Madrid, and Wendy Hunter, 77–97. New York: Cambridge University Press.

Huber, Evelyne, and John D. Stephens. 2012. *Democracy and the Left: Social Policy and Inequality in Latin America*. Chicago: University of Chicago Press.

Hufbauer, Gary Clyde, and Kati Suominen. 2010. *Globalization at Risk: Challenges to Finance and Trade*. New Haven, CT: Yale University Press.

Hung, Ho-Fung. 2011. "Sinomania: Global Crisis, China's Crisis?" In *Socialist Register 2012: The Crisis and the Left*, edited by Leo Panitch, Greg Albo, and Vivek Chibber, 217–34. New York: Monthly Review.

Hunter, Wendy. 2010. *The Transformation of the Workers' Party in Brazil, 1989–2009*. New York: Cambridge University Press.

———. 2011. "Brazil: The PT in Power." In *The Resurgence of the Latin American Left*, edited by Steven Levitsky and Kenneth Roberts, 306–24. Baltimore, MD: Johns Hopkins University Press.

Hurst, William, and Christian Sorace. 2011. "Recession and the Politics of Class and Production in China." *New Political Science* 33 (December): 509–24.

Hutton, Will. 2010. *Them and Us: Changing Britain—Why We Need a Fair Society*. London: Little, Brown.

Ide, Eisaku, and Sven Steinmo. 2009. "The End of the Strong State? On the Evolution of Japanese Tax Policy." In *The New Fiscal Sociology: Taxation in Comparative and Historical Perspective*, edited by Isaac William Martin, Ajay K. Mehrotra, and Monica Prasad, 119–37. New York: Cambridge University Press.

ILO (International Labour Organization). 2013. *World of Work Report 2013: Repairing the Economic and Social Fabric*. Geneva: International Institute for Labour Studies.

IMF (International Monetary Fund). 2012a. *International Financial Statistics Yearbook 2012*. Washington, DC: International Monetary Fund.

———. 2012b. *World Economic Outlook: Coping with High Debt and Sluggish Growth*, no. 2 (October). Washington, DC: International Monetary Fund.

Ingham, Geoffrey. 2008. *Capitalism*. Cambridge: Polity.

Inglehart, Ronald, and Christian Welzel. 2009. "How Development Leads to Democracy: What We Know about Modernization." *Foreign Affairs* 88 (March/April): 33–48.

Irvin, George. 2011. "Inequality and Recession in Britain and the USA." *Development and Change* 42 (January): 154–82.

Ivanova, Maria. 2007. "Inequality and Government Policies in Central and Eastern Europe." *East European Quarterly* 41 (June): 167–204.

Iversen, Torben. 2009. "Capitalism and Democracy." In *Oxford Handbook of Political Science*, edited by Robert E. Goodin, 826–48. New York: Oxford University Press.

Iyengar, Shanto. 2011. *Media Politics: A Citizen's Guide*. 2nd ed. New York: W. W. Norton.

Iyengar, Sheena. 2010. *The Art of Choosing*. New York: Hachette.

Jacobs, Andrew. 2010. "Workers Let Go by China's Banks Putting Up Fight." *New York Times*, August 16, A1, A6.

———. 2012. "Protesters Become Voters in Chinese Village." *New York Times*, February 2, A4.

Jaeger, Mads Meier. 2009. "United but Divided: Welfare Regimes and the Level and Variance in Public Support for Redistribution." *European Sociological Review* 25 (December): 723–37.

Jenkins, Patrick, John Gapper, and Brooke Masters. 2012. "The Gathering Storm." *Financial Times*, June 30/July 1, 7.

Jenkins, Patrick, and Brooke Masters. 2011. "Banks: Again under Strain." *Financial Times*, July 8, 7.

Jenkins, Patrick, Brooke Masters, and Tom Braithwaite. 2011. "The Future of Banking: Hunt for a Common Front." *Financial Times*, September 8, 9.

Jensen, Carsten. 2008. "Worlds of Welfare Services and Transfers." *Journal of European Social Policy* 18 (May): 151–62.

———. 2010. "Issue Compensation and Right-Wing Government Social Spending." *European Journal of Political Research* 49 (March): 282–99.

———. 2011. "Conditional Contraction: Globalisation and Capitalist Systems." *European Journal of Political Research* 50 (March): 168–99.

Jie, Lei, and Alan Walker. 2013. "The Big Society in China: A Failed Experiment." *Social Policy & Society* 12 (January): 17–30.

Jiménez-Huerta, Mariana. 2008. "Neoliberal Restructuring, Financialisation and Socio-political Competition in Argentina: The Convertibility System and the Contradictory Outcomes of Dollarisation, 1989–2001." *Contemporary Politics* 14 (September): 335–55.

Joas, Hans, and Wolfgang Knöbl. 2009. *Social Theory: Twenty Introductory Lectures*. Translated by Alex Skinner. New York: Cambridge University Press.

Johnston, Hank. 2009. "Protest Cultures: Performance, Artifacts, and Ideations." In *Culture, Social Movements, and Protest*, edited by Hank Johnston, 3–29. Surrey, UK: Ashgate.

Jones, Michael D. 2011. "Leading the Way to Compromise? Cultural Theory and Climate Change Opinion." *PS: Political Science & Politics* 44 (October): 720–25.

Jones, Robert P., Daniel Cox, E. J. Dionne Jr., William A. Galston, and Juhem Navarro-Rivera. 2012. *The 2012 American Values Survey*. Washington, DC: Public Religion Research Institute. http://publicreligion.org/site/wp-content/uploads/2012/10/AVS-2012-Pre-election-Report-for-Web.pdf.

Jost, John T., Christopher M. Federico, and Jaime L. Napier. 2009. "Political Ideology: Its Structure, Functions, and Elective Affinities." *Annual Review of Psychology* 60: 307–37.

Jost, John T., and Aaron C. Kay. 2010. "Social Justice." In *Handbook of Social Psychology*, 5th ed., edited by Susan T. Fiske, Daniel T. Gilbert, and Gardner Lindzey, 1122–65. Hoboken, NJ: Wiley.

Joyce, Joseph P. 2009a. "International Monetary Fund (IMF)." In *Princeton Encyclopedia of the World Economy*, edited by Kenneth A. Reinert and Ramkishen S. Rajan, 686–90. Princeton, NJ: Princeton University Press.

———. 2009b. "International Monetary Fund Conditionality." In *Princeton Encyclopedia of the World Economy*, edited by Kenneth A. Reinert and Ramkishen S. Rajan, 690–93. Princeton, NJ: Princeton University Press.

Jung, Chang Lyul, and Alan Walker. 2009. "The Impact of Neo-liberalism on South Korea's Public Pension: A Political Economy of Pension Reform." *Social Policy & Administration* 43 (October): 425–44.

Kääriäinen, Juha, and Heikki Lehtonen. 2006. "The Variety of Social Capital in Welfare State Regimes—A Comparative Study of 21 Countries." *European Societies* 8 (March): 27–57.

Kahneman, Daniel. 2011. *Thinking, Fast and Slow*. New York: Farrar, Straus & Giroux.

Kalinowski, Thomas. 2009. "The Politics of Market Reform: Korea's Path from Chaebol Republic to Market Democracy and Back." *Contemporary Politics* 15 (September): 287–304.

Kalleberg, Arne L. 2006. "Nonstandard Employment Relations and Labour Market Inequality: Cross-national Patterns." In *Inequalities of the World*, edited by Göran Therborn, 136–62. London: Verso.

———. 2009. "Precarious Work, Insecure Workers: Employment Relations in Transition." *American Sociological Review* 74 (February): 1–22.

Kang, Susan L. 2012. *Human Rights and Labor Solidarity: Trade Unions in the Global Economy*. Philadelphia: University of Pennsylvania Press.

Kaplan, Steven N., and Joshua Rauh. 2010. "Wall Street and Main Street: What Contributes to the Rise in the Highest Incomes?" *Review of Financial Studies* 23 (March): 1004–50.

Karapin, Roger. 2007. *Protest Politics in Germany: Movements on the Left and Right since the 1960s*. University Park: Pennsylvania State University Press.

Karpowitz, Christopher F., J. Quin Monson, Kelly D. Patterson, and Jeremy C. Pope. 2011. "Tea Time in America? The Impact of the Tea Party Movement on the 2010 Midterm Elections." *PS: Political Science & Politics* 44 (April): 303–9.

Karriem, Abdurazack. 2009. "The Brazilian Landless Movement: Mobilization for Transformative Politics." In *Hegemonic Transitions, the State and Crisis in Neoliberal Capitalism*, edited by Yildiz Atasoy, 262–80. London: Routledge.

Kaufman, Robert R. 2007. "Market Reform and Social Protection: Lessons from the Czech Republic, Hungary, and Poland." *East European Politics and Societies* 21 (February): 111–25.

Kay, Cristóbal. 2008. "Latin America's Rural Transformation: Unequal Development and Persistent Poverty." In *Capital, Power, and Inequality in Latin America and the Caribbean*, new ed., edited by Richard L. Harris and Jorge Nef, 24–48. Lanham, MD: Rowman & Littlefield.

Kaya, Yunus. 2008. "Proletarianization with Polarization: Industrialization, Globalization, and Social Class in Turkey, 1980–2005." *Research in Social Stratification and Mobility* 26 (June): 161–81.

Kazmin, Amy. 2012. "Little Reward in Sight for Army of Poor Labourers Building the New India." *Financial Times*, November 1, 8.

Kelly, Gavin. 2011. "The Recession Is Over. The Real Pain Starts Now." *New Statesman* 140 (January 10): 24–27.

Kentor, Jeffrey, Andrew K. Jorgenson, and Edward Kick. 2012. "The 'New' Military and Income Inequality: A Cross National Analysis." *Social Science Research* 41 (May): 514–26.

Kenworthy, Lane. 2008. *Jobs with Equality*. New York: Oxford University Press.

———. 2009. "The Effect of Public Opinion on Social Policy Generosity." *Socio-Economic Review* 7 (October): 727–40.

———. 2011. *Progress for the Poor*. New York: Oxford University Press.

Keyder, Caglar. 2011. "Crisis, Underconsumption, and Social Policy." In *Business as Usual: The Roots of the Global Financial Meltdown*, edited by Craig Calhoun and Georgi Derluguian, 159–83. New York: New York University Press.

Keynes, John Maynard. 1924. "Alfred Marshall, 1842–1924." *Economic Journal* 34 (September): 311–72.

———. 1971a. *A Tract on Monetary Reform*. Vol. 4 of *Collected Writings of John Maynard Keynes*. London: Macmillan.

———. 1971b. *A Treatise on Money*. Vol. 5 of *Collected Writings*. London: Macmillan.

———. 1972. *Essays in Persuasion*. Vol. 9 of *Collected Writings*. London: Macmillan.

———. 1973a. *The General Theory and After: Part I, Preparation*. Vol. 13 of *Collected Writings*. Edited by Donald Moggridge. London: Macmillan.

———. 1973b. *The General Theory and After: Part II, Defence and Development*. Vol. 14 of *Collected Writings*. Edited by Donald Moggridge. London: Macmillan.

———. 1973c. *The General Theory of Employment, Interest, and Money*.Vol. 7 of *Collected Writings*. London: Macmillan.

———. 1978. *Activities 1939–1945: Internal War Finance*. Vol. 22 of *Collected Writings*. Edited by Donald Moggridge. London: Mamcillan.

———. 1979. *The General Theory and After: A Supplement*. Vol. 29 of *Collected Writings*. Edited by Donald Moggridge. London: Macmillan.

———. 1980a. *Activities 1940–1944: Shaping the Post-war World: The Clearing Union*. Vol. 25 of *Collected Writings*. Edited by Donald Moggridge. London: Macmillan.

———. 1980b. *Activities 1940–1946: Shaping the Post-War World: Employment and Commodities*. Vol. 27 of *Collected Writings*. Edited by Donald Moggridge. London: Macmillan.

———. 1980c. *Activities 1941–1946: Shaping the Post-war World: Bretton Woods and Reparations*. Vol. 26 of *Collected Writings*. Edited by Donald Moggridge. London: Macmillan.

———. 1980d. *Activities 1944–1946: The Transition to Peace*. Vol. 24 of *Collected Writings*. Edited by Donald Moggridge. London: Macmillan.

———. 1981a. *Activities 1922–1929: The Return to Gold and Industrial Policy*. Vol. 19 of *Collected Writings*. Edited by Donald Moggridge. London: Macmillan.

———. 1981b. *Activities 1929–1931: Rethinking Employment and Unemployment Policies*. Vol. 20 of *Collected Writings*. Edited by Donald Moggridge. London: Macmillan.

———. 1982a. *Activities 1931–1939: World Crises and Policies in Britain and America*. Vol. 21 of *Collected Writings*. Edited by Donald Moggridge. London: Macmillan.

———. 1982b. *Social, Political and Literary Writings*. Vol. 28 of *Collected Writings*. Edited by Donald Moggridge. London: Macmillan.

———. 1983. *Economic Articles and Correspondence Investment and Editorial*. Vol. 12 of *Collected Writings*. Edited by Donald Moggridge. London: Macmillan.

Kiely, Ray. 2007. "Poverty Reduction through Liberalisation? Neoliberalism and the Myth of Global Convergence." *Review of International Studies* 33 (July): 415–34.

Kim, Hee-Kang. 2009. "Analyzing the Gender Division of Labor: The Cases of the United States and South Korea." *Asian Perspective* 33 (2): 181–229.

Kim, Myunghee, and Mychal Voorhees. 2011. "Government Effectiveness and Institutional Trust in Japan, South Korea, and China." *Asian Politics & Policy* 3 (July): 413–32.

Kim, Pil Ho. 2010. "The East Asian Welfare State Debate and Surrogate Social Policy: An Exploratory Study on Japan and South Korea." *Socio-Economic Review* 8 (July): 411–35.

Kim, Richard. 2011. "The Audacity of Occupy Wall Street." *Nation* 293 (November 21): 15–21.

Kim, Sangjoon. 2010. "Globalisation and Individuals: The Political Economy of South Korea's Educational Expansion." *Journal of Contemporary Asia* 40 (May 2010): 309–28.

Kim, Taekyoon. 2008. "The Social Construction of Welfare Control: A Sociological Review on State-Voluntary Sector Links in Korea." *International Sociology* 23 (November): 819–44.

Kim, Taekyoon, Huck-Ju Kwon, Jooha Lee, and Ilcheong Yi. 2012. "'Mixed Governance' and Welfare in South Korea." In *Poverty, Inequality, and Democracy*, edited by Francis Fukuyama, Larry Diamond, and Marc F. Plattner, 168–82. Baltimore, MD: Johns Hopkins University Press.

Kinder, Donald R., and Cindy D. Kam. 2009. *Us against Them: Ethnocentric Boundaries of American Opinion*. Chicago: University of Chicago Press.

King, Brayden G., and Nicholas A. Pearce. 2010. "The Contentiousness of Markets: Politics, Social Movements, and Institutional Change in Markets." *Annual Review of Sociology* 36: 249–67.

Kisby, Ben. 2010. "The Big Society: Power to the People?" *Political Quarterly* 81 (October–December): 484–91.

Kivinen, Markku. 2006. "Classes in the Making? The Russian Social Structure in Transition." In *Inequalities of the World*, edited by Göran Therborn, 247–94. London: Verso.

Klandermans, Bert, Jojanneke van der Toorn, and Jacquelien van Stekelenburg. 2008. "Embeddedness and Identity: How Immigrants Turn Grievances into Action." *American Sociological Review* 73 (December): 992–1012.

Klasen, Stephan, and Felicitas Nowak-Lehmann. 2009. "Poverty, Inequality, and Policy in Latin America: An Introduction." In *Poverty, Inequality, and Policy in Latin America*, edited by Stephan Klasen and Felicitas Nowak-Lehmann, 1–16. Cambridge, MA: MIT Press.

Kogan, Irena. 2006. "Labor Markets and Economic Incorporation among Recent Immigrants in Europe." *Social Forces* 85 (December): 697–721.

Kohli, Atul. 2012. *Poverty Amid Plenty in the New India*. New York: Cambridge University Press.

Kohn, Margaret. 2013. "Privatization and Protest: Occupy Wall Street, Occupy Toronto, and the Occupation of Public Space in a Democracy." *Perspectives on Politics* 11 (March): 99–110.

Kolb, Felix. 2007. *Protest and Opportunities: The Political Outcomes of Social Movements*. New York: Campus Verlag.

Kollmeyer, Christopher. 2009. "Explaining Deindustrialization: How Affluence, Productivity Growth, and Globalization Diminish Manufacturing Employment." *American Journal of Sociology* 114 (May): 1644–74.

Kontogiannis, Dimitris. 2010. "Athens Hopes Deep Cuts Will Restore Confidence." *Financial Times*, March 4, 2.

Koopmans, Ruud, Ines Michalowski, and Stine Waibel. 2012. "Citizenship Rights for Immigrants: National Political Processes and Cross-national Convergence in Western Europe, 1980–2008." *American Journal of Sociology* 117 (January): 1202–45.

Korzeniewicz, Roberto Patricio, and Timothy Patrick Moran. 2009. *Unveiling Inequality: A World-Historical Perspective*. New York: Russell Sage Foundation.

Kotz, David M., and Terrence McDonough. 2010. "Global Neoliberalism and the Contemporary Social Structure of Accumulation." In *Contemporary Capitalism and Its Crises: Social Structure of Accumulation Theory for the 21st Century*, edited by Terrence McDonough, Michael Reich, and David M. Kotz, 93–120. New York: Cambridge University Press.

Kouvelakis, Stathis. 2011. "The Greek Cauldron." *New Left Review*, no. 72 (November–December): 17–32.

Kramer, Andrew E., and David M. Herszenhorn. 2012. "Midas Touch in St. Petersburg: Friends of Putin Glow Brightly." *New York Times*, March 2, A1, A10.

Kramer, Andrew E., and Floyd Norris. 2013. "G-20 Backs Plan to Curb Corporate Tax Strategy." *New York Times*, July 20, B1, B2.

Kregel, Jan. 2009. "Bretton Woods System." In *Princeton Encyclopedia of the World Economy*, edited by Kenneth A. Reinert and Ramkishen S. Rajan, 141–45. Princeton, NJ: Princeton University Press.

Krishna, Anirudh. 2009. "Why Don't 'the Poor' Make Common Cause? The Importance of Subgroups." *Journal of Development Studies* 45 (July): 947–65.

Krishnan, Raghu, and Adrien Thomas. 2007. "Resistance to Neoliberalism in France." In *Socialist Register 2008: Global Flashpoints*, edited by Leo Panitch and Colin Leys, 295–314. New York: Monthly Review.

Kristal, Tali. 2010. "Good Times, Bad Times: Postwar Labor's Share of National Income in Capitalist Democracies." *American Sociological Review* 75 (October): 729–63.

Krugman, Paul. 2009. *The Return of Depression Economics and the Crisis of 2008*. New York: W. W. Norton.

———. 2012. *End This Depression Now!* New York: W. W. Norton.

———. 2013. "How the Case for Austerity Has Crumbled." *New York Review of Books* 60 (June 6): 67–68, 72–73.

Kuk, Min-Ho. 2010. "Consolidation of the Developmental State and Chaebols in Korea: After the 1997 Economic Crisis." *Korean Journal of Sociology* 44 (June): 91–110.

Kulin, Joakim, and Stevan Svallfors. 2013. "Class, Values, and Attitudes towards Redistribution: A European Comparison." *European Sociological Review* 29 (April): 155–67.

Kurtz, Marcus J., and Sarah M. Brooks. 2008. "Embedding Neoliberal Reform in Latin America." *World Politics* 60 (January): 231–80.

Kuttner, Robert. 2011. "History's Missed Moment." *American Prospect* 22 (October): 18–25.

Kwack, Sung Yeung, and Young Sun Lee. 2007. "The Distribution and Polarization of Income in Korea, 1965–2005: A Historical Analysis." *Journal of Economic Development* 32 (December): 1–39.

Kyrrä, Tomi, and Mika Maliranta. 2008. "The Micro-level Dynamics of Declining Labour Share: Lessons from the Finnish Great Leap." *Industrial and Corporate Change* 17 (December): 1147–72.

Lacey, Nicola. 2010. "American Imprisonment in Comparative Perspective." *Daedalus* 139 (Summer): 102–14.

Lafer, Gordon. 2013. "The Legislative Attack on American Wages and Labor Standards, 2011–2012." EPI Briefing Paper, no. 364. Washington, DC: Economic Policy Institute.

LaFraniere, Sharon. 2011. "Lead Poisoning in China: The Hidden Scourge." *New York Times*, June 15, A1, A10.

Lahusen, Christian. 2013. "The Protests of the Unemployed in France, Germany, and Sweden (1994–2004): Protest Dynamics and Political Contexts." *Social Movement Studies* 12 (January): 1–22.

Lakoff, George. 2008. *The Political Mind*. New York: Viking.

Lamont, James. 2011a. "Farmers Reap Little Despite Rising Food Crises." *Financial Times*, March 1, 7.

———. 2011b. "Strong Growth Yet to Improve Lives of the Poor." *Financial Times Special Report*, January 27, 1.

Lamont, James, and James Fontanella-Khan. 2011. "Writing Is on the Wall." *Financial Times*, March 22, 7.

Lanchester, John. 2010. *I.O.U.: Why Everyone Owes Everyone and No One Can Pay*. New York: Simon & Schuster.

———. 2013a. "Are We Having Fun Yet? On the Banks' Barely Believable Behaviour." *London Review of Books* 35 (July 4): 3–8.

———. 2013b. "Let's Consider Kate: What Is to Be Done about the Banks." *London Review of Books* 35 (July 18): 3–8.

Lansley, Stewart. 2011. *The Cost of Inequality*. London: Gibson Square.

Lanzaro, Jorge. 2011. "Uruguay: A Social Democratic Government in Latin America." In *The Resurgence of the Latin American Left*, edited by Steven Levitsky and Kenneth M. Roberts, 348–74. Baltimore, MD: Johns Hopkins University Press.

Larsen, Christian Albrekt, and Jørgen Goul Andersen. 2009. "How New Economic Ideas Changed the Danish Welfare State: The Case of Neoliberal Ideas and Highly Organized Social Democratic Interests." *Governance* 22 (April): 239–61.

Lavaca Collective. 2007. *Sin Patrón: Stories from Argentina's Worker-Run Factories*. Chicago: Haymarket.

Lawson, Tony. 2009. "The Current Economic Crisis: Its Nature and the Course of Academic Economics." *Cambridge Journal of Economics* 33 (July): 759–77.

Leahy, Joe. 2013. "Brazil: The Power of the Streets." *Financial Times*, June 22/23, 5.

Leamer, Edward E. 2010. "What Have Changes to the Global Markets for Goods and Services Done to the Viability of the Swedish Welfare State?" In *Reforming the Welfare State: Recovery and Beyond in Sweden*, edited by Richard B. Freeman, Birgitta Swedenborg, and Robert Topel, 285–325. Chicago: University of Chicago Press.

LeBaron, Genevieve, and Adrienne Roberts. 2012. "Confining Social Insecurity: Neoliberalism and the Rise of the 21st Century Debtors' Prison." *Politics & Gender* 8 (March): 25–49.

Ledeneva, Alena V. 2013. *Can Russia Modernise? Sistema, Power Networks and Informal Governance*. New York: Cambridge University Press.

Lee, Chang Hee, and Mingwei Liu. 2011. "Collective Bargaining in Transition: Measuring the Effects of Collective Voice in China." In *The Role of Collective Bargaining in the Global Economy: Negotiating for Social Justice*, edited by Susan Hayter, 205–26. Cheltenham, UK: Edward Elgar.

Lee, Cheol-Sung, Young-Bum Kim, and Jae-Mahn Shim. 2011. "The Limit of Equality Projects: Public-Sector Expansion, Sectoral Conflicts, and Income Inequality in Postindustrial Economies." *American Sociological Review* 76 (February): 100–124.

Lee, Cheol-Sung, François Nielsen, and Arthur S. Alderson. 2007. "Income Inequality, Global Economy, and the State." Social Forces 86 (Spring): 77–111.

Lee, Ching Kwan. 2010. "Workers and the Quest for Citizenship." In *Reclaiming Chinese Society: The New Social Activism*, edited by You-tien Hsing and Ching Kwan Lee, 42–63. London: Routledge.

Lee, Ching Kwan, and Yonghong Zhang. 2013. "The Power of Instability: Unraveling the Microfoundations of Bargained Authoritarianism in China." *American Journal of Sociology* 118 (May): 1475–1508.

Lee, Taeku, and Nicole Willcoxon. 2011. "Race, Public Opinion, the Media." In *Oxford Handbook of American Public Opinion and the Media*, edited by Robert Y. Shapiro and Lawrence R. Jacobs, 605–21. New York: Oxford University Press.

Lee, Yeonho, Sukku Chung, and Haehyun Jang. 2008. "Labor and Politics in East Asia: The Case of Failure of the Encompassing Labor Organization in Korea." *Asian Perspective* 32 (3): 111–38.

Legatum Institute. 2010. *Legatum Prosperity Index*. London: Legatum Institute.

Leigh, Andrew. 2009. "Top Incomes." In *Oxford Handbook of Economic Inequality*, edited by Wiemer Salverda, Brian Nolan, and Timothy M. Smeeding, 150–74. New York: Oxford University Press.

Leiva, Fernando Ignacio. 2008. *Latin American Neostructuralism: The Contradictions of Post-Neoliberal Development*. Minneapolis: University of Minnesota Press.

Lepianka, Dorota, John Gelissen, and Wim van Oorschot. 2010. "Popular Explanations for Poverty in Europe: Effects of Contextual and Individual Characteristics across 28 European Countries." *Acta Sociologica* 53 (March): 53–72.

Lethbridge, Robert. 1993. Introduction to *Germinal* by Émile Zola, vii–xxviii. New York: Oxford University Press.

Levine, Lawrence W., and Cornelia R. Levine. 2010. *The Fireside Conversations: America Responds to FDR during the Great Depression*. Berkeley: University of California Press.

Levitsky, Steven, and Kenneth M. Roberts. 2011. "Latin America's 'Left Turn': A Framework for Analysis." In *The Resurgence of the Latin American Left*, edited by Steven Levitsky and Kenneth M. Roberts, 1–28. Baltimore, MD: Johns Hopkins University Press.

Levy, Santiago, and Norbert Schady. 2013. "Latin America's Social Policy Challenge: Education, Social Insurance, Redistribution." *Journal of Economic Perspectives* 27 (Spring): 193–218.

Lewis-Beck, Michael S., William G. Jacoby, Helmut Norpoth, and Herbert F. Weisberg. 2008. *The American Voter Revisited*. Ann Arbor: University of Michigan Press.

Li, Lianjiang, and Kevin J. O'Brien. 2010. "Protest Leadership in Rural China." In *Chinese Politics: State, Society and the Market*, edited by Peter Hays Gries and Stanley Rosen, 85–108. London: Routledge.

Lim, Haeran. 2009. "Democratization and the Transformation Process in East Asian Developmental States: Financial Reform in Korea and Taiwan." *Asian Perspective* 33 (1): 75–110.

———. 2010. "The Transformation of the Developmental State and Economic Reform in Korea." *Journal of Contemporary Asia* 40 (May): 188–210.

Lin, Ken-Hou, and Donald Tomaskovic-Devey. 2013. "Financialization and U.S. Income Inequality, 1970–2008." *American Journal of Sociology* 118 (March): 1284–1329.

Lin, Tun, Juzhong Zhuang, Damaris Yarcia, and Fen Lin. 2008. "Income Inequality in the People's Republic of China and Its Decomposition: 1990–2004." *Asian Development Review* 25 (June–December): 119–36.

———. 2010. "Decomposing Income Inequality: People's Republic of China, 1990–2005." In *Poverty, Inequality, and Inclusive Growth in Asia: Measurement, Policy Issues, and Country Studies*, edited by Juzhong Zhuang, 367–86. London: Anthem.

Lindvall, Johannes. 2012. "Politics and Policies in Two Economic Crises: The Nordic Countries." In *Coping with Crisis: Government Reactions to the Great Recession*, edited by Nancy Bermeo and Jonas Pontusson, 233–60. New York: Russell Sage Foundation.

Lipset, Seymour Martin, and Jason M. Lakin. 2004. *The Democratic Century*. Norman: University of Oklahoma Press.

Liptak, Adam. 2010. "Justices Offer Receptive Ear to Business Interests." *New York Times*, December 19, 1, 32.

Liptak, Adam, and Allison Kopicki. 2012. "Public's Opinion of Supreme Court Drops after Health Care Law Decision." *New York Times*, July 19, A21.

Lloyd-Sherlock, Peter. 2009. "Social Policy and Inequality in Latin America: A Review of Recent Trends." *Social Policy & Administration* 43 (August): 347–63.

Loera, Nashieli Rangel. 2010. "'Encampment Time': An Anthropological Analysis of the Land Occupations in Brazil." *Journal of Peasant Studies* 37 (April): 285–318.

López-Calva, Luis F., and Nora Lustig. 2010. "Explaining the Decline in Inequality in Latin America: Technological Change, Educational Upgrading, and Democracy." In *Declining Inequality in Latin America: A Decade of Progress?* edited by Luis F. López-Calva and Nora Lustig, 1–24. Washington, DC: Brookings.

Loveless, Matthew, and Stephen Whitefield. 2011. "Being Unequal and Seeing Inequality: Explaining the Political Significance of Social Inequality in New Market Economies." *European Journal of Political Research* 50 (March): 239–66.

Loveman, Brian. 2001. *Chile: The Legacy of Hispanic Capitalism*. 3rd ed. New York: Oxford University Press.

———. 2010. *No Higher Law: American Foreign Policy and the Western Hemisphere since 1776*. Chapel Hill: University of North Carolina Press.

Loveman, Mara. 1998. "High-Risk Collective Action: Defending Human Rights in Chile, Uruguay, and Argentina." *American Journal of Sociology* 104 (September): 477–525.

Lovett, Frank. 2009. "Domination and Distributive Justice." *Journal of Politics* 71 (July): 817–30.

Loyalka, Michelle Dammon. 2012. *Eating Bitterness: Stories from the Front Lines of China's Great Urban Migration*. Berkeley: University of California Press.

Lum, Thomas. 2011. *Human Rights in China and U.S. Policy*. Washington, DC: Congressional Research Service.

Lund, Roger D. 1982. "Genteel Fictions: Caricature and Satirical Design in *Little Dorrit*." In *Dickens Studies Annual: Essays on Victorian Fiction*, vol. 10, edited by Michal Timko, Fred Kaplan, and Edward Guiliano, 45–66. New York: AMS.

Lundestad, Geir. 2012. *The Rise & Decline of the American "Empire": Power and Its Limits in Comparative Perspective*. New York: Oxford University Press.

Lustig, Nora, Luis F. López-Calva, and Eduardo Ortiz-Juarez. 2013. "Declining Inequality in Latin America in the 2000s: The Cases of Argentina, Brazil, and Mexico." *World Development* 44 (April): 129–41.

Lustig, Nora, Carola Pessino, and John Scott. 2013. "The Impact of Taxes and Social Spending on Inequality and Poverty in Argentina, Bolivia, Brazil, Mexico, Peru and Uruguay: An Overview." CEQ Working Paper No. 13. Washington, DC: Commitment to Equity Project. http://www.commitmentoequity.org.

Lutz, Catherine. 2009. "Introduction: Bases, Empire, and Global Response." In *The Bases of Empire: The Global Struggle against U. S. Military Bases*, edited by Catherine Lutz, 1–44. New York: New York University Press.

Lyall, Sarah, and Alan Cowell. 2010. "Britain Plans Deepest Cuts to Spending in 60 Years." *New York Times*, October 21, A6.

Lynch, James P., and William Alex Pridemore. 2011. "Crime in International Perspective." In *Crime and Public Policy*, edited by James Q. Wilson and Joan Petersilia, 5–52. New York: Oxford University Press.

MacKenzie, Donald. 2013. "The Magic Lever: How the Big Banks Get Away with It." *London Review of Books* 35 (May 9): 16–19.

Maddison, Angus. 2006. *The World Economy*. Paris: OECD.

———. 2007a. *Chinese Economic Performance in the Long Run*. 2nd rev. ed. Paris: OECD.

———. 2007b. *Contours of the World Economy, 1–2030 AD: Essays in Macro-Economic History*. New York: Oxford University Press.

Madrid, Raúl L., Wendy Hunter, and Kurt Weyland. 2010. "The Policies and Performance of the Contemporary and Moderate Left." In *Leftist Governments in Latin America: Successes and Shortcomings*, edited by Kurt Weyland, Raúl Madrid, and Wendy Hunter, 140–80. New York: Cambridge University Press.

Mahoney, James. 2010. *Colonialism and Postcolonial Development: Spanish America in Comparative Perspective*. New York: Cambridge University Press.

Mainwaring, Scott, and Timothy R. Scully. 2010. "Democratic Governance in Latin America: Eleven Lessons from Recent Experience." In *Democratic Governance in Latin America*, edited by Scott Mainwaring and Timothy R. Scully, 365–97. Stanford, CA: Stanford University Press.

Majumder, Rajarshi. 2007. "Earning Differentials across Social Groups: Evidence from India." *Indian Journal of Labour Economics* 50 (October–December): 943–53.

Makarenko, Boris I. 2012. "The Post-Soviet Party of Power: United Russia in Comparative Perspective." *Russian Social Science Review* 53 (July–August): 27–56.

Malleson, Tom. 2013. "Economic Democracy: The Left's Big Idea for the Twenty-First Century?" *New Political Science* 35 (March): 84–108.

Mallet, Victor, Lionel Barber, and Mark Mulligan. 2010. "A Legacy in Limbo." *Financial Times*, April 12, 7.

Mann, Michael, and Dylan Riley. 2007. "Explaining Macro-regional Trends in Global Income Inequalities, 1950–2000." *Socio-Economic Review* 5 (January): 81–115.

Mann, Thomas E., and Norman J. Ornstein. 2012. *It's Even Worse Than It Looks: How the American Constitutional System Collided with the New Politics of Extremism*. New York: Basic.

Mannathukkaren, Nissim. 2011. "Redistribution and Recognition: Land Reforms in Kerala and the Limits of Culturalism." *Journal of Peasant Studies* 38 (March): 379–411.

Manzetti, Luigi. 2009. *Neoliberalism, Accountability, and Reform Failures in Emerging Markets: Eastern Europe, Russia, Argentina, and Chile in Comparative Perspective*. University Park: Pennsylvania State University Press.

Markus, Stanislav. 2007. "Capitalists of All Russia, Unite! Business Mobilization under Debilitated Dirigisme." *Polity* 39 (July): 277–304.

Martínez, Miguel. 2007. "The Squatters' Movement: Urban Counter-Culture and Alter-Globalization Dynamics." *South European Society and Politics* 12 (September): 379–98.

Martínez-Torres, María, and Peter M. Rosset. 2010. "La Vía Campesina: The Birth and Evolution of a Transnational Social Movement." *Journal of Peasant Studies* 37 (January): 149–75.

Marx, Karl. 1974. *The First International and After: Political Writings*, vol. 3. Edited by David Fernbach. New York: Vintage.

———. 1975. *Early Writings*. Translated by Rodney Livingstone and Gregor Benton. New York: Vintage.

Mastanduno, Michael. 2009. "System Maker and Privilege Taker: U.S. Power and the International Political Economy." *World Politics* 61 (January): 121–54.

Masters, Brooke, and Philip Stafford. 2013. "Scandal-Plagued Libor Moves to NYSE as Part of Reforms." *Financial Times*, July 10, 1.

Mastoor, Maryam. 2008. "Dalits in Indian Polity—A Survey." *Regional Studies* 26 (Spring): 85–112.

Mavris, Yiannis. 2012. "Greece's Austerity Election." *New Left Review*, no. 76 (July–August): 95–107.

Mazzuca, Sebastián. 2010. "Macrofoundations of Regime Change: Democracy, State Formation, and Capitalist Development." *Comparative Politics* 43 (October): 1–19.

McAdam, Doug, Sidney Tarrow, and Charles Tilly. 2001. *Dynamics of Contention*. New York: Cambridge University Press.

McCall, Leslie. 2013. *The Undeserving Rich: American Beliefs about Inequality, Opportunity, and Redistribution*. New York: Cambridge University Press.

McCarty, Nolan, and Jonas Pontusson. 2009. "The Political Economy of Inequality and Redistribution." In *Oxford Handbook of Economic Inequality*, edited by Wiemer Salverda, Brian Nolan, and Timothy M. Smeeding, 665–92. New York: Oxford University Press.

McDonald, Ronald H., and Martin Weinstein. 2011. "Uruguay." In *Latin American Politics and Development*, 7th ed., edited by Howard J. Wiarda and Harvey F. Kline, 304–24. Boulder, CO: Westview.

McGuire, James W. 2012. "Social Policies in Latin America: Causes, Characteristics, and Consequences." In *Routledge Handbook of Latin American Politics*, edited by Peter Kingstone and Deborah J. Yashar, 200–223. New York: Routledge.

McKibbin, Ross. 2013. "Anything but Benevolent: On the Remodelling of the Welfare State." *London Review of Books* 35 (April 25): 3, 5.

McLeod, Darryl, and Nora Lustig. 2011. "Inequality and Poverty under Latin America's New Left Regimes." Working paper for the Society for Study of Economic Inequality (ECINEQ), no. 208. Palma de Mallorca, Spain: Society for the Study of Economic Inequality. http://www.ecineq.org.

Mehta, Suketu. 2013. "India's Speech Impediments." *New York Times*, February 6, A23.

Meschi, Elena, and Marco Vivarelli. 2009. "Trade and Income Inequality in Developing Countries." *World Development* 37 (February): 287–302.

Mettler, Suzanne. 2011. *The Submerged State: How Invisible Government Policies Undermine American Democracy*. Chicago: University of Chicago Press.

Meyer, Laura, and María Chaves. 2009. "Winds of Freedom: An Argentine Factory under Workers' Control." *Socialism and Democracy* 23 (November): 167–79.

Milanovic, Branko. 2011. *The Haves and the Have-Nots: A Brief and Idiosyncratic History of Global Inequality*. New York: Basic.

———. 2012. "Global Income Inequality by the Numbers: In History and Now." World Bank Development Research Group, Policy Research working paper no. 6259. Washington, DC: World Bank.

Milne, Alistair. 2009. *The Fall of the House of Credit: What Went Wrong in Banking and What Can Be Done to Repair the Damage?* Cambridge: Cambridge University Press.

Milne, Richard, and Andrew Ward. 2009. "Illuminating Outline: The Nordic Model." *Financial Times*, July 30, 7.

Minder, Raphael. 2012. "Spain's Crisis Reignites an Old Social Conflict: Jobless Farmworkers vs. Landowners." *New York Times*, August 24, A11.

Minder, Raphael, and Stephen Castle. 2010. "Workers in Europe Protest Austerity Measures." *New York Times*, September 30, A6.

Mirowski, Philip. 2013. *Never Let a Serious Crisis Go to Waste: How Neoliberalism Survived the Financial Meltdown*. London: Verso.

Mitchell, Jack. 1969. *Robert Tressell and "The Ragged Trousered Philanthropists."* London: Lawrence & Wishart.

Mitchell, Tom. 2011. "Truckers' Strike Alerts Beijing to Dangers of High Inflation." *Financial Times*, April 25, 2.

Mohanty, Ranjita. 2010. "Contesting Development, Reinventing Democracy: Grassroots Social Movements in India." In *Citizenship and Social Movements Perspectives from the Global South*, edited by Lisa Thompson and Chris Tapscott, 239–59. London: Zed.

Mondak, Jeffery J., Damarys Canache, Mitchell A. Seligson, and Matthew V. Hibbing. 2011. "The Participatory Personality: Evidence from Latin America." *British Journal of Political Science* 41 (January): 211–21.

Monsiváis, Carlos. 1997. *Mexican Postcards*. Edited and translated by John Kraniauskas. London: Verso.

Moolakkattu, John S. 2007. "Land Reform and Peaceful Change in Kerala." *Peace Review* 19 (January–March): 87–94.

Morgan, Jamie. 2009. "The Limits of Central Bank Policy: Economic Crisis and the Challenge of Effective Solutions." *Cambridge Journal of Economics* 33 (July): 581–608.

Morgan, Jana, and Nathan J. Kelly. 2010. "Explaining Public Attitudes toward Fighting Inequality in Latin America." *Poverty & Public Policy* 2: 79–111.

———. 2013. "Market Inequality and Redistribution in Latin America and the Caribbean." *Journal of Politics* 75 (July): 672–85.

Morton, Adam David. 2007. "Global Capitalism and the Peasantry in Mexico: The Recomposition of the Class Struggle." *Journal of Peasant Studies* 34 (July/October): 441–73.

Moschonas, Gerassimas. 2011. "Historical Decline or Change of Scale? The Electoral Dynamics of European Social Democratic Parties, 1950–2009." In *What's Left of the Left? Democrats and Social Democrats in Challenging Times*, edited by James Cronin, George Ross, and James Shoch, 50–85. Durham, NC: Duke University Press.

Mosley, Layna. 2011. *Labor Rights and Multinational Production*. New York: Cambridge University Press.

Mudde, Cas. 2013. "Three Decades of Populist Radical Right Parties in Western Europe: So What?" *European Journal of Political Research* 52 (March): 1–19.

Muir, Kathie, and David Peetz. 2010. "Not Dead Yet: The Australian Union Movement and the Defeat of a Government." *Social Movement Studies* 9 (April): 215–28.

Mukherji, Rahul. 2009. "The State, Economic Growth, and Development in India." *India Review* 8 (January–March): 81–106.

Mulheirn, Ian. 2013. "The Truth about Welfare." *New Statesman* 142 (May 17–23): 32–34.

Mullard, Maurice, and Raymond Swaray. 2010. "New Labour Legacy: Comparing the Labour Governments of Blair and Brown to Labour Governments since 1945." *Political Quarterly* 81 (October–December): 511–21.

Murphy, Megan, and Patrick Jenkins. 2011. "Ahead in the Clouds: Banking." *Financial Times*, March 15, 7.

Muthyala, John. 2008. "Whose World Is Flat? Mapping the Globalization of Information Technology." *New Global Studies* 2 (January): article 3.

Nadeem, Shehzad. 2011. *Dead Ringers: How Outsourcing Is Changing the Way Indians Understand Themselves*. Princeton, NJ: Princeton University Press.

Nakamoto, Michiyo. 2010. "Displacement Activity: Asia." *Financial Times*, August 23, 7.

Narrain, Siddharth. 2011. "'Disaffection' and the Law: The Chilling Effect of Sedition Laws in India." *Economic & Political Weekly* 46 (February 19): 33–37.

Navlakha, Gautam. 2011. "On Ending the War against Our Own People." *Economic & Political Weekly* 46 (February 19): 24–28.

Ndikumana, Léonce. 2009. "Capital Flight." In *Princeton Encyclopedia of the World Economy*, edited by Kenneth A. Reinert and Ramkishen S. Rajan, 156–58. Princeton, NJ: Princeton University Press.

Neckerman, Kathryn M., and Florencia Torche. 2007. "Inequality: Causes and Consequences." *Annual Review of Sociology* 33: 335–57.

Nef, Jorge, and Alejandra Roncallo. 2010. "Latin America and the New Pax Americana." In *Latin American Identities after 1980*, edited by Gordana Yovanovich and Amy Huras, 3–25. Waterloo, ON: Wilfred Laurier University Press.

Nelson, Kenneth. 2013. "Social Assistance and EU Poverty Thresholds 1990–2008: Are European Welfare Systems Providing Just and Fair Protection against Low Income?" *European Sociological Review* 29 (April): 386–401.

Newman, Katherine S., and Elisabeth S. Jacobs. 2010. *Who Cares? Public Ambivalence and Government Activism from the New Deal to the Second Gilded Age*. Princeton, NJ: Princeton University Press.

Newport, Frank. 2011. "Americans Prioritize Economy over Reducing Wealth Gap." http://www.gallup.com/poll/151568/americans-prioritize-growing-economy-reducing-wealth-gap.aspx.

Noah, Timothy. 2012. *The Great Divergence: America's Growing Inequality Crisis and What We Can Do about It*. New York: Bloomsbury.

Noble, Josh. 2013. "Spectre of 1990s Crisis Looms Large as Debt Grows." *Financial Times*, August 21, 3.

Norris, Floyd. 2012. "How the Public Sees Business Rules." *New York Times*, January 28, B3.

———. 2013. "Wage Disparity Continues to Grow." *New York Times*, April 27, B3.

Norris, Pippa. 2011. *Democratic Deficit: Critical Citizens Revisited*. New York: Cambridge University Press.

Norton, Michael I., and Dan Ariely. 2011. "Building a Better America—One Wealth Quintile at a Time." *Perspectives on Psychological Science* 6 (January): 9–12.

Oatley, Thomas, W. Kindred Winecoff, Andrew Pennock, and Sarah Bauerle Danzman. 2013. "The Political Ecology of Global Finance: A Network Model." *Perspectives on Politics* 11 (March): 133–53.

Ocampo, José Antonio. 2011. "Latin American Development after the Global Financial Crisis." In *New Ideas on Development after the Financial Crisis*, edited by Nancy Birdsall and Francis Fukuyama, 133–57. Baltimore, MD: Johns Hopkins University Press.

OECD (Organization for Economic Cooperation and Development). 2006. *OECD in Figures 2006–2007*. Paris: Organization for Economic Cooperation and Development.

———. 2008. *Growing Unequal? Income Distribution and Poverty in OECD Countries*. Paris: OECD.

———. 2010a. *Latin American Economic Outlook 2011: How Middle Class Is Latin America?* Paris: OECD.

———. 2010b. *OECD Economic Surveys: China*. Paris: OECD.

———. 2011a. *Divided We Stand: Why Inequality Keeps Rising*. Paris: OECD.

———. 2011b. *How's Life: Measuring Well-Being*. Paris: OECD.

———. 2011c. *OECD Economic Surveys: Estonia*. Paris: OECD.

———. 2011d. *OECD Economic Surveys: France*. Paris: OECD.

———. 2011e. *OECD Reviews of Labour Market and Social Policies: Russian Federation 2011*. Paris: OECD.

———. 2011f. *Society at a Glance: Asia/Pacific 2011*. Paris: OECD.

———. 2011g. *Society at a Glance 2011: OECD Social Indicators*. Paris: OECD.

———. 2012a. *Economic Policy Reforms: Going for Growth*. Paris: OECD.

———. 2012b. *OECD Economic Surveys: Norway*. Paris: OECD.

———. 2012c. *Revenue Statistics 1965–2011*. Paris: OECD.

———. 2013a. "Crisis Squeezes Income and Puts Pressure on Inequality and Poverty." Report for OECD Income Distribution Database. Paris: OECD.

———. 2013b. *OECD Economic Surveys: China*. Paris: OECD.

———. 2013c. *OECD Factbook: Economic, Environmental and Social Statistics*. Paris: OECD.

OECD/ECLAC. 2011. *Latin American Economic Outlook 2012: Transforming the State for Development*. Paris: OECD; New York: UN-ECLAC.

OECD/ECLAC/CIAT (Inter-American Center of Tax Administration). 2012. *Revenue Statistics in Latin America 1990–2010*. Paris: OECD.

O'Hearn, Denis. 2009. "Repression and Solidary Cultures of Resistance: Irish Political Prisoners on Protest." *American Journal of Sociology* 115 (September): 491–526.

Olesker, Daniel. 2009a. *Crecimiento e inclusión: Logros del gobierno frenteamplista*. Montevideo, Uruguay: Ediciones Trilce.

———. 2009b. "Un modèle économique en mutation? L'Uruguay dans le context économique régionale et international." *Problèmes d'Amérique latine*, no. 74 (Autumn): 63–78.

Oliver, Christian, and Kang Buseong. 2012. "South Korea's Graduates Struggle in Jobs Market." *Financial Times* April 27, 2.

Ondetti, Gabriel. 2008. *Land, Protest, and Politics: The Landless Movement and the Struggle for Agrarian Reform in Brazil*. University Park: Pennsylvania State University Press.

Opp, Karl-Dieter. 2009. *Theories of Political Protest and Social Movements: A Multidisciplinary Introduction, Critique, and Synthesis*. New York: Routledge.

Opp, Karl-Dieter, and Bernhard Kittel. 2010. "The Dynamics of Political Protest: Feedback Effects and Interdependence in the Explanation of Protest Participation." *European Sociological Review* 26 (February): 97–109.

Ormerod, Paul. 2012. *Positive Linking: How Networks Can Revolutionise the World*. London: Faber and Faber.

Osberg, Lars, and Timothy Smeeding. 2006. "'Fair' Inequality? Attitudes toward Pay Differentials: The United States in Comparative Perspective." *American Sociological Review* 71 (June): 450–73.

Osburg, John. 2013. *Anxious Wealth: Money and Morality among China's New Rich*. Stanford, CA: Stanford University Press.

Ost, David. 2009. "The End of Postcommunism: Trade Unions in Eastern Europe's Future." *East European Politics and Societies* 23 (February): 13–33.

Osterloh, Steffen, and Marc Debus. 2012. "Partisan Politics in Corporate Taxation." *European Journal of Political Economy* 28 (June): 192–207.

Page, Benjamin I., Larry M. Bartels, and Jason Seawright. 2013. "Democracy and the Policy Preferences of Wealthy Americans." *Perspectives on Politics* 11 (March): 51–73.

Page, Benjamin I., and Lawrence R. Jacobs. 2009a. *Class War? What Americans Really Think about Economic Inequality*. Chicago: University of Chicago Press.

———. 2009b. "No Class War: Economic Inequality and the American Public." In *The Unsustainable American State*, edited by Lawrence Jacobs and Desmond King, 135–66. New York: Oxford University Press.

Pai, Sudra. 2010. "Farmers' Movements." In *Oxford Companion to Politics in India*, edited by Niraja Gopal Jayal and Pratap Bhana Mehta, 391–408. New Delhi, India: Oxford University Press.

Palan, Ronen, Richard Murphy, and Christian Chavagneux. 2010. *Tax Havens: How Globalization Really Works*. Ithaca, NY: Cornell University Press.

Palma, José Gabriel. 2009. "The Revenge of the Market on the Rentiers: Why Neo-liberal Reports of the End of History Turned Out to Be Premature." *Cambridge Journal of Economics* 33 (July): 829–69.

———. 2011. "Homogeneous Middles vs. Heterogeneous Tails, and the End of the 'Inverted-U': It's All about the Share of the Rich." *Development and Change* 42 (January): 87–153.

Paloni, Alberto. 2009. "Structural Adjustment." In *Princeton Encyclopedia of the World Economy*, edited by Kenneth A. Reinert and Ramkishen S. Rajan, 1039–43. Princeton, NJ: Princeton University Press.

Panayotakis, Costas. 2013. "The State of Anti-Austerity Struggles in Greece." *New Politics* 14 (Winter): 16–21.

Pande, Rekha. 2007. "Gender, Poverty and Globalization in India." *Development* 50 (June): 134–40.

Panić, Mica. 2007. "Does Europe Need Neoliberal Reforms?" *Cambridge Journal of Economics* 31 (January): 145–69.

Panitch, Leo, and Sam Gindin. 2012. *The Making of Global Capitalism: The Political Economy of American Empire*. London: Verso.

Paredes, Ricardo, and Juan Ignacio Pinto. 2009. "¿El fin de la educación pública en Chile?" *Estudios de economía* 36 (June): 47–66.

Park, Juyoung, and Jai S. Mah. 2011. "Neo-liberal Reform and Bipolarisation of Income in Korea." *Journal of Contemporary Asia* 41 (May): 249–65.

Park, Yong Soo. 2008. "Revisiting the Welfare State System in the Republic of Korea." *International Social Security Review* 61 (April–June): 3–19.

———. 2011. "The Social Welfare Reform during the Progressive Regimes of South Korea: Theoretical Implications." *Social Science Journal* 48 (January): 13–28.

Parker, Christopher S., and Matt A. Barreto. 2013. *Change They Can't Believe In: The Tea Party and Reactionary Politics in America*. Princeton, NJ: Princeton University Press.

Parker, George, and David Oakley. 2010. "Finance Minister Pledges to Press On with Spending Curbs." *Financial Times*, October 22, 3.

Parthasarathy, D. 2012. "Planning and the Fate of Democracy: State, Capital, and Governance in Post-Independence India." In *State Capitalism, Contentious Politics, and Large-Scale Social Change*, edited by Vincent Kelly Pollard, 81–118. Chicago: Haymarket.

Patroni, Viviana. 2008. "Economic Restructuring, Neoliberalism, and the Working Class." In *Capital, Power, and Inequality in Latin America and the Caribbean*, new ed., edited by Richard L. Harris and Jorge Nef, 96–117. Lanham, MD: Rowman & Littlefield.

Pautz, Hartwig, and Margarita Kominou. 2013. "Reacting to 'Austerity Politics': The Tactic of Collective Expropriation in Greece." *Social Movement Studies* 12 (January): 103–10.

Pearson, Samantha. 2013. "Slogans Made into Protest Songs." *Financial Times*, June 27, 10.

Peck, Don. 2011. *Pinched: How the Great Recession Has Narrowed Our Futures & What We Can Do about It*. New York: Crown.

Pérez Caldentey, Esteban. 2012. "Income Convergence, Capability Divergence, and the Middle Income Trap: An Analysis of the Case of Chile." *Studies in Comparative International Development* 47 (June): 185–207.

Pérez Caldentey, Esteban, and Matías Vernengo. 2010. "How Stimulative Has Fiscal Policy Been around the World?" *Challenge* 53 (May–June): 6–31.

Peston, Robert, and Laurence Knight. 2012. *How Do We Fix This Mess? The Economic Price of Having It All and the Route to Lasting Prosperity*. London: Hodder & Stoughton.

Petersen, Michael Bang. 2012. "Social Welfare as Small-Scale Help: Evolutionary Psychology and the Deservingness Heuristic." *American Journal of Political Science* 56 (January): 1–16.

Petras, James, and Henry Veltmeyer. 2007. "The 'Development State' in Latin America: Whose Development, Whose State?" *Journal of Peasant Studies* 34 (July/October): 371–407.

———. 2009. *What's Left in Latin America? Regime Change in New Times*. Surrey, England: Ashgate.

Pettit, Philip. 2009. "Varieties of Public Representation." In *Political Representation*, edited by Ian Shapiro, Susan C. Stokes, Elisabeth Jean Wood, and Alexander S. Kirshner, 61–89. New York: Cambridge University Press.

Pevear, Richard. 2005. Introduction to *"The Double" and "The Gambler"* by Fyodor Dostoevsky, ix–xviii. New York: Vintage.

Pew Research Center. 2012. *Trends in American Values 1987–2012: Partisan Polarization Surges in Bush, Obama Years*. Washington, DC: Pew Research Center for the People & the Press. http://www.people-press.org/2012/06/04/partisan-polarization-surges-in-bush-obama-years/.

———. 2013. *As Sequester Deadline Looms, Little Support for Cutting Most Programs*. Washington, DC: Pew Research Center for People & the Press. http://www.people-press.org/2013/02/22/as-sequester-deadline-looms-little-support-for-cutting-most-programs/.

Pfeffer, Jeffrey. 2010. "Power Play." *Harvard Business Review* 88 (July–August): 84–92.

Philpotts, Trey. 1993. "Trevelyan, Treasury, and Circumlocution." In *Dickens Studies Annual: Essays on Victorian Fiction*, vol. 22, edited by Michael Timko, Fred Kaplan, and Edward Guiliano, 283–301. New York: AMS.

Piketty, Thomas, and Nancy Qian. 2009. "Income Inequality and Progressive Income Taxation in China and India, 1986–2015." *American Economic Journal: Applied Economics* 1 (April): 53–63.

Pilger, John. 2010. "Chile's Ghosts Are Not Being Rescued." *New Statesman* 139 (October 18): 19.

Piñera, Sebastian. 2011. "Piñera Faced with Healing Deep Wound of Inequality." *Financial Times*, September 15, 5.

Pitkin, Hanna Fenichel. 2004. "Representation and Democracy: Uneasy Alliance." *Scandinavian Political Studies* 27 (September): 335–42.

Piven, Frances Fox. 2008. "Can Power from Below Change the World?" *American Sociological Review* 73 (February): 1–14.

Platt, Matthew B. 2008. "Participation for What? A Policy-Motivated Approach to Political Activism." *Political Behavior* 30 (September): 391–413.

Ponniah, Thomas. 2011. "The Space as Actor: The Form and Content of the Social Forum Process." In *Handbook on World Social Forum Activism*, edited by Jackie Smith, Scott Byrd, Ellen Reese, and Elizabeth Smythe, 378–96. Boulder, CO: Paradigm.

Pontusson, Jonas. 2011. "Once Again a Model: Nordic Social Democracy in a Globalized World." In *What's Left of the Left: Democrats and Social Democrats in Challenging Times*, edited by James Cronin, George Ross, and James Shoch, 89–115. Durham, NC: Duke University Press.

Pontusson, Jonas, and David Rueda. 2010. "The Politics of Inequality: Voter Mobilization and Left Parties in Advanced Industrial States." *Comparative Political Studies* 43 (June): 675–705.

Popov, Vladimir. 2012. "Russia: Austerity and Deficit Reduction in Historical and Comparative Perspective." *Cambridge Journal of Economics* 36 (January): 313–34.

Popper, Nathaniel. 2013. "NYSE Euronext to Take Over Administration of Libor." *New York Times*, July 10, B3.

Posner, Richard A. 2009. *A Failure of Capitalism: The Crisis of '08 and the Descent into Depression*. Cambridge, MA: Harvard University Press.

———. 2010. *The Crisis of Capitalist Democracy*. Cambridge, MA: Harvard University Press.

Pötzsch, Janelle. 2012. "Market and Society—Are They Really Separate Spheres?" *Challenge* 55 (July–August): 50–62.

Prasad, Monica. 2005. "Why Is France So French? Culture, Institutions, and Neoliberalism, 1974–1981." *American Journal of Sociology* 111 (September): 357–407.

Prasad, Monica, and Yingying Deng. 2009. "Taxation and the Worlds of Welfare." *Socio-Economic Review* 7 (July): 431–57.

Pribble, Jennifer. 2011. "Worlds Apart: Social Policy Regimes in Latin America." *Studies in Comparative International Development* 46 (June): 191–216.

———. 2013. *Welfare and Party Politics in Latin America*. New York: Cambridge University Press.

Pribble, Jennifer, and Evelyne Huber. 2011. "Social Policy and Redistribution: Chile and Uruguay." In *The Resurgence of the Latin American Left*, edited by Steven Levitsky and Kenneth M. Roberts, 117–38. Baltimore, MD: Johns Hopkins University Press.

Pringle, Tim. 2011. *Trade Unions in China: The Challenge of Labour Unrest*. London: Routledge.

Pringle, Tim, and Simon Clarke. 2011. *The Challenge of Tradition: Trade Unions in Russia, China and Vietnam*. New York: Palgrave Macmillan.

ProQuest. 2012. *ProQuest Statistical Abstract of the United States 2013*. Bethesda, MD: Bernan.

Pryor, Frederic L. 2010. *Capitalism Reassessed*. New York: Cambridge University Press.

Przeworski, Adam. 2010. *Democracy and the Limits of Self-Government*. New York: Cambridge University Press.

Psimitis, Michalis. 2011. "The Protest Cycle of Spring 2010 in Greece." *Social Movement Studies* 10 (April): 191–97.

Puga, Ana Elena. 2008. Introduction to *Finished from the Start and Other Plays* by Juan Radrigán, xxvii–lxix. Evanston, IL: Northwestern University Press.

Puryear, Jeffrey, and Mariellen Malloy Jewers. 2009. *How Poor and Unequal Is Latin America and the Caribbean?* Policy brief no. 1. Washington, DC: Inter-American Dialogue.

Rabinovitch, Simon. 2012. "China's Lending Laboratory." *Financial Times*, May 23, 9.

———. 2013. "China Wealth Gap Data Challenged." *Financial Times*, January 19/20, 3.

Radrigán. Juan. 2008. *Finished from the Start and Other Plays*. Translated by Ana Elena Puga with Mónica Núñez-Parra. Evanston, IL: Northwestern University Press.

Ramos, Joseph. 2010. "Trade Unions in the 'South' in the Era of Globalization." *CEPAL Review*, no. 100 (April): 97–120.

Rao, Rahul. 2010. *Third World Protest: Between Home and the World*. New York: Oxford University Press.

Reese, Ellen, Christopher Chase-Dunn, Kadambari Anantram, Gary Coyne, Matheu Kaneshiro, Ashley N. Koda, Roy Kwon, and Preeta Saxena. 2011. "Surveys of World Social Forum Participants Show Influence of Place and Base in the Global Public Sphere." In *Handbook on World Social Forum Activism*, edited by Jackie Smith, Scott Byrd, Ellen Reese, and Elizabeth Smythe, 64–81. Boulder, CO: Paradigm.

Rehm, Philipp, Jacob S. Hacker, and Mark Schlesinger. 2012. "Insecure Alliances: Risk, Inequality, and Support for the Welfare State." *American Political Science Review* 106 (May): 386–406.

Reich, Robert B. 2012. *Beyond Outrage*. New York: Vintage.

Reinecke, Gerhard, and María Elena Valenzuela. 2011. "Illustrating the Gap: Collective Bargaining and Income Distribution in Chile." In *The Role of Collective Bargaining in the Global Economy: Negotiating for Social Justice*, edited by Susan Hayter, 187–204. Cheltenham, UK: Edward Elgar.

Reinhart, Carmen M., and Kenneth S. Rogoff. 2009. *This Time Is Different: Eight Centuries of Financial Folly*. Princeton, NJ: Princeton University Press.

Reis, Elisa. 2011. "Elite Perceptions of Poverty and Inequality in Brazil." In *The Great Gap: Inequality and the Politics of Redistribution in Latin America*, edited by Merike Blofield, 89–108. University Park: Pennsylvania State University Press.

Remington, Thomas F. 2011. *The Politics of Inequality in Russia*. New York: Cambridge University Press.

Rénique, Gerardo. 2009. "Latin America: The New Neoliberalism and Popular Mobilization." *Socialism and Democracy* 23 (November): 1–26.

Reygadas, Luis, and Fernando Filgueira. 2010. "Inequality and the Incorporation Crisis: The Left's Social Policy Toolkit." In *Latin America's Left Turns: Politics, Policies, and Trajectories of Change*, edited by Maxwell A. Cameron and Eric Hershberg, 171–208. Boulder, CO: Rienner.

Roberts, Alasdair. 2010. *The Logic of Discipline: Global Capitalism and the Architecture of Government*. New York: Oxford University Press.

Roberts, Kenneth M. 2008. "The Mobilization of Opposition to Economic Liberalization." *Annual Review of Political Science* 11: 327–49.

———. 2011. "Chile: The Left after Neoliberalism." In *The Resurgence of the Latin American Left*, edited by Steven Levitsky and Kenneth M. Roberts, 325–47. Baltimore, MD: Johns Hopkins University Press.

Robinson, Austin. 1947. "John Maynard Keynes, 1883–1946." *Economic Journal* 57 (March): 1–68.

Robinson, William I. 2008. *Latin America and Global Capitalism: A Critical Globalization Perspective*. Baltimore, MD: Johns Hopkins University Press.

Rocca, Jean-Louis. 2009. "'Old-Working Class' Resistance in Capitalist China: A Ritualised Social Management (1995–2006)." In *Social Movements in China and Hong Kong: The Expansion of Protest Space*, edited by Khun Eng Kuah-Pearce and Gilles Guiheuix, 117–34. Amsterdam, Netherlands: Amsterdam University Press.

Rodrik, Dani. 2011. *The Globalization Paradox: Democracy and the Future of the World Economy*. New York: W. W. Norton.

Roemer, John E. 2009. "Prospects for Achieving Equality in Market Economies." In *Oxford Handbook of Economic Inequality*, edited by Wiemer Slverda, Brian Nolan, and Timothy M. Smeeding, 693–708. New York: Oxford University Press.

Rogers, Joel, and Laura Dresser. 2011. "Business Domination Inc." *Nation* 293 (August 1/8): 17–20.

Romero, Simon. 2013a. "Brazil's Leftist Ruling Party, Born of Protests, Is Perplexed by Revolt." *New York Times*, June 20, A8.

———. 2013b. "Protests Widen As Brazilians Chide Leaders." *New York Times*, June 19, Al, A8.

———. 2013c. "Uruguay Lawmakers to Vote on Legalizing Marijuana." *New York Times*, August 1, A8.

———. 2013d. "With Rise of Video Game Start-Ups, Uruguay Enters a New Level." *New York Times*, February 22, A10.

Rosenfeld, Jake, and Meredith Kleykamp. 2012. "Organized Labor and Racial Wage Inequality in the United States." *American Journal of Sociology* 117 (March): 1460–1502.

Rosengarten, Frank. 1994. Introduction to *Letters from Prison*, vol. 1, by Antonio Gramsci, 1–32. New York: Columbia University Press.

Roth, Guenther. 2005. "Max Weber, Scion of the Cosmopolitan Bourgeoisie: Historical Context and Present-Day Relevance." In *Max Weber's Economy and Society: A Critical Companion*, edited by Charles Camic, Philip S. Gorski, and David M. Trubek, 31–46. Stanford, CA: Stanford University Press.

Rothstein, Bo. 2010. "Happiness and the Welfare State." *Social Research* 77 (Summer): 441–68.

———. 2011. *The Quality of Life: Corruption, Social Trust, and Inequality in Comparative Perspective*. Chicago: University of Chicago Press.

Roubini, Nouriel, and Stephen Mihm. 2010. *Crisis Economics: A Crash Course in the Future of Finance*. New York: Penguin.

Rueschemeyer, Dietrich. 2009. *Usable Theory: Analytic Tools for Social and Political Research*. Princeton, NJ: Princeton University Press.

Sachs, Jeffrey D. 2011. *The Price of Civilization: Reawakening American Virtue and Prosperity*. New York: Random House.

Sachweh, Patrick. 2012. "The Moral Economy of Inequality: Popular Views on Income Differentiation, Poverty and Wealth." *Socio-Economic Review* 10 (July): 419–45.

Saez, Emmanuel. 2006. "Income and Wealth Concentration in a Historical and International Perspective." In *Public Policy and the Income Distribution*, edited by Alan J. Auerbach, David Card, and John M. Quigley, 221–58. New York: Russell Sage Foundation.

Şahin, Sevgi Balkan. 2010. "Privatization as a Hegemonic Process in Turkey." *Journal of Contemporary European Studies* 18 (December): 483–98.

Sahoo, Sarbeswar. 2010. "Political Mobilisation, the Poor and Democratisation in Neo-liberal India." *Journal of Contemporary Asia* 40 (August): 487–508.

Sainsbury, Diane. 2006. "Immigrants' Social Rights in Comparative Perspective: Welfare Regimes, Forms of Immigration and Immigration Policy Regimes." *Journal of European Social Policy* 16 (August): 229–44.

Saint-Exupéry, Antoine de. 1940. *Wind, Sand and Stars*. Translated by Lewis Galantière. New York: Harcourt, Brace & World.

———. 1948. *Citadelle*. Paris: Gallimard.

———. 1986. *Wartime Writings 1939–1944*. Translated by Norah Purcell. New York: Harcourt Brace Jovanovich.

Sandbrook, Richard, Marc Edelman, Patrick Heller, and Judith Teichman. 2007. *Social Democracy in the Global Periphery: Origins, Challenges, Prospects*. New York: Cambridge University Press.

Sandel, Michael J. 2009. *Justice: What's the Right Thing to Do?* New York: Farrar, Straus & Giroux.

Sang-Hun, Choe. 2012. "In Changing South Korea, Who Counts as 'Korean'?" *New York Times*, December 7, A10.

Santiso, Javier, and Pablo Zoido. 2011. "Fiscal Legitimacy, Inequalities, and Democratic Consolidation in Latin America." In *Oxford Handbook of Latin American Economics*, edited by José Antonio Ocampo and Jaime Ros, 293–313. New York: Oxford University Press.

Santos, Boaventura de Sousa. 2006. *The Rise of the Global Left: The World Social Forum and Beyond*. London: Zed.

Santucci, Antonio A. 2010. *Antonio Gramsci*. Translated by Graziella Di Mauro with Salvatore Engel-Di Mauro. New York: Monthly Review.

Sarai, David. 2009. "The US Treasury and the Re-emergence of Global Finance." In *Hegemonic Transitions, the State and Crisis in Neoliberal Capitalism*, edited by Yildiz Atasoy, 87–103. London: Routledge.

Sarkar, Sandip, and Balwant Singh Mehta. 2010. "Income Inequality in India: Pre- and Post-Reform Periods." *Economic & Political Weekly* 45 (September 11): 45–55.

Save the Children. 2011. *State of the World's Mothers 2011*. Westport, CT: Save the Children Federation.

Savoie, Donald J. 2010. *Power: Where Is It?* Montreal: McGill-Queen's University Press.

Scalon, Celi. 2007. "Justiça como igualdade? A percepção da elite e do povo brasileiro." *Sociologias*, no. 18 (July–December): 126–49.

Scerri, Andy. 2013. "The World Social Forum: Another World Might Be Possible." *Social Movement Studies* 12 (January): 111–20.

Scheve, Kenneth, and David Stasavage. 2009. "Institutions, Partisanship, and Inequality in the Long Run." *World Politics* 61 (April): 215–53.

Schlozman, Kay Lehman, Sidney Verba, and Henry E. Brady. 2012. *The Unheavenly Chorus: Unequal Political Voice and the Broken Promise of American Democracy*. Princeton, NJ: Princeton University Press.

Schmitter, Philippe C. 2004. "The Ambiguous Virtues of Accountability." *Journal of Democracy* 15 (October): 47–60.

Schneider, Ben Ross. 2008. "Economic Liberalization and Corporate Governance: The Resilience of Business Groups in Latin America." *Comparative Politics* 40 (July): 379–97.

———. 2012. "Contrasting Capitalisms: Latin America in Comparative Perspective." In *Oxford Handbook of Latin American Political Economy*, edited by Javier Santiso and Jeff Dayton-Johnson, 149–67. New York: Oxford University Press.

Schneider, Ben Ross, and David Soskice. 2009. "Inequality in Developed Countries and Latin America: Coordinated, Liberal and Hierarchical Systems." *Economy and Society* 38 (February): 17–52.

Schneider, Carsten Q., and Philippe C. Schmitter. 2004. "Liberalization, Transition and Consolidation: Measuring the Components of Democratization." *Democratization* 11 (December): 59–90.

Schneider, Nathan. 2012. "Occupy, after Occupy." *Nation* 295 (September 24): 13–17.

Schucher, Günter. 2009. "China's Employment Crisis—A Stimulus for Policy Change?" *Journal of Current Chinese Affairs* 38 (2): 121–44.

Schwartz, Mattathias. 2011. "Pre-Occupied: The Origins and Future of Occupy Wall Street." *New Yorker* (November 28): 28–35.

Schwartz, Shalom H. 2012. "Basic Personal Values and Political Orientations." In *Improving Public Opinion Surveys: Interdisciplinary Innovation and the American National Election Studies*, edited by John H. Aldrich and Kathleen M. McGraw, 63–82. Princeton, NJ: Princeton University Press.

Scruggs, Lyle. 2008. "Social Rights, Welfare Generosity, and Inequality." In *Democracy, Inequality, and Representation: A Comparative Perspective*, edited by Pablo Beramendi and Christopher J. Anderson, 62–90. New York: Russell Sage Foundation.

Sehnbruch, Kirsten. 2010. "Unresolved Conflicts within the Consensus: Bachelet's Inheritance of Labor and Employment Issues." In *The Bachelet Government: Conflict and Consensus in Post-Pinochet Chile*, edited by Silvia Borzutzky and Gregory B. Weeks, 136–57. Gainesville: University of Florida Press.

Sejersted, Francis. 2011. *The Age of Social Democracy: Norway and Sweden in the Twentieth Century*. Princeton, NJ: Princeton University Press.

Semyonov, Moshe, Rebeca Raijman, and Anatasia Gorodzeisky. 2007. "On the Relations between Right-Wing Parties and Anti-foreigner Sentiment." *American Sociological Review* 72 (October): 841–49.

Sen, Abhijit, and Himanshu. 2005. "Poverty and Inequality in India." In *The Great Indian Poverty Debate*, edited by Angus Deaton and Valerie Kozel, 306–70. New Delhi: Macmillan.

Sender, Henny. 2011. "A Shadowy Presence: Chinese Finance." *Financial Times*, April 1, 9.

Sennett, Richard. 2012. "New Ways of Thinking about Space." *Nation* 295 (September 24): 24–26.

Şenses, Fikret. 2012. "Turkey's Experience with Neoliberal Policies since 1980 in Retrospect and Prospect." *New Perspectives on Turkey*, no. 47 (Fall): 11–31.

Shaw, George Bernard. 2008. *"Pygmalion" and "Major Barbara."* New York: Bantam Classics.

Shaxson, Nicholas. 2011. *Treasure Islands: Tax Havens and the Men Who Stole the World*. London: Bodley Head.

———. 2013. "The Zombies of Mayfair." *New Statesman* 142 (June 28–July 4): 31–35.

Shayo, Moses. 2009. "A Model of Social Identity with an Application to Political Economy: Nation, Class, and Redistribution." *American Political Science Review* 103 (May): 147–74.

Sheehan, Brendan. 2009. *Understanding Keynes' General Theory*. Houndmills, Basingstoke, England: Palgrave Macmillan.

Sheng, Andrew. 2009. *From Asian to Global Financial Crisis: An Asian Regulator's View of Unfettered Finance in the 1990s and 2000s*. New York: Cambridge University Press.

Shin, Kwang-Yeong. 2010. "Globalisation and the Working Class in South Korea: Contestation, Fragmentation and Renewal." *Journal of Contemporary Asia* 40 (May): 211–29.

Shlapentokh, Vladimir. 2008. "Big Money as an Obstacle to Democracy in Russia." *Journal of Communist Studies and Transition Politics* 24 (December): 512–30.

Siegel, David A. 2009. "Social Networks and Collective Action." *American Journal of Political Science* 53 (January): 122–38.

———. 2011. "When Does Repression Work? Collective Action in Social Networks." *Journal of Politics* 73 (October): 993–1010.

Sinha, Aseema. 2010. "Business and Politics." In *Oxford Companion to Politics in India*, edited by Niraja Gopal Jayal and Pratap Bhanu Mehta, 459–76. New York: Oxford University Press.

Sinn, Hans-Werner. 2010. *Casino Capitalism: How the Financial Crisis Came About and What Needs to Be Done Now*. New York: Oxford University Press.

SIPRI (Stockholm International Peace Research Institute). 2012. *SIPRI Yearbook 2012: Armaments, Disarmament and International Security*. Oxford, UK: Oxford University Press.

Skidelsky, Robert. 2009. *Keynes: The Return of the Master*. New York: Public Affairs.

———. 2011. "The Relevance of Keynes." *Cambridge Journal of Economics* 35 (January): 1–13.

Skocpol, Theda, and Lawrence R. Jacobs. 2012. "Accomplished and Embattled: Understanding Obama's Presidency." *Political Science Quarterly* 127 (Spring): 1–24.

Skocpol, Theda, and Vanessa Williamson. 2012. *The Tea Party and the Remaking of Republican Conservatism*. New York: Oxford University Press.

Slater, Michael. 2009. *Charles Dickens*. New Haven, CT: Yale University Press.

Słomczyński, Kazimierz M., and Krystyna Janicka. 2008. "Polarized Social-Class Structure: On the Matthew Effect and Increasing Inequality." *Polish Sociological Review*, no. 164: 341–57.

Smith, Jackie. 2008. *Social Movements for Global Democracy*. Baltimore, MD: Johns Hopkins University Press.

———. 2009. "Contested Globalizations: Social Movements and the Struggle for Global Democracy." In *Unsettled Legitimacy: Political Community, Power, and Authority in a Global Era*, edited by Steven Bernstein and William D. Coleman, 300–316. Vancouver, BC: University of British Columbia Press.

Smith, Jackie, and Dawn Wiest. 2012. *Social Movements in the World-System: The Politics of Crisis and Transformation*. Washington, DC: Russell Sage Foundation.

Smith, Peter H., and Melissa R. Ziegler. 2007. "Governmental Performance and Political Regimes: Latin America in Comparative Perspective, 1990–2004." *Taiwan Journal of Democracy* 3 (December): 101–17.

Snel, Erik, Jack Burgers, and Arjen Leerkes. 2007. "Class Position of Immigrant Workers in a Post-industrial Economy: The Dutch Case." *Journal of Ethnic and Migration Studies* 33 (November): 1323–42.

So, Alvin Y. 2007a. "Globalization and the Transition from Neoliberal Capitalism to State Developmentalism in China." Special issue, *International Review of Modern Sociology* 33: 61–76.

———. 2007b. "Peasant Conflict and the Local Predatory State in the Countryside." *Journal of Peasant Studies* 34 (July/October): 560–81.

———. 2010. "Globalization and China: From Neoliberal Capitalism to State Developmentalism in East Asia." In *Globalization in the 21st Century: Labor, Capital, and the State on a World Scale*, edited by Berch Berberoglu, 133–54. Houndmills, Basingstoke, UK: Palgrave Macmillan.

Solimano, Andrés. 2012. *Chile and the Neoliberal Trap: The Post-Pinochet Era*. New York: Cambridge University Press.

Song, Hae-Yung. 2013. "Democracy against Labour: The Dialectic of Democratisation and Dedemocratisation in Korea." *Journal of Contemporary Asia* 43 (May): 338–62.

Song, Jesook. 2009. *South Koreans in the Debt Crisis: The Creation of a Neoliberal Welfare Society*. Durham, NC: Duke University Press.

Song, Zheng, Kjetil Storesletten, and Fabrizio Zilibotti. 2011. "Growing Like China." *American Economic Review* 101 (February): 196–223.

Sorkin, Andrew Ross. 2012. "Gun Reform Not a Cause on Wall Street." *New York Times*, December 18, B1, B4.

Soroka, Stuart N., and Christopher Wlezien. 2010a. *Degrees of Democracy: Politics, Public Opinion, and Policy*. New York: Cambridge University Press.

———. 2010b. "Public Opinion and Public Policy." In *Oxford Handbook of Canadian Politics*, edited by John C. Courtney and David E. Smith, 263–80. New York: Oxford University Press.

Soskice, David. 2010. "American Exceptionalism and Comparative Political Economy." In *Labor in the Era of Globalization*, edited by Clair Brown, Barry Eichengreen, and Michael Reich, 51–93. New York: Cambridge University Press.

Sperber, Jonathan. 2013. *Karl Marx: A Nineteenth-Century Life*. New York: Liveright.

Spilerman, Seymour. 2009. "How Globalization Has Impacted Labor: A Review Essay." *European Sociological Review* 25 (February): 73–86.

Staerklé, Christian, Tiina Likki, and Régis Scheidegger. 2012. "A Normative Approach to Welfare Attitudes." In *Contested Welfare States: Welfare Attitudes in Europe and Beyond*, edited by Stefan Svallfors, 81–118. Stanford, CA: Stanford University Press.

Stahler-Sholk, Richard. 2007. "Resisting Neoliberal Homogenization: The Zapatista Autonomy Movement." *Latin American Perspectives* 34 (March): 48–63.

Stallings, Barbara. 2007. "The Globalization of Capital Flows: Who Benefits?" *Annals of the American Academy of Political and Social Science* 610 (March): 202–16.

Stallings, Barbara, and Wilson Peres. 2011. "Is Economic Reform Dead in Latin America? Rhetoric and Reality since 2000." *Journal of Latin American Studies* 43 (November): 755–86.

Standing, Guy. 2008. "How Cash Transfers Promote the Case for Basic Income." *Basic Income Studies* 3 (April): article 5.

———. 2011. *The Precariat: The New Dangerous Class*. London: Bloomsbury Academic.

Stanford, Jim. 2008. *Economics for Everyone: A Short Guide to the Economics of Capitalism*. London: Pluto.

Starr, Amory, Luis Fernandez, and Christian Scholl. 2011. *Shutting Down the Streets: Political Violence and Social Control in the Global Era*. New York: New York University Press.

Stédile, João Pedro. 2007. "The Class Struggle in Brazil: The Perspective of the MST." In *Socialist Register 2008: Global Flashpoints*, edited by Leo Panitch and Colin Leys, 193–216. London: Merlin.

Steen, Michael. 2013. "Eurozone Divergence Raises Contradictions." *Financial Times*, July 27/28, 2.

Steger, Debra, and Natalia Shpilkovskaya. 2010. "Internal Management of the WTO: Room for Improvement." In *Redesigning the World Trade Organization for the Twenty-First Century*, edited by Debra P. Steger, 129–61. Waterloo, ON: Wilfrid Laurier University Press.

Steger, Manfred B., and Ravi K. Roy. 2010. *Neoliberalism: A Very Short Introduction*. New York: Oxford University Press.

Stephens, Philip. 2013. "Prosperity Fuels Protest in the New Age of Unrest." *Financial Times*, June 28, 9.

Stevens, John Paul. 2013. "The Court & the Right to Vote: A Dissent." *New York Review of Books* 60 (August 15): 37–39.

Stevis, Dimitris, and Terry Boswell. 2008. *Globalization and Labor: Democratizing Global Governance*. Lanham, MD: Rowman & Littlefield.

Stiglitz, Joseph E. 2008. "Is There a Post-Washington Consensus Consensus?" In *The Washington Consensus Reconsidered: Towards a New Global Governance*, edited by Narcís Serra and Joseph E. Stiglitz, 41–56. New York: Oxford University Press.

———. 2010. *Free Fall: America, Free Markets, and the Sinking of the World Economy*. New York: W. W. Norton.

———. 2011. "Of the 1%, by the 1%, for the 1%." *Vanity Fair* 53 (May): 126–29.

———. 2012. *The Price of Inequality: How Today's Divided Society Endangers Our Future*. New York: W. W. Norton.

Stiglitz, Joseph E., and Linda J. Bilmes. 2008. *The Three Trillion Dollar War: The True Cost of the Iraq Conflict*. New York: W. W. Norton.

Stiglitz, Joseph E., and UN Commission of Financial Experts. 2010. *The Stiglitz Report: Reforming the International Monetary and Financial Systems in the Wake of the Global Crisis*. New York: New Press.

Stimson. James A. 2011. "The Issues in Representation." In *Who Gets Represented?* edited by Peter K. Enns and Christopher Wlezien, 347–60. New York: Russell Sage Foundation.

Stinchcombe, Arthur L. 2005. *The Logic of Social Research.* Chicago: University of Chicago Press.

Streeck, Wolfgang. 2011. "The Crises of Democratic Capitalism." *New Left Review*, no. 71 (September–October): 5–29.

———. 2012a. "Citizens as Customers: Considerations on the New Politics of Consumption." *New Left Review*, no. 76 (July–August): 27–47.

———. 2012b. "On Fred Block, Varieties of What? Should We Still Be Using the Concept of Capitalism?" In *Political Power and Social Theory*, vol. 23, edited by Julian Go, 311–21. Bingley, UK: Emerald Group.

Street, Paul, and Anthony DiMaggio. 2011. *Crashing the Tea Party: Mass Media and the Campaign to Remake American Politics*. Boulder, CO: Paradigm.

Strøm, Kaare, Hanne Marthe Narud, and Henry Valen. 2007. "A More Fragile Chain of Governance in Norway." In *Norway in Transition: Transforming a Stable Democracy*, edited by Øyvind Østerud, 77–102. London: Routledge.

Strømmen, Øyvimd. 2012. *La Toile brune*. Translated by Loup-Maëlle Besançon. Paris: Actes Sud.

Suárez, Sandra, and Robin Kolodny. 2011. "Paving the Road to 'Too Big to Fail': Business Interests and the Politics of Financial Deregulation in the United States." *Politics & Society* 39 (March): 74–102.

Sukiassyan, Grigor. 2007. "Inequality and Growth: What Does the Transition Data Say?" *Journal of Comparative Economics* 35 (March): 35–56.

Svallfors, Stefan. 2007. "Class and Attitudes to Market Inequality: A Comparison of Sweden, Britain, Germany, and the United States." In *The Political Sociology of the Welfare State: Institutions, Social Cleavages, and Orientations*, edited by Stefan Svallfors, 189–222. Stanford, CA: Stanford University Press.

———. 2010. "Public Attitudes." In *Oxford Handbook of the Welfare State*, edited by Francis G. Castles, Stephan Leibfried, Jane Lewis, Herbert Obinger, and Christopher Pierson, 241–51. New York: Oxford University Press.

———. 2012a. "Welfare Attitudes in Context." In *Contested Welfare States: Welfare Attitudes in Europe and Beyond*, edited by Stefan Svallfors, 222–39. Stanford, CA: Stanford University Press.

———. 2012b. "Welfare States and Welfare Attitudes." In *Contested Welfare States: Welfare Attitudes in Europe and Beyond*, edited by Stefan Svallfors, 1–24. Stanford, CA: Stanford University Press.

Svallfors, Stefan, Joakim Kulin, and Annette Schnabel. 2012. "Age, Class, and Attitudes toward Government Responsibilities." In *Contested Welfare States: Welfare Attitudes in Europe and Beyond*, edited by Stefan Svallfors, 158–92. Stanford, CA: Stanford University Press.

Swain, Ashok. 2010. *Struggle against the State: Social Network and Protest Mobilization in India*. Surrey, UK: Ashgate.

Swedlow, Brendon. 2011. "A Cultural Theory of Politics." *PS: Political Science & Politics* 44 (October): 703–10.

Tabb, William K. 2010. "Financialization in the Contemporary Social Structure of Accumulation." In *Contemporary Capitalism and Its Crises: Social Structure of Accumulation Theory for the 21st Century*, edited by Terrence McDonough, Michael Reich, and David M. Kotz, 145–67. New York: Cambridge University Press.

———. 2012. *The Restructuring of Capitalism in Our Time*. New York: Columbia University Press.

Tabuchi, Hiroko. 2010. "Indentured Workers in Distress: Job Program in Japan Brings Migrants and Problems." *New York Times*, July 21, B1, B5.

Taibbi, Matt. 2012. "The Slow, Painful Death of Dodd-Frank." *Rolling Stone*, no. 1157 (May 24): 62–67, 86–87.

Tanzi, Vito. 2011. *Government versus Markets: The Changing Economic Role of the State*. New York: Cambridge University Press.

Tarrow, Sidney. 2011. *Power in Movement: Social Movements and Contentious Politics*. 3rd ed. New York: Cambridge University Press.

Taylor, Astra. 2012. "Occupy 2.0: Strike Debt." *Nation* 295 (September 24): 17–20.

Taylor, John B. 2012. *First Principles: Five Keys to Restoring America's Prosperity*. New York: W. W. Norton.

Taylor-Gooby, Peter. 2013. "Riots, Demonstrations, Strikes and the Coalition Programme." *Social Policy & Society* 12 (January): 1–15.

Taylor-Gooby, Peter, and Gerry Stoker. 2011. "The Coalition Programme: A New Vision for Britain or Politics as Usual?" *Political Quarterly* 62 (January–March): 4–15.

Taylor-Robinson, Michelle M. 2010. *Do the Poor Count? Democratic Institutions and Accountability in a Context of Poverty*. University Park: Pennsylvania State University Press.

Teichman, Judith A. 2012. *Social Forces and States: Poverty and Distributional Outcomes in South Korea, Chile, and Mexico*. Stanford, CA: Stanford University Press.

Teorell, Jan. 2006. "Political Participation and Three Theories of Democracy: A Research Inventory and Agenda." *European Journal of Political Research* 45 (August): 787–810.

Thomas, Landon, Jr. 2013. "Tall Monuments to End of Boom and Easy Credit." *New York Times*, August 21, A1, B2.

Thompson, Jennifer. 2012. "Compound Interest: The Global Probe into Rate-Rigging." *Financial Times*, December 10, 6.

Thompson, Noel. 2008. "Hollowing Out the State: Public Choice Theory and the Critique of Keynesian Social Democracy." *Contemporary British History* 22 (September): 355–82.

Thomson, Adam. 2012. "Mexico: North of the Border." *Financial Times*, August 23, 5.

Thorp, Rosemary. 2012. "A Historical Perspective on the Political Economy of Inequality in Latin America." In *Oxford Handbook of Latin American Political Economy*, edited by Javier Santiso and Jeff Dayton-Johnson, 149–67. New York: Oxford University Press.

Tikhonova, N. E. 2011. "The Causes and Prospects of Low-Income Poverty in Russia Today." *Sociological Research* 50 (January–February): 24–43.

Titunik, Regina F. 2005. "Democracy, Domination, and Legitimacy in Max Weber's Political Thought." In *Max Weber's Economy and Society: A Critical Companion*, edited by Charles Camic, Philip S. Gorski, and David M. Trubek, 143–63. Stanford, CA: Stanford University Press.

Tokman, Victor E. 2011. "Employment: The Dominance of the Informal Economy." In *Oxford Handbook of Latin American Economics*, edited by José Antonio Ocampo and Jaime Ros, 767–89. New York: Oxford University Press.

Tonkiss, Fran. 2006. *Contemporary Economic Sociology: Globalisation, Production, Inequality*. London: Routledge.

Toshiaki, Tachibanaki. 2010. *The New Paradox for Japanese Women: Greater Choice, Greater Inequality*. Tokyo: International House of Japan.

Traxler, Franz. 2010. "The Long-Term Development of Organised Business and Its Implications for Corporatism: A Cross-National Comparison of Membership, Activities and Governing Capacities of Business Interest Associations, 1980–2003." *European Journal of Political Research* 49 (March): 151–73.

Traxler, Franz, and Bernd Brandl. 2011. "The Economic Impact of Collective Bargaining Coverage." In *The Role of Collective Bargaining in the Global Economy: Negotiating for Social Justice*, edited by Susan Hayter, 227–53. Cheltenham, UK: Edward Elgar.

Tremlett, Giles, and Martin Roberts. 2012. "Can Spain Survive Austerity?" *Guardian Weekly*, October 5, 1–2.

Tressell, Robert. 1962. *The Ragged Trousered Philanthropists*. New York: Monthly Review.

Tridico, Pasquale. 2012a. "Financial Crisis and Global Imbalances: Its Labour Market Origins and the Aftermath." *Cambridge Journal of Economics* 36 (January): 17–42.

———. 2012b. "Varieties of Capitalism and Development in Transition Economies Since the Fall of the Berlin Wall." *Challenge* 55 (May/June): 90–128.

Trilling, Daniel. 2013. "All That Glitters." *New Statesman* 142 (June 21–27): 30–33.

Tyler, Tom R. 2011. *Why People Cooperate: The Role of Social Motivations*. Princeton, NJ: Princeton University Press.

Uba, Katrin, 2008. "Labor Union Resistance to Economic Liberalization in India: What Can National and State Level Protests against Privatization Tell Us?" *Asian Survey* 43 (September/October): 860–84.

UNCTAD (United Nations Conference on Trade and Development). 2012. *Trade and Development Report, 2012: Policies for Inclusive and Balanced Growth*. New York: United Nations.

UNDP (United Nations Development Program). 2010. *Human Development Report 2010*. New York: Palgrave Macmillan.

UNODC (United Nations Office on Drugs and Crime). 2011. *2011 Global Study on Homicide: Trends, Contexts, Data*. New York: United Nations Office on Drugs and Crime. http://www.unodc.org/documents/data-and-analysis/statistics/Homicide/Globa_study_on_homicide_2011_web.pdf.

Vakulabharanam, Vamsi. 2010. "Does Class Matter? Class Structure and Worsening Inequality in India." *Economic & Political Weekly* 45 (July 17): 67–76.

Valenzuela, Jonay Martín. 2012. "A Social Awakening: History of the Protests against Evictions." In *From Cairo to Wall Street: Voices from the Global Spring*, edited by Anya Schiffrin and Eamon Kircher-Allen, 133–40. New York: New Press.

Van Hiel, Alain. 2012. "A Psycho-Political Profile of Party Activists and Left-Wing and Right-Wing Extremists." *European Journal of Political Research* 51 (March): 166–203.

Van Spanje, Joost. 2011. "The Wrong and the Right: A Comparative Analysis of 'Anti-Immigration' and 'Far Right' Parties." *Government and Opposition* 46 (July): 293–320.

Varley, John. 2010. "Casino Gibes That Do Our Banks No Justice." *Financial Times*, September 24, 9.

Vergara, Eva. 2009. "Mapuche Unrest Provokes Revival of Dictator Tactics." *San Francisco Chronicle*, November 18, A4.

Verhulst, Joris, and Stefaan Walgrave. 2009. "The First Time Is the Hardest? A Cross-national and Cross-issue Comparison of First-Time Protest Participants." *Political Behavior* 31 (September): 455–84.

Vieira, Mónica Brito, and David Runciman. 2008. *Representation*. Cambridge: Polity.

Visser, Jelle, and Danielle Checchi. 2009. "Inequality and the Labor Market: Unions." In *Oxford Handbook of Economic Inequality*, edited by Wiemer Salverda, Brian Nolan, and Timothy M. Smeeding, 230–56. New York: Oxford University Press.

Volscho, Thomas W., and Nathan J. Kelly. 2012. "The Rise of the Super-Rich: Power Resources, Taxes, Financial Markets, and the Dynamics of the Top 1 Percent, 1949 to 2008." *American Sociological Review* 77 (October): 679–99.

Vos, Rob. 2011. "Economic Insecurity and Development in Latin America and the Caribbean." In *Oxford Handbook of Latin American Economics*, edited by José Antonio Ocampo and Jaime Ros, 741–66. New York: Oxford University Press.

Wacquant, Loïc. 2008a. "The Militarization of Urban Marginality: Lessons from the Brazilian Metropolis." *International Political Sociology* 2 (March): 56–74.

———. 2008b. *Urban Outcasts: A Comparative Sociology of Advanced Marginality*. Cambridge: Polity.

———. 2009. *Punishing the Poor: The Neoliberal Government of Social Insecurity*. Durham, NC: Duke University Press.

———. 2010. "Crafting the Neoliberal State: Workfare, Prisonfare, and Social Insecurity." *Sociological Forum* 25 (June): 197–220.

Wade, Robert. 2008. "The First-World Debt Crisis of 2007–2010 in Global Perspective." *Challenge* 51 (July/August): 23–54.

———. 2009. "From Global Imbalances to Global Reorganisations." *Cambridge Journal of Economics* 33 (July): 539–62.

———. 2010. "The State of the World Bank." *Challenge* 53 (July/August): 43–67.

———. 2011a. "The Economy Has Not Solved Its Problems." *Challenge* 54 (March/April): 5–41.

———. 2011b. "Global Trends in Income Inequality: What Is Happening, and Should We Worry?" *Challenge* 54 (September/October): 54–75.

———. 2012. "Why Has Income Inequality Remained on the Sidelines of Public Policy for So Long?" *Challenge* 55 (May–June): 21–50.

———. 2013. "The Art of Power Maintenance: How Western States Keep the Lead in Global Organizations." *Challenge* 56 (January/February): 5–39.

Walder, Andrew G. 2009. "Political Sociology and Social Movements." *Annual Review of Sociology* 35: 393–412.

Walder, Andrew G., and Songhua Hu. 2009. "Revolution, Reform, and Status Inheritance: Urban China, 1949–1996." *American Journal of Sociology* 114 (March): 1395–1427.

Wall, Stephen, and Helen Small. 2003. Introduction to *Little Dorrit*, rev. ed., by Charles Dickens, xi–xxvii. New York: Penguin.

Walls, Marion. 2008. "The Whited Sepulchre: Christianity and Philosophy in *The Ragged Trousered Philanthropists*." In *Revisiting Robert Tressell's Mugsborough: New Perspectives on "The Ragged Trousered Philanthropists,"* edited by Julie Cairnie and Marion Wells, 151–71. Amherst, NY: Cambria.

Wang, Chen, Koen Caminada, and Kees Goudswaard. 2012. "The Redistributive Effect of Social Transfer Programmes and Taxes: A Decomposition across Countries." *International Social Security Review* 65 (July–September): 27–48.

Wang, Feng. 2008. *Boundaries and Categories: Rising Inequality in Post-Socialist Urban China*. Stanford, CA: Stanford University Press.

Wapshott, Nicholas. 2011. *Keynes Hayek: The Clash That Defined Modern Economics*. New York: W. W. Norton.

Weaver, Catherine. 2008. *Hypocrisy Trap: The World Bank and the Poverty of Reform*. Princeton, NJ: Princeton University Press.

Webber, Jude. 2013. "Plain-Spoken Mujica Looks North to Boost Uruguay's Trade." *Financial Times*, May 17, 5.

Weber, Max. 2012. *Max Weber: Collected Methodological Writings*. Edited by Hans Henrik Bruun and Sam Whimster, translated by Hans Henrik Bruun. New York: Routledge.

Weeks, Gregory, and Silvia Borzutzky. 2012. "Michelle Bachelet's Government: The Paradoxes of a Chilean President." *Journal of Politics in Latin America* 4 (3): 97–121.

Wegren, Stephen K. 2007. "The State and Agrarian Reform in Post-communist Russia." *Journal of Peasant Studies* 34 (July/October): 498–526.

Weisbrot, Mark. 2013. "Latin America Must Support Honduran Fight for Freedom." *Guardian Weekly*, November 8, 9.

Weisbrot, Mark, and Juan Montecino. 2010. *The IMF and Economic Recovery: Is Fund Policy Contributing to Downside Risks?* Washington, DC: Center for Economic and Policy Research.

Weisman, Jonathan. 2013. "House G.O.P. Sets a New Offensive on Obama Goals." *New York Times*, July 24, A1, A3.

Weiss, Barbara. 1982. "Secret Pockets and Secret Breasts: *Little Dorrit* and the Commercial Scandals of the Fifties." In *Dickens Studies Annual: Essays on Victorian Fiction*, vol. 10, edited by Stanley Friedman, Edward Guiliano, Anne Humpherys, Natalie McKnight, and Michal Timko, 67–76. New York: AMS.

Weldon, S. Laurel. 2011. *When Protest Makes Policy: How Social Movements Represent Disadvantaged Groups*. Ann Arbor: University of Michigan Press.

Welzel, Christian, and Franziska Deutsch. 2012. "Emancipative Values and Non-Violent Protest: The Importance of 'Ecological' Effects." *British Journal of Political Science* 42 (April): 465–79.

Welzel, Christian, and Ronald Inglehart. 2005. "Democratization as the Growth of Freedom: The Human Development Perspective." *Japanese Journal of Political Science* 6 (December): 313–43.

———. 2010. "Agency, Values, and Well-Being: A Human Development Model." *Social Indicators Research* 97 (May): 43–63.

Western, Bruce, and Becky Pettit. 2010. "Incarceration & Social Inequality." *Daedalus* 139 (Summer): 8–19.

Westra, Richard. 2010. "South Korea *Déjà Vu*." *Journal of Contemporary Asia* 40 (May): 329–36.

Wheeler, William. 2012. "Europe's New Fascists." *New York Times* Sunday Review, November 18, 7.

White, Jonathan. 2009. "The Social Theory of Mass Politics." *Journal of Politics* 71 (January): 96–112.

Whyte, Martin King. 2010a. "Do Chinese Citizens Want the Government to Do More to Promote Equality?" In *Chinese Politics: State, Society and the Market*, edited by Peter Hays Gries and Stanley Rosen, 129–59. London: Routledge.

———. 2010b. *Myth of the Social Volcano: Perceptions of Inequality and Distributive Justice in Contemporary China*. Stanford, CA: Stanford University Press.

———. 2010c. "The Paradoxes of Rural-Urban China Inequality in Contemporary China." In *One Country, Two Societies: Rural-Urban Inequality in Contemporary China*, edited by Martin King Whyte, 1–25. Cambridge, MA: Harvard University Press.

Whyte, Martin King, and Chunping Han. 2008. "Popular Attitudes toward Distributive Injustice: Beijing and Warsaw Compared." *Journal of Chinese Political Science* 13 (April): 29–51.

Wildavsky, Aaron. 1998. *Culture and Social Theory*. Edited by Sun-Ki Chai and Brendon Swedlow. New Brunswick, NJ: Transaction.

Wilensky, Harold L. 2012. *American Political Economy in Global Perspective*. New York: Cambridge University Press.

Wilkinson, Frank. 2007. "Neo-liberalism and New Labour Policy: Economic Performance, Historical Comparisons and Future Prospects." *Cambridge Journal of Economics* 31 (November): 817–43.

Wilkinson, Richard, and Kate Pickett. 2009. *The Spirit Level: Why More Equal Societies Almost Always Do Better*. London: Allen Lane.

Williams, Michelle. 2008. *The Roots of Participatory Democracy: Democratic Communists in South Africa and Kerala, India*. New York: Palgrave Macmillan.

Williamson, Jeffrey G. 2011. *Trade and Poverty: When the Third World Fell Behind*. Cambridge, MA: MIT Press.

Wilson, James, and Gerrit Wiesmann. 2011. "Visibility Needed: Banking." *Financial Times*, April 6, 9.

Wolf, Martin. 2010. *Fixing Global Finance*. Baltimore, MD: Johns Hopkins University Press.

———. 2012. "The Union Outlived de Tocqueville." *Financial Times*, April 18, 9.

Wolff, Richard. 2012. *Democracy at Work: A Cure for Capitalism*. Chicago: Haymarket.

Wolford, Wendy. 2010. "Participatory Democracy by Default: Land Reform, Social Movements and the State in Brazil." *Journal of Peasant Studies* 37 (January): 91–109.

Wolin, Richard. 2011. "Ghosts of a Tortured Past: Europe's Right Turn." *Dissent* 58 (Winter): 58–65.

Wolin, Sheldon S. 2004. *Politics and Vision: Continuity and Innovation in Western Political Thought*. Expanded ed. Princeton, NJ: Princeton University Press.

———. 2008. *Democracy Incorporated: Managed Democracy and the Specter of Inverted Totalitarianism*. Princeton, NJ: Princeton University Press.

Woll, Cornelia. 2007. "Leading the Dance? Power and Political Resources of Business Lobbyists." *Journal of Public Policy* 27 (January–April): 57–78.

Wong, Edward. 2013. "Survey in China Shows a Wide Gap in Income." *New York Times*, July 20, A9.

Wood, Tony. 2012. "Collapse as Crucible: The Reforging of Russian Society." *New Left Review*, no. 74 (March–April): 5–38.

World Bank. 2011. *World Development Indicators 2011*. Washington, DC: International Bank for Reconstruction and Development.

Wright, Erik Olin. 2005. "The Shadow of Exploitation in Weber's Class Analysis." In *Max Weber's Economy and Society: A Critical Companion*, edited by Charles Camic, Philip S. Gorski, and David M. Trubek, 204–36. Stanford, CA: Stanford University Press.

Yadav, Vineeta. 2011. *Political Parties, Business Groups, and Corruption in Developing Countries*. New York: Oxford University Press.

Young, Alfred F. 2011. "The People and the Patriots: Who Led Whom in the American Revolution?" *Boston Review* 36 (November/December): 30–37.

Yun, Ji-Whan. 2009. "Regulatory Contradictions: The Political Determinants of Labor Market Inequality in Korea and Japan." *Governance* 22 (January): 1–25.

———. 2010. "Unequal Japan: Conservative Corporatism and Labour Market Disparities." *British Journal of Industrial Relations* 48 (March): 1–25.

Zaidi, Salman. 2009. "Main Drivers of Income Inequality in Central European and Baltic Countries: Some Insights from Recent Household Survey Data." Policy Research working paper no. 4815. Washington, DC: World Bank.

Zakarian, Richard H. 1972. *Zola's "Germinal": A Critical Study of Its Primary Sources.* Geneva: Librairie Droz.

Zandi, Mark. 2008. *Financial Shock: A 360° Look at the Subprime Mortgage Implosion and How to Avoid the Next Financial Crisis.* Upper Saddle River, NJ: Pearson Education.

Zaslove, Andrej. 2008. "Exclusion, Community, and a Populist Political Economy: The Radical Right as an Anti-Globalization Movement." *Comparative European Politics* 6 (July): 169–89.

Zehavi, Amos. 2012. "Welfare State Politics in Privatization of Delivery: Linking Constituencies to Left and Right." *Comparative Political Studies* 45 (February): 194–219.

Zeng, Zhen, and Yu Xie. 2008. "A Preference-Opportunity-Choice Framework with Applications to Intergroup Friendship." *American Journal of Sociology* 114 (November): 615–48.

Zhang, Xiaoke. 2010. "Global Forces and Corporate Reforms in Korea." *International Political Science Review* 31 (January): 59–76.

Zhou, Yanqiu Rachel. 2008. "Economic Reform, Neoliberal Globalization and Social Policy: Reconstructing the Relationship between the State, the Market and Citizens in China." *Global Social Policy* 8 (April): 115–28.

Zola, Émile. 1954. *Germinal.* Translated by Leonard Tancock. London: Penguin.

———. 1979. *Germinal.* Edited by Colette Becker. Paris: Éditions Garnier Frères.

———. 2007. *Germinal.* Translated by Larry Duffy. London: Wordsworth.

Index

About the Author

Charles F. Andrain, an emeritus professor of political science, taught at San Diego State University for more than thirty years. There he offered classes in comparative policy analysis, political systems, and the developing nations. He has published numerous books about public policy, including ones that focused on income distribution, health, and religion. Several of his publications covered not only industrialized societies but also countries in Asia, Latin America, the Middle East, and Central and Eastern Europe. Written with David E. Apter, *Political Protest and Social Change* was selected by *Choice* magazine as an outstanding academic book issued in 1995.

CPSIA information can be obtained at www.ICGtesting.com
Printed in the USA
BVOW07*1234020214

343436BV00004B/6/P

9 781442 229464